Jon E. Lewis is the author of numerous books in the Autobiography series, including *Engl*  *London: The Autobiography* and *Spitfir* books have been published in langua and Portuguese Brazilian, and have copies.

Praise for his previous books:

England: The Autobiography:
'A triumph' Saul David, author of *Victoria's Army*

The British Soldier: The Autobiography:
'This thoughtful compilation . . . almost unbearably moving'
Guardian

'Compelling Tommy's eye view of war' *Daily Telegraph*

'What a book. Five stars' *Daily Express*

SAS

Britain's Elite Special Forces in their Own Words

Edited by Jon E. Lewis

A Herman Graf Book
Skyhorse Publishing

Skyhorse Publishing books may be purchased in bulk at special discounts for sales promotion, corporate gifts, fund-raising, or educational purposes. Special editions can also be created to specifications. For details, contact the Special Sales Department, Skyhorse Publishing, 307 West 36th Street, 11th Floor, New York, NY 10018 or info@skyhorsepublishing.com.

Skyhorse® and Skyhorse Publishing® are registered trademarks of Skyhorse Publishing, Inc.®, a Delaware corporation.

www.skyhorsepublishing.com

10 9 8 7 6 5 4 3 2 1

Library of Congress Cataloging-in-Publication Data is available on file.

ISBN 978-1-61608-452-3

Printed and bound in the UK

CONTENTS

INTRODUCTION

AN INFANT IN ARMS

The Birth of the Special Air Service Regiment, 1941

1941. Of all unlikely places, the Special Air Service – destined to become the world's most famous and most feared special forces unit – was conceived in a hospital bed in Egypt. Injured while undertaking some unofficial parachute training, David Stirling, a twenty-six-year-old subaltern in No. 8 (Guards) Commando, used his enforced sojourn in 15 Scottish Military Hospital in Cairo to conjure a scheme for hit-and-run operations against the Germans in the North African desert.

On his release from hospital in July, Stirling decided to take his idea to the top. To present the plan through the usual channels would only mean it getting buried in what Stirling thought of as 'fossilized shit' – bureaucracy, in other, politer words. Although generals are not, by and large, in the habit of granting interviews to second-lieutenants, Stirling hobbled on crutches to General Headquarters Middle East in Cairo's leafy Tonbalat Street; after failing to show a pass at the security barrier, he went around the corner, jumped over the fence and careered inside the building, the warden's bellowed alarms close behind him. Up on the third floor, Stirling found his way into the office of Major General Neil Ritchie, Claude Auchinleck's Deputy Chief of Staff. Stirling breathlessly apologized to the surprised Ritchie for the somewhat unconventional nature of his call, but insisted that he had something of 'great operational importance' to show him. Stirling then pulled out the pencilled memo on small-scale desert raiding he had prepared in hospital. 'He [Ritchie] was very courteous,' Stirling remembered years later, 'and he settled down to read it. About halfway through, he got very engrossed, and had forgotten the rather irregular way it had been presented.'

It was Stirling's turn to be surprised. Looking up, Ritchie said matter-of-factly, 'I think this may be the sort of plan we are looking for. I will discuss it with the Commander-in-Chief and let you know our decision in the next day or so.' The Commander-in-Chief was General Claude Auchinleck, new to his post, and under immense pressure from Churchill to mount offensive operations. Stirling's plan was a gift for Auchinleck; it required few resources, it was original, and it dovetailed neatly with Churchill's own love of commandos. Stirling's memo went under the cumbersome title of 'Case for the retention of a limited number of special service troops, for employment as parachutists', but there was nothing ungainly about its concept; on the contrary, Stirling understood that small can be beautifully lethal in wartime. The unit Stirling proposed was to operate behind enemy lines and attack vulnerable targets such as supply lines and airfields at night. What is more, the raids were to be carried out by groups of five to ten men, rather than the hundreds of a standard commando force, the very numbers of which made them susceptible to detection by the enemy. Since these special service commandos were to be inserted by air, they had greater range than seaborne troops and did not require costly (and reluctant) Royal Navy support. Stirling wrote later:

I argued the advantage of establishing a unit based on the principle of the fullest exploitation of surprise and of making the minimum demands on manpower and equipment . . . a sub-unit of five men to cover a target previously requiring four troops of commando, i.e. about two hundred men. I sought to prove that, if an aerodrome or transport park was

2

the objective of an operation, then the destruction of fifty aircraft or units of transport was more easily accomplished by a sub-unit of five men than by a force of two hundred.

While Auchinleck pondered Stirling's memo, Ritchie looked into David Stirling's background. He was equally pleased and displeased by what he found. On graduation from the Guards' depot at Pirbright, David Stirling had been classed as an 'irresponsible and unremarkable soldier'. He was dismissive of authority. He overslept so much he was nicknamed 'The Great Sloth'. In Egypt his partying had become legendary, and he had more than once revived himself from hangovers by inhaling oxygen begged from nurses at the 15 Scottish Military Hospital.

But it wasn't all bad. David Stirling, born in 1915, came from 'good stock'; he was the youngest son of Brigadier Archibald Stirling of Keir; his mother was the daughter of the 16th Baron Lovat. After Ampleforth and three years at Cambridge, Stirling had enthusiastically calls joined the Scots Guards, before transferring to No. 8 Commando. Like many a commando officer, he was recruited over a pink gin at White's Club by Lieutenant Colonel Bob Laycock, 8 Commando's Commanding Officer. As part of the 'Layforce' brigade, No. 8 Commando had been dispatched to North Africa, where its seaborne raids had been embarrassing wash-outs. On the disbandment of Layforce, Stirling had jumped – literally – at the chance of joining an unofficial parachute training session organized by another officer in No. 8 Commando. Many people over the years mistook Stirling's diffidence, abetted by the slight stoop common to the very tall (Stirling was six feet six) for a lack of ambition; on the contrary, Stirling possessed a core of steely resolve. (Churchill, who met Stirling later in the war, borrowed an apposite couplet from *Don Juan* for his pen portrait of the SAS leader as 'the mildest manner'd man that ever scuttled ship or cut a throat'.) This inner determination was the reason why Stirling participated in the impromptu parachute-jumping trials at Fuka: he wanted to get on with the war. Unfortunately, the aircraft used, a lumbering Valencia bi-plane, was not equipped for parachuting and the men had secured the static lines which opened the silk canopies to seat legs. Stirling's parachute caught on the door and snagged; he descended far too rapidly and hit the ground so hard that he was temporarily paralysed from the waist down. Thus he had ended up as a bed patient in the Scottish Military Hospital.

Three days after his meeting with Ritchie, Stirling was back at Middle East Headquarters, this time with a pass. Auchinleck saw him in person. Stirling was given permission to recruit a force of sixty officers and men. The unit was to be called 'L Detachment, SAS Brigade'. The 'SAS' stood for 'Special Air Service', a force which was wholly imaginary and whose nomenclature was devised by Brigadier Dudley Clarke, a staff Intelligence officer, to convince the Germans that Britain had a large airborne force in North Africa. To mark his new appointment as the Commanding Officer of L Detachment, Stirling was promoted to captain.

There were two particular officers Stirling wanted for his outfit. The first was John 'Jock' Lewes, whom Stirling found at Tobruk, where he was leading raids on the Axis lines. British by birth, Lewes had been brought up in Australia, and was an Oxford rowing 'blue' who had led his university eight to a historic win over Cambridge. It had been Lewes who had organized the parachute jump at Fuka during which Stirling had crashed. Lewes' influence on the formation of the SAS was paramount; on a visit to Stirling in hospital, Lewes had voiced proposals and queries which did much to further the embryonic idea of a desert raiding force that was circling around in Stirling's head. Stirling said later: 'The chat with Jock was the key to success. I knew I had to have all the answers to the questions he raised if I was to get anywhere.'

When Stirling asked Lewes to become the first recruit of 'L Detachment' Lewes refused point blank. He did not trust

4

Stirling's commitment. But Stirling, as everyone agreed, could be very persuasive. Besides, he was displaying more grit than Lewes had seen in the party boy hitherto. After a month of cajoling, Lewes agreed to join. So did Captain R. B. 'Paddy' Mayne.

Before the war, Mayne had been a rugby player of international rank, capped six times for Ireland and once for the British Lions. He was also a useful boxer and had reached the final of the British Universities' Championship heavyweight division. Unfortunately, when taken by drink Mayne was not too fussy whom he fought; in June 1941 he'd been returned to unit from 11 Commando for attacking his commanding officer.

However, Paddy Mayne was much more than a six-foot-two drinker and brawler. A former law student, he had a 'Dr Jekyll' side, and was sensitive, literate, modest and painfully shy. Unquestionably he was brave; he'd won a Mention in Dispatches for his baptismal combat – 1 Commando's raid on the Litani River in Syria. He would end up as one of the four most decorated British officers of the Second World War, with a Distinguished Service Order (DSO) and three Bars (the other being Lieutenant Col Alistair Pearson of the Parachute Regiment). As 'brave as ten lions, a tactical genius', is how George Jellicoe, a fellow SAS officer (and later a commanding officer of the Special Boat Squadron), remembered Mayne. Nevertheless, before accepting Mayne into L Detachment, Stirling extricated a promise that he would not attack his new commanding officer. As Stirling noted years later, Mayne 'kept the promise, at least in respect of myself, though not with others'.

Like Lewes and Mayne, most of the rest of the officers and men of L Detachment, who would later be known as 'The Originals', were volunteers recruited from commandos beached at the Infantry Base Depot at Geneifa following the disbandment of Layforce. Selection was based on Stirling's personal impression of the men at brief interviews. He also told them that if they failed to make the grade in training they would have to return to their units. Why did they join? Captain Malcolm Pleyell, L Detachment's first medical officer, wrote, doubtless accurately:

> This sort of warfare possessed a definite flavour of romance. It conjured up visions of dashing deeds which might become famous overnight.

By August 1941, Stirling had established a base at Kabrit, 100 miles south of Cairo in the Canal Zone. Equipment was conspicuous by its absence, due to the parsimony of Q Branch. Arriving by truck at Kabrit, Johnny Cooper, recruited from No. 8 Commando, found:

> only two medium-sized marquees and three 180-lb tents piled up in the middle of the strip of bare desert allocated to us. No camp, none of the usual facilities, not even a flagpole.

A wooden sign bearing the words 'L Detachment – SAS' was the sole clue that this was base camp. Being, in his own words, a 'cheekie laddie', Stirling had a plan to secure the necessary equipment to complete the camp – which was to 'borrow' it from a New Zealand camp down the road. Thus the first – and highly unofficial – attack of L Detachment was a night raid on the camp of 2 New Zealand Division, filling up L Detachment's one and only three-ton truck with anything useful that could be found. Including tents and a piano for the sergeants' mess. The next day, L Detachment boasted one of the smartest and most luxuriously furnished British camps in the Canal Zone.

Training then began in earnest. From the outset, Stirling insisted on a high standard of discipline, equal to that of the Brigade of Guards. In his opening address to L Detachment on 4 September, he told the men: 'We can't afford to piss about disciplining anyone who is not a hundred per cent devoted to having a crack at the Hun.' L Detachment required a special discipline: self-discipline.

Stirling told the L Detachment volunteers that control of self was expected at all times, even on leave:

> When anyone is on leave in Cairo or Alexandria, please remember that there's to be no bragging or scrapping in bars or restaurants. Get this quite clear. In the SAS, all toughness is reserved exclusively for the enemy.

In return, the usual Army 'bullshit' of parades, saluting officers every time they loomed into sight was to be dropped. This informal style was to become a hallmark of the SAS. He expected personal initiative, independence and modesty. Any 'passengers' would be returned to their units.

David Stirling also demanded the utmost physical fitness, but it was Jock Lewes who translated the master's ideas into practicalities. The early L Detachment training devised by Lewes was, in essence, commando training adapted to desert conditions, especially those encountered at night. The emphasis was on navigation, weapons training, demolition training and punishing physical training sessions. Endurance marches became marathons of up to thirty miles a night, carrying packs crammed with sand or bricks.

Everyone joining the SAS had to be a parachutist, since Stirling envisaged insertion by air for his force. No parachute training instructors were available (the only British parachute-training schools extant were Ringway, near Manchester, and Delhi, in India), so the SAS under Jock Lewes developed its own parachute training techniques. These involved jumping from ever higher scaffold towers and from the tailboard of a 112-pound Bedford truck moving at 30 miles per hour across the desert. More than half the 'Originals' of L Detachment sustained injuries launching themselves off the back of the Bedford. After this very basic parachute training, the L Detachment recruits made their first live drop, from a Bristol Bombay aircraft. There were no reserve parachutes. Two men, Ken Warburton and Joseph Duffy, died when the snap-links connecting the strops on their parachutes to the static rail in the Bombay twisted apart. Consequently, when they jumped they were no longer attached to the aircraft – and there was nothing to pull the canopies out. Afterwards, Bob Bennett recalled:

> . . . we went to bed with as many cigarettes as possible, and smoked until morning. Next morning, every man (led by Stirling himself) jumped; no one backed out. It was then that I realized that I was with a great bunch of chaps.

The drop on the morning of 17 October was a key moment in SAS history. Stirling displayed leadership; he took the men through the doubt and the darkness.

To replace the faulty clips on the Bombay had been straight-forward; however, another engineering problem before L Detachment proved harder to solve. What bomb should the patrols carry to blow up German aircraft? The bomb had to be small enough to be easily transportable but powerful enough to do the job of destruction. Most SAS men infiltrating on foot from a drop zone could only be expected to carry two of the widely available five-pound charges, which would only inflict superficial damage. Once again it was Jock Lewes to the rescue. After weeks of experiments in a small hut at Kabrit, Lewes invented the requisite device – henceforth known as the 'Lewes bomb' – which was a mixture of plastic explosive, thermite and aluminium turnings rolled in engine oil. Likened to a 'nice little black pudding' by L Detachment's Sergeant John Almonds (known to all as 'Gentleman Jim'), the Lewes bomb was sticky and could quickly be placed onto the side of an aircraft. Just a pound of 'Lewes bomb' could annihilate an aircraft, meaning that each trooper could carry the means of dispatching ten aircraft.

By the end of August, L Detachment was ready for its final

exercise, a dummy attack on the large RAF base at Heliopolis, outside Cairo. Stirling had been bluntly told by an RAF Group Captain that his plan to sabotage German aircraft on the ground was far-fetched. So far-fetched, indeed, that he bet Stirling $16 that L Detachment could not infiltrate the Heliopolis base and place labels representing bombs on the parked aircraft. Now, Stirling decided, it was time to pay up. The entire orbat of L Detachment, six officers and fifty-five men, trekked ninety miles across the desert from Kabrit over four days, on four pints of water each, and carrying weights to simulate Lewes bombs. Although the RAF knew the SAS were coming, and even set up air patrols, Stirling and his men successfully infiltrated the base on the fourth night and adorned the parked aircraft with sticky labels marked 'BOMB'.

Stirling collected his $16.

The first operational raid by the SAS was planned for the night of 17 November 1941. Five parties were to be dropped from Bristol Bombays, to attack Axis fighter and bomber strips at Gazala and Timini. The drop zones were about twelve miles from the objective, and the teams were to spend a day in a lying-up position observing their targets before a night attack with Lewes bombs, to be detonated by time-delay pencils. After the attack, the teams were to rendezvous south of Trig al' Abd track with a motor patrol of the Long Range Desert Group (LRDG). Reconnaissance behind enemy lines was the stock-in-trade of the LRDG, which had been founded by Major Ralph Bagnold, an amateur pre-war explorer of the Sahara.

Stirling's attack had a purpose behind the destruction of enemy aircraft; it was designed to divert enemy attention on the eve of Operation Crusader, Auchinleck's offensive to push Rommel out of Cyrenaica in North Africa. The same evening was to see No. 11 Commando attack Rommel's house in Beda Littoria (now Al Baydá).

Like so many previous commando raids, that on Rommel's

headquarters was a seamless disaster, resulting in the loss of thirty men for no gain whatsoever; the house raided by 11 Commando had never even been used by Rommel.

Not that Stirling's debut raid garnered a better result, though. Following a Met Office forecast of 30-knot winds and rain in the target area, Stirling toyed with cancelling the *Squatter mission*, since airborne operations in anything above 15 knots invariably ended in the scattering and injuring of the parachutists. On further thought, though, Stirling decided to go ahead, as he believed that a cancellation would affect L Detachment's bubbling-over morale. Moreover, in his sales talk on behalf of his intended parachute force, Stirling had promised general headquarters that the unique quality of his unit was that 'the weather would not restrict their operations to the same extent that it had done in the case of seaborne special service troops'. To Stirling's relief, the officers of L Detachment, assembled ready to go at Baggush airfield, backed his decision to go ahead. So did the enlisted men. 'We'll go because we've got to,' Stirling told them. Any man who wanted to could leave. No one did.

Of the fifty-four SAS men who jumped out into the windswept night of 16 November, only twenty-one made the rendezvous with the Long Range Desert Group. The plane carrying Lieutenant Charles Bonnington's stick was hit by flak, after which a Me-109 fighter delivered the *coup de grâce*; all the SAS men aboard were injured, one fatally. Meanwhile, Lieutenant Eoin McGonigal had been killed on landing, and when his stick set out towards the rendezvous they were captured by an Italian patrol. Nearly every man in Stirling's, Mayne's and Lewes' sticks suffered concussion, sprains or broken bones; Mayne's troop sergeant, Jock Cheyne, broke his back. Since all their gear had been dropped separately, even the walking able found themselves lacking bombs and fuses. What fuses were recovered were then wrecked by the driving rain. The storm of 16 and 17 November 1942 was one of the worst of the war in the western desert. Demoralized, the survivors trekked to the rendezvous not through blistering heat, as they had expected, but through mud and floods. Stirling and Bob Tait were among the last to arrive. Waiting for them on the Trig al'Abd was Captain David Lloyd Owen of the LRDG's Y patrol:

One very interesting thing arose from my meeting with David Stirling that morning. David told me all about the operation and that it had been a total failure. He was a remarkable man. He never gave in to failure and was determined to make the next operation a success. I turned over in my mind, 'Why the hell do this ridiculous parachuting, why didn't they let us take them to where they wanted to go? We could take them like a taxi to do the job. We could push off while they did their task, and then pick them up at an agreed rendezvous.' We discussed this while having a mug of tea laced with rum in the dawn. He was a little doubtful. I then took him to the next RV to meet up with Jake Easonsmith who was detailed to take him to Siwa and thence to Cairo. A week or so later David told me he had been so immensely impressed by Jake and his patrol, he decided that he would work with us, and they did until the end of 1942, when they got their own transport. These were months of great success.

They were. Although Stirling thought his L Detachment SAS might be killed off as a result of *Squatter*'s failure, no one at general headquarters seemed to care much. General headquarters had bigger problems on its collective mind than the loss of thirty-four parachutists; Rommel was making his famous 'dash to the wire' and a counter-thrust was needed. It would help the counter-thrust if the Axis aircraft at Tamet, Sirte, Aghayala and Agedabia aerodromes were destroyed. Stirling was given another chance and he took it with both hands. This time there was to be no parachute drop; the SAS were to be taxied to the target by the LRDG.

On 8 December, Stirling, Mayne and eleven other SAS men

11

departed their temporary headquarters at Jalo oasis accompanied by the LRDG's Rhodesian patrol under the command of Captain Gus Holliman. Stirling and Mayne were set to raid Sirte and Tamet airfields, which were about 350 miles from Jalo, on the night of 14 December. At the same time, Jock Lewes was to lead a section in an attack on Aghayla. A fourth SAS patrol, comprising four men under Lieutenant Bill Fraser, was to raid Agedabia a week later.

Sitting aboard the LRDG's stripped-down Ford trucks, the SAS men were overcome by the vastness of the Sahara. There was no sign of life, and Stirling found the brooding solitude like being on the high seas. Courtesy of dead-on navigation by the LRDG's Corporal Mike Sadler, the SAS were just forty miles south of Sirte by noon on 11 December. Then their luck changed: an Italian Ghibli spotter plane appeared out of the haze to strafe and bomb them. Holliman ordered the patrol to make for cover in a thorn scrub two miles back, and there they lay as two more Ghiblis came hunting, but failed to see the patrol. The element of surprise, the *sine qua non* of the SAS, was lost. Even so, Stirling determined to press on, and the obliging LRDG dropped the SAS off not the agreed twenty miles from Sirte, but a mere three. Knowing that a reception committee was likely to be waiting, Stirling chose not to risk his whole section but to instead infiltrate the airfield with just one companion, Sergeant Jimmy Brough. The rest of the team, under Mayne, was sent to a satellite airfield five miles away at Wadi Tamet.

Unfortunately, during their recce of the airfield Stirling and Brough stumbled over two Italian sentries, one of whom began firing off bullets, causing the SAS men to sprint away into the desert night. Next day, as they lay up near the base, Stirling and Brough watched in bitter frustration as Italian Caproni bomber after bomber flew away. Alerted and suspicious, the Italians were evacuating the airfield.

At nightfall, Stirling and Brough tramped in silence to the rendezvous with the LRDG. Once again, an SAS operation had been a washout. Stirling knew that unless Mayne and Lewes triumphed, the disbandment of the SAS was likely. Mayne's attack was to take place at eleven; the hour came and went, unlit by explosions, and then there was a great *whumph* and a bolt flame in the west, followed by explosion upon explosion. The SAS was in the sabotage business. Stirling and Brough almost danced with delight. 'It almost makes the army worthwhile,' shouted Brough.

There had, it turned out, been a good reason for Mayne's slight delay at Wadi Tamet. Approaching the airfield, Mayne had noticed a chink of light and the sound of laughter coming from a hut; on putting his ear to the door he realized that it was the pilots' mess and a party was in full swing. Deciding that the party should come to an end, Mayne kicked open the door and hosed the room with bullets from his .45-calibre Tommy gun. For good measure, he shot out the lights, leaving the room in chaos. Crouching outside were the rest of his section – McDonald, Hawkins, Besworth, Seekings and White. Reg Seekings recalled:

As soon as Paddy cut loose . . . the whole place went mad – [they fired] everything they had including tracer . . . They had fixed lines of fire about a couple of feet from the ground. We had either to jump over or crawl under them . . . Besworth came slithering over to us on all fours. I can still see him getting to his feet, pulling in his arse as the tracer ripped past his pack, missing him by inches. On a signal from Paddy, we got the hell out of it.

They dashed to the airfield, setting Lewes bombs as they passed down the rows of aircraft. Finding himself a bomb short, Mayne clambered into one aircraft's cockpit and tore out the instrument panel with his bare hands. Corporal Seekings takes up the story:

We had not gone fifty yards when the first plane went up. We stopped to look but the second one went up near us and we began to run. After a while we felt fairly safe and stopped to take another glance. What a sight! Planes exploding all over, and the terrific roar of petrol and bombs going up.

Jock Lewes had not enjoyed good hunting, but when Bill Fraser's party reached their rendezvous they reported the most astounding success of all. They had blown up thirty-seven aircraft at Agedabia aerodrome. In this sequence of week-long raids, the SAS had accounted for no less than sixty-one enemy aircraft destroyed, together with petrol, stores and transport.

His tail up, Stirling could not wait to have another go at the enemy. On the presumption that the enemy would not expect another attack so soon, Stirling and Mayne set off from their Jalo desert base on Christmas Day 1941 to revisit Tamet and Sirte. Their second attack was a mirror image of the first. Mayne destroyed twenty-seven aircraft at Tamet; Stirling was unable to reach the airfield because of the crush of German armour and vehicles around it. He was fortunate to escape with his life; an Italian guard tried to shoot him, only to discover he had a faulty round in the barrel of his rifle.

Meanwhile, Fraser and Lewes were taken by Lieutenant Morris's LRDG patrol to raid airstrips at Nofilia and Ras Lanuf. At the latter location, Mussolini had built a grandiose triumphal arch to commemorate his African conquests; to the Tommies it looked similar to the arch at the end of Oxford Street, and 'Marble Arch' it became known to one and all throughout the British Army.

Lewes had a difficult time at Nofilia when a bomb he was placing on an aircraft exploded prematurely. Withdrawing under heavy fire, Lewes and his party were picked up by their LRDG escort, only to come under attack by Messerschmitts and Stukas in the open desert. Jock Lewes was killed, the survivors scattered. The death of Lewes was a heavy blow to Stirling, as there was no one else on whom he so heavily relied. There was more bad news: Captain Fraser's patrol was missing.

To this episode, at least, there was a happy ending. On finding the Marble Arch strip bereft of aircraft, Fraser and his section had waited for Morris's LRDG patrol. When, after six days, Morris failed to arrive, the SAS men decided to walk the 200 burning miles to Jalo. Their walk, which took eight days, was the first of several epic peregrinations in the SAS annals, to rank alongside that of Trooper John Sillito the following year (again, 200 miles in eight days, drinking his own urine for hydration) and that of Chris Ryan during the Gulf War.

Fraser's walk and the unit's bag of nearly ninety aircraft in a month were an emphatic vindication of Stirling's concept of small-scale raiding by a volunteer elite. The 'Originals' of L Detachment looked forward to even better hunting in the new year of 1942.

PART I

GOING TO THE WARS

The SAS, 1942–5

It was Stirling's gift as a leader to see the big picture, and where the SAS fitted into that scene. He was also, due to his social background and boundless confidence, possessed of friends in the highest places. Both attributes came together in early January 1942, when Stirling sought a personal interview with Auchinleck, the Commander-in-Chief, during which he proposed that L Detachment should switch from striking airfields to ports. Although the *Crusader* operation had pushed Rommel westwards, the Afrika Korps remained a potent force, not least because it continued to receive supplies of Panzers through the coastal harbour. Stirling pointed out to Auchinleck that Bouerat would become the likely main supply harbour for the Afrika Korps, and that the fuel dumps there could and should be blown up. Auchinleck agreed. When Stirling asked for men for L Detachment, Auchinleck gave him permission to recruit a further six officers and thirty to forty men, some of whom could be drawn from the Special Boat Section of No. 8 Commando. For good measure, Auchinleck promoted Stirling to major.

There was one final thing: Stirling's enemies in general head-quarters (who were the sort of literal-minded men who thought irregular forces were a diversion from the 'real' war) had bluntly informed him that L Detachment, because it was a temporary unit, could not have its own badge. Nonetheless, Stirling brashly wore

SAS wings and cap badge to meet the Commander-in-Chief. Stirling had calculated correctly; Auchinleck liked and approved the badge. The SAS badge was more than a mark of an elite unit, it was a debt Stirling felt he owed Lewes, who had been instrumental in its design. The so-called 'Winged Dagger' was modelled by Bob Tait on King Arthur's sword Excalibur, while the wings were probably taken from an ibis on a fresco in Shepheard's Hotel. The colors of the wings, Oxford and Cambridge blue, were selected because Lewes had rowed for Oxford, and Tom Langton, another early L-Detachment officer, for Cambridge. It was Stirling himself who came up with the motto 'Who Dares Wins'. The badge was worn on berets – which at first were white, but when these attracted wolf whistles they were changed to a sand color, which they still are.

On the way back to Jalo, Stirling came across fifty French parachutists at Alexandria who, after some vigorous appeals to the Free French commander in Cairo, General Catroux, Stirling annexed for the SAS. He also recruited Captain Bill Cumper of the Royal Engineers, a Cockney explosives expert who would take on the vacancy of demolitions instructor left open by Lewes' death. But Cumper could not take on the whole gamut of training the SAS recruits who were now so numerous the camp at Kabrit was overflowing with them; that mantle, Stirling resolved, should be taken by Paddy Mayne. Sitting in his tent, Stirling explained his thinking to Mayne, who accepted with bad grace verging on insubordination. He would only 'do his best', and then only on a temporary basis. Mayne even hinted that Stirling was green-eyed about his success in blowing up aircraft, and pinning him to a desk was a way of stealing the glory.

With a moody Mayne left sulking in Kabrit, Stirling launched a raid on Bouerat from Jalo on 17 January. Taxiing the SAS team out was the Guards patrol of the LRDG, led by Captain Anthony Hunter. As on previous missions, Stirling seemed chained to ill luck. On the sixth day out, the patrol was strafed and bombed in the Wadi Tamrit, with the loss of the radio truck and three men. Then Stirling instructed the two Special Boat Section men in the party to assemble their *folbot* (a type of collapsible canoe) before the final approach – the plan being for the SBS men to paddle out and set limpet mines on ships in the harbour. As their 1,680-pound Ford truck neared Bouerat, it lurched down a pothole and the *folbot* shattered. Not that it mattered; there were no ships in the port. Instead, Stirling had to satisfy himself with detonating petrol bowsers and the wireless station.

Picked up by a LRDG truck driven by Corporal 'Flash' Gibson, Stirling and his crew rode around, stopping to plant bombs on parked trucks. They then made off to the main rendezvous. Mounted on the back of the Ford V-8 truck was a novelty – a Vickers K aircraft-type machine gun, whose .303-inch barrels could spew out bullets at 1,200 rounds per minute. Johnny Cooper was the man with his finger on the trigger:

As we motored at speed along the track, we suddenly noticed flashing lights up ahead of us and a few isolated shots whizzed through the air. Whether they were warning shots or the enemy clearing their guns we did not know, but as our truck accelerated down a slight incline it became painfully obvious that an ambush had been set up . . . I slipped off the safety catch and let fly with a devastating mixture of tracer and incendiary, amazed at the firepower of the Vickers. At the same time, Reg [Seekings] opened up with his Thompson, and we ploughed through the ambush, completely outgunning and demoralizing the Italians. Gibson, with great presence of mind, switched on the headlamps and roared away at about 40 mph, driving with absolute efficiency and coolness to extricate us from a difficult position.

Gibson was awarded the Military Medal (MM) for the operation, and Johnny Cooper the Distinguished Conduct Medal (DCM). The

Vickers K, fired for the first time in action by the SAS, became the unit's weapon of choice for the rest of the war.

On the way back to Jalo, Stirling discovered why Bouerat had been free of shipping. Rommel had ordered the Afrika Korps to advance and, in what became known as the 'Msus Stakes', had rolled the British back to Gazala line. He now had a port closer to the front line – Benghazi.

With his head full of a plan to attack Benghazi, Stirling returned to the SAS base at Kabrit, only to find that Mayne had virtually abandoned all administration and training. He had even let the estimable Cumper be posted away. Stirling went into Mayne's tent. 'Paddy was surrounded by bottles, reading James Joyce,' Stirling recalled. A furious row ensued, only resolved when Mayne was returned to the orbat. Old hands, however, noticed a continued tension between Stirling and Mayne, which was not cooled by Stirling appointing a complete outsider, Lieutenant George, Earl Jellicoe, as his second-in-command. Probably Mayne's contrived incompetence as an administrator ruled him out of the job, but doubtless too Stirling wanted as his right hand someone less combustible than Mayne, whose aggression when drunk was notorious. Mayne's role as training officer was taken over by Sergeant Major 'Big Pat' Riley. It was Riley who inducted Reg Seekings, Bob Bennett and 'Young Johnny' Cooper, all recently promoted, into the sergeants' mess. Cooper recalled:

Once you were promoted you had to go to the bar on first entering the mess and drink a pint of whatever drink you designated without taking your lips from the glass. One Saturday morning, Reg and I entered the mess tent and were welcomed by Pat Riley. To me he said, 'Well, young Cooper, I know you don't drink alcohol, so you had better have a non-alcoholic drink.' 'Yes, Sergeant Major,' I replied, somewhat overawed by the whole occasion. Pat continued, 'We have a drink here which is definitely non-alcoholic – it's called

19

cherry brandy.' A tankard was filled with red liquid and handed to me. At first it was quite sweet and enjoyable but then I found it sickly and thick. I only just managed to get it down before bolting from the tent in the nick of time to get rid of the contents of my stomach. For the next two days I had a permanent hangover and have never touched the stuff since.

The good tidings that awaited Stirling at Kabrit were that Bill Fraser and four men, missing since the Yuletide attack on the 'Marble Arch' airfield, had been picked up by British troops. Second Lieutenant Fitzroy Maclean, an SAS new boy, was just settling into his tent when Fraser turned up at Kabrit:

As I was unpacking my kit, the flap of the tent was pulled back and a wild-looking figure with a beard looked in. 'My tent,' he said. It was the owner, Bill Fraser. He was not dead at all. Finding himself cut off, he had walked back across two-hundred-odd miles of desert to our lines, keeping himself alive by drinking rusty water from the radiators of derelict trucks. It showed what could be done.

Prevented from military service by his profession of diplomat, Maclean had obviated the ruling by getting himself elected to Parliament and thus out of the Foreign Office. (Churchill quipped that Maclean had 'used the Mother of Parliaments as a public convenience'.) Maclean had been on his way to join the 2nd Camerons in the desert when a chance meeting with the persuasive David Stirling in Cairo resulted in him transferring to the SAS. For all Stirling's promotion of meritocracy in the SAS, he was always most comfortable in recruiting officers from his own set. Maclean and Stirling's brother, Peter, the Secretary at the British Embassy in Cairo, were old friends. Another acquaintance brought into the SAS by Stirling was the Prime Minister's son, Captain

Randolph Churchill, 4 Hussars. Pinguescent and overbearing, Churchill was not standard SAS material, but, as Stirling knew, Randolph wrote to his father daily. In the Machiavellian world of Army politics, with its shifting loyalties and competing empires, Stirling understood the importance of gaining, even indirectly, the Prime Minister's ear.

Maclean and Churchill both accompanied Stirling on the raid against Benghazi on 21 May 1942. The intention was to penetrate the harbour, where the team – which also included Cooper, Rose and Lieutenant Gordon Alston – would lay limpet mines on Axis ships. An earlier SAS venture against Benghazi had come to grief when the *folbot* collapsible canoe proved impossible to fit together; for this operation, Stirling had secured inflatable recce craft from the Royal Engineers.

Escorted by an LRDG patrol, the SAS team set off for Benghazi in the 'Blitz Buggy'. This was a Ford V8 utility vehicle Stirling had poached in Cairo and had then modified by removing the roof and windows and installed a water condenser, an extra-large fuel tank and a sun compass. It also had a single Vickers K machine gun at the front and twin Vickers at the rear. The 'Blitz Buggy' was painted in olive grey to look like a German staff car. Alas, on the long run into Benghazi the Blitz Buggy developed a distinctly attention-seeking fault. Maclean recalled:

Once we had left the desert and were on the smooth tarmac road, we noticed that the car was making an odd noise. It was more than a squeak; it was a high-pitched screech with two notes in it. Evidently one of the many jolts which they had received had damaged the track rods. Now the wheels were out of alignment and this was the result.

We laid down on our backs in the road and tinkered. It was no use. When we got back into the car and drove off again, the screech was louder than ever. We could hardly have made more noise if we had been in a fire engine with its bell clanging. It was awkward, but there was nothing we could do about it now. Fortunately, it did not seem to affect the speed of the car.

Soon we were passing the high wire fence round the Regina aerodrome. We were not far from Benghazi now. We were going at a good speed and expected to be there in five or ten minutes. I hoped that the Intelligence Branch were right in thinking there was no road block. It was cold in the open car. Feeling in my greatcoat pocket I found a bar of milk chocolate that had been forgotten there. I unwrapped it and ate it. It tasted good.

Then, suddenly, we turned a corner and I saw something that made me sit up and concentrate. A hundred yards away, straight ahead of us, a red light was showing right in the middle of the road.

David slammed on the brakes and we slithered to a standstill. There was a heavy bar of wood across the road with a red lantern hanging from the middle of it. On my side of the road stood a sentry who had me covered with his Tommy gun. He was an Italian. I bent down and picked up a heavy spanner from the floor of the car. Then I beckoned to the sentry to come nearer, waving some papers at him with my free hand as if I wanted to show them to him. If only he would come near enough I could knock him on the head and we could drive on.

He did not move but kept me covered with his Tommy gun. Then I saw that beyond him in the shadows were two or three more Italians with Tommy guns and what looked like a guardroom or a machine-gun post. Unless we could bluff our way through there would be nothing for it but to shoot it out, which was the last thing we wanted at this stage of the expedition.

There was a pause and then the sentry asked who we were. 'Staff officers,' I told him, and added peremptorily, 'in a hurry.' I had not spoken a word of Italian for three years and I hoped devoutly that my accent sounded convincing. Also that he would not notice in the dark that we were all wearing British uniforms.

He did not reply immediately. It looked as though his suspicions were aroused. In the car behind me I heard a click, as the safety catch of a Tommy gun slid back. Someone had decided not to take any chances.

Then, just as I had made my mind up that there was going to be trouble, the sentry pointed at our headlights. 'You ought to get those dimmed,' he said, saluting sloppily, opened the gate and stood aside to let us pass. Screeching loudly, we drove on towards Benghazi.

Soon we were on the outskirts of the town.

Coming towards us were the headlights of another car. It passed us. Then, looking back over our shoulders, we saw that it had stopped and turned back after us. This looked suspicious. David slowed down to let it pass. The car slowed down too. He accelerated; the car accelerated. Then he decided to shake it off. He put his foot down on the accelerator, and, screeching louder than ever, we drove into Benghazi at a good eighty miles an hour with the other car after us.

Once in the town, we turned the first corner we came to and, switching off our headlights, stopped to listen. The other car shot past and went roaring off into the darkness. For the moment our immediate troubles were over.

But only for a moment. As we sat listening a rocket sailed up into the sky, then another, then another. Then all the air-raid sirens in Benghazi started to wail. We had arranged with the RAF before we started that they should leave Benghazi alone that night; so this could not be an air-raid warning. It looked very much as though the alert was being given in our honour . . .

Clearly the battle wagon, with its distinctive screech, was no longer an asset now that the alarm had been given. We decided to get rid of it at once and take a chance escaping on foot. Planting a detonator timed to go off in thirty minutes amongst the explosives in the back, we started off in single file through the darkness.

We were in the Arab quarter of town, which had suffered most heavily from the RAF raids. Every other house was in ruins and, threading our way over the rubble through one bombed-out building after another, we had soon put several blocks between ourselves and the place where we had left the car to explode. Once or twice we stopped to listen. We could hear people walking along the adjacent streets, but no one seemed to be following us.

Then, passing through a breach in a wall, we emerged unexpectedly in a narrow side street, to find ourselves face to face with an Italian Carabiniere.

There was no avoiding him and it seemed better to take the initiative and accost him before he accosted us. The rockets and sirens provided a ready-made subject for conversation. 'What,' I asked, 'is all this noise about?' 'Oh, just another of those damned English air raids,' he said gloomily. 'Might it be,' I inquired anxiously, 'that enemy ground forces are raiding the town and that they are the cause of the alert?' 'No,' he said, 'there's no need to be nervous about that, not with the English almost back on the Egyptian frontier.'

I thanked him for his reassuring remarks and wished him good night. Although we had been standing under a street light, he did not seem to have noticed that I was in British uniform.

This encounter put a different complexion on the situation. We seemed to have been unduly pessimistic. We might have a go at the harbour yet. And save ourselves a long walk back to the Jebel.

We hurried back to the car. Our watches showed that about twenty-five minutes had elapsed since we had set off the time pencil. If it was an accurate one, there should still be five minutes to go before it detonated and blew up the car . . . Nervously, we extricated it from the back of the car and threw it over the nearest wall. A minute or two later we heard it go off with a sharp crack. We had not been a moment too soon.

The next thing was to make our way to the harbour, which was about a mile off. The screech made it inadvisable to take the car. Accordingly we left Randolph and Corporal Rose to find somewhere to hide it, while David, Corporal Cooper and myself, with Alston as guide, started off for the harbour, armed with Tommy guns and carrying one of the boats and a selection of explosives in a kitbag. Soon we had left the dark alleyways of the Arab quarter behind us and were in the European part of the town. High white buildings loomed up round us, and our footsteps echoed noisily in the broad paved streets. Then, just as we were coming to the barbed-wire fence which surrounded the harbour, I caught sight of a sentry.

Laden as we were, we made a suspicious-looking party, and once again I thought it better to try to set his suspicions at rest by accosting him, rather than attempting to slink on unnoticed. 'We have,' I said, thinking quickly, 'just met with a motor accident. All this is our luggage. Can you direct us to a hotel where we can spend the night?'

The sentry listened politely. Then he said he was afraid that all the hotels had been put out of action by the accursed English bombing, but perhaps, if we went on trying, we would find somewhere to sleep. He seemed well disposed and was an apparently unobservant man. We wished him good night and trudged off.

As soon as we were out of sight, we started to look for a place to get through the wire. Eventually we found one and dragged the boat and explosives through it. Then, dodging between cranes and railway trucks, we made our way down to the water's edge. Looking round at the dim outlines of the jetties and buildings, I realized with a momentary feeling of satisfaction that we were on the identical strip of shingle which we had picked on as a likely starting point on the wooden model at Alexandria. So far, so good.

David, who possesses the gift of moving slowly and invisibly by night, now set off on a tour of the harbour with Alston, leaving Cooper and myself to inflate the boat. Crouching under a low sea wall, we unpacked the kitbag and set to work with the bellows. There was no moon, but brilliant starlight. The smooth, shining surface of the harbour was like a sheet of quicksilver, and the black hulls of the ships seemed no more than a stone's throw away. They would make good targets, if only we could reach them unobserved. At any rate, we should not have far to paddle, though I could have wished for a better background than this smooth expanse of water. Diligently we plugged away at the bellows, which squeaked louder than I liked, and seemed to be making little or no impression on the boat. Several minutes passed. The boat was still as flat as a pancake. We verified the connection and went on pumping.

Then suddenly we were hailed from one of the ships. It was a sentry. *'Chi va la?'* he challenged. *'Militari!'* I shouted back. There was a pause and we resumed pumping. But still the sentry was suspicious. 'What are you up to over there?' he inquired. 'Nothing to do with you,' I answered, with a show of assurance which I was far from feeling. After that there was silence.

Meanwhile, the boat remained flat. There could only be one explanation: somehow, since we had inspected it in the wadi that morning, it had got punctured. There was nothing for it but to go and fetch another. It was fortunate we had two. Hiding the first boat as best we could under the shadow of the wall, we crossed the docks, slipping unseen through the hole in the wire, and walked back through the silent streets to where we had left the car. There we found Randolph and Rose in fine fettle, trying with the utmost unconcern to maneuver the car through a hole in the wall of a bombed-out house. Occasionally passers-by, Arabs for the most part, gaped at them with undisguised interest and admiration.

Wishing them luck, we pulled the second boat out of the car and started back to the harbour. Once again we got safely through the wire and down to the water's edge, but only to find that the second boat, like the first, was uninflatable. It was heart-rending. Meanwhile, there was no sign of David. We decided to go and look for him.

As we reached the hole in the wire we saw, to our disgust, someone standing on the other side of it. I was just thinking what to say in Italian, when the unknown figure spoke to me in English. It was David, who had been down to the water to look for us and had been as alarmed at not finding us as we had been at not finding him.

There followed a hurried council of war. All this tramping backwards and forwards had taken time and our watches showed that we had only another half-hour's darkness. Already the sky was beginning to lighten. We debated whether or not to plant our explosives haphazardly in the railway trucks with which the quays were crowded, but decided that, as targets, they were not important enough to justify us in betraying our presence in the harbour and thus prejudicing the success of an eventual large-scale raid. If we were to blow them up, the alarm would be given. We should probably be able to get away in the confusion, but another time we should stand a much poorer chance of raiding the harbour unnoticed. Our present expedition must thus be regarded as reconnaissance.

27

Stirling's disappointed party were not out of the harbour yet, though. After an altercation with a Somali sentry, the SAS team collected their equipment and were making for the hole in the perimeter wire when two Italian sentries fell in behind them. Realizing that massive bluffing was now the only option, Maclean led the party to the main gate, where with 'as pompous a manner as my ten days' beard and shabby appearance allowed,' he demanded to speak to the guard commander. A sleepy sergeant, pulling on his trousers, appeared. Maclean upbraided the sergeant for not keeping a proper guard. What if he had been leading a band of British saboteurs? Maclean demanded. The guard commander tittered at such an improbability.

With a final warning to the sergeant to improve his security, Maclean dismissed him and they briskly walked out through the main gate. After lying up in a deserted house for the day, Stirling gave the order to leave Benghazi and rendezvous with the LRDG.

On the way out of Benghazi a notion to bomb two motor torpedo boats had to be abandoned due to the watchfulness of enemy guards. All that could be said for the Benghazi raid was that it provided useful reconnaissance and taught the SAS a valuable lesson in the virtue of bluffing. In the words of Corporal Johnny Cooper: 'If you think of something the enemy would consider an impossible stupidity, and carry it out with determination, you can get away with it by sheer blatant cheek.'

Otherwise, the ill star over the Benghazi mission continued to dog us. On reaching their own lines, Stirling struck a truck on the road to Cairo and rolled the 'Blitz Buggy'. Arthur Merton, the *Daily Telegraph* journalist who had hitched a ride, was killed, Maclean suffered a fractured skull and was *hors de combat* for three months, Rose broke an arm, and Churchill damaged his spine so severely that he had to be invalided to Britain. Stirling himself escaped with a broken wrist, which prevented him from getting behind the wheel for a time. As many muttered silently, this was no bad thing, as Stirling's driving was atrocious.

Stirling had little time to nurse his injury, even if he had wanted to. Aside from the constant struggle with Middle East Headquarters to preserve, let alone expand, L Detachment, Stirling threw himself into the planning of another raid – one which tested the soundness of his strategic vision. This raid was intended to assist in the battle of Malta. Perched in the middle of the Mediterranean, British-controlled Malta posed a mortal threat to Rommel's line of supply back to Italy. Consequently, the Axis was trying to bomb and blockade the island into submission. Announcing that the loss of Malta would be 'a disaster of the first magnitude to the British Empire, and probably fatal in the long run to the defence of the Nile Valley,' Churchill decreed that two supply convoys must get through in the June dark-phase. Since these convoys would almost certainly be attacked by Axis aircraft operating from Cyrenaica and Crete, Stirling proposed that L Detachment would mount a synchronized attack on Axis aerodromes in these locations on 13 and 14 June. Fortunately for L Detachment, its ranks had been modestly enlarged by the annexation of the Special Interrogation Group. This had been formed by Captain Buck and consisted of German-speaking Jews and a couple of Afrika Korps deserters, all of whom were prepared to masquerade in German uniform, knowing all too well their fate if caught.

The various L Detachment teams who were to carry out the raids in North Africa gathered at Siwa, before being escorted to within striking distance of their targets by the LRDG. Stirling, accompanied by his familiars, Cooper and Seekings, headed for Benina aerodrome. For once, Stirling had good hunting. Johnny Cooper later wrote:

We were about a thousand feet above the airfield and were able to look down on the coastal plain towards Benghazi. We lay up during the day in a patch of scrub and bushes, making our plans and checking compass bearings for the night approach. David told us that he had laid on an RAF raid on Benghazi that night to act as a diversion, and that this would determine the time of our attack. At last light the three of us, with David in the lead, started to descend the escarpment. This was quite difficult as our way was criss-crossed by numerous small wadis. Slithering and stumbling over the rocks, grabbing hold where we could in order not to break our necks or legs, we managed to complete this section before total darkness fell. We got on to the airfield without difficulty and simply walked out into the middle. Dead on time, the RAF arrived over the town and started their bombing runs, while we sat there in the dark. As we were a long way from the main buildings we were able to talk quite freely about all sorts of subjects. David gave us a long lecture on deer stalking, including methods of getting into position to stalk, the problems of wind and the necessity for camouflage and stealthy movement. Absorbed in his Highland exploits we could forget the job in hand and time passed very quickly.

Glancing at his watch, David brought the lecture to a close. 'Right,' he said, 'squeeze the time pencils. We're ready to go.' We each had twenty bombs and the whole operation only took a few minutes. We crept forward for about five hundred yards when we found ourselves in the middle of a dug-in dump of aviation fuel which was about six feet deep and extended over quite a large area. We left two bombs there so that we would have illumination later, then moved on. Reg suddenly grabbed David by the arm. We all heard the heavy tread of a sentry on the tarmacadam perimeter track between the hangars and the office block. He was ambling along quite nonchalantly and his hobnailed boots gave us plenty of warning. We crouched down and waited until he had passed the hangars and then crept up to the closed doors. Reg and I managed to prise them open rather noisily, but no alarm was given. Leaving Reg outside with his Tommy gun, David and I went inside. As our eyes grew accustomed to the darkness we saw that the hangar was full of German aircraft. Motioning me to go to the right, David set off to the left, and we busily placed our bombs on the Stukas and Messerschmitts that were in there for repair.

I came across a Me110, a large twin-engined fighter-bomber, and had to stand on tiptoe to try to place my bomb on the wing. But David, who was so much taller than I, stole up from behind. 'All right, Cooper, this one's mine. You go into the far corner and fix that JU52.' I reluctantly withdrew my bomb and went over to do justice to the Junkers. We then continued to the second hangar and dealt with more aircraft while Reg discovered a mass of spare aero engines and highly technical-looking equipment. All this accounted for our full stock of sixty bombs. As each weighed nearly two pounds, fifteen were all that could be carried easily, in addition to personal weapons and other kit. Further down the track between the hangars we came across a small guard house and we observed that occasionally the door opened as the sentries were changed. David said that he would give them something to remember us by, and with Reg and myself covering him, he kicked open the door. We saw that the room was crowded with Germans, many of whom were asleep. David calmly bowled a grenade along the floor, saying 'Share this among you.' He slammed the door and jumped clear. The delay was only four seconds and the explosion shattered the guard house while we rapidly made our escape behind the hangars. We never knew what casualties we had caused, but they must have been considerable in such a confined space.

While still behind the last hangar we heard our first bomb go off, to be followed in rapid succession by all the rest. Although all the time pencils had been activated at the same time, there was always a slight difference due to differing

31

acid strengths. Almost deafened by the noise, we struggled through a gap in the wire, crossed the main road and scrambled up the escarpment.

Climbing up the escarpment on the edge of the Jebel, Stirling called a halt; he was suffering one of his frequent migraine attacks. Eventually Cooper and Seekings led Stirling, staggering and half blind, into a concealed position in the scrub, where they watched 'the fantastic fireworks display'. Cooper thought it difficult to believe that such destruction could be wrought by just three men and the contents of their knapsacks.

At the rendezvous, Stirling fortified himself with rum in his tea. He was elated that he had finally emulated Paddy Mayne. Two days later, Mayne himself arrived at the rendezvous; for once Mars had not smiled on the Ulsterman, and his attack on Berka Satellite field had failed to destroy a single aircraft. Mayne's pride took another buffeting with the news that Lieutenant Zirnheld and a team of French SAS had knocked out eleven aircraft at Berka Main aerodrome. Unable to resist pouring salt into the wound of Mayne's cut ego, Stirling foolhardily proposed driving back to Benina to view the damage, and perhaps do some drive-along shootings at the same time. Jollying along the coastal road in a Chevrolet truck borrowed from the LRDG, they came across a road block. Although they talked their way through the road-block, thanks to Karl Kahane, one of Buck's SIG who was aboard, the suspicious Italian sentries raised the alarm. Further along the road, the SAS men were intercepted by Italian troops waving rifles. Mayne put his foot down, and Seekings dispersed the enemy with a burst of Vickers fire. Then, after placing bombs on enemy trucks at a roadside filling station, Stirling decided to high-tail it back to the rendezvous with the LRDG by cutting across the coastal plain. Nearing the top of the escarpment, Bob Lilley yelled for everyone to jump out. He had smelled burning and realized that one of the time pencils in the bombs had activated. Mere seconds after they scrambled out, the truck blew up. Bruised and subdued, they set off for the rendezvous on foot, Stirling wondering how he was going to explain the loss of the Chevrolet to the LRDG.

The other SAS raids had met with mixed fortune. Although one French SAS group had succeeded in destroying the ammunition dumps at Barce, the party sent to attack Derna had been betrayed by one of Captain Buck's Afrika Korps prisoners and almost all the party were captured. The SAS raid on the Cretan airfields was in the charge of George Jellicoe and Captain Georges Bergé. Jellicoe takes up the story.

About three weeks before the German offensive which led to the disorderly retreat to Alamein, I was evacuated to the CCS at Tobruk and from there to the General Hospital Alexandria. We had a really beautiful nurse who was only 24 years old, she nearly became the Duchess of Wellington, but she married really well. Then David Stirling asked me to join him. I went to Beirut on sick leave and got malaria. Then I got sent to an Australian Hospital with male nurses, no beautiful nurses. I don't think I've ever got out of a hospital quicker. I then joined L Detachment of the SAS.

Stirling required me as his 2ic, to try to get the organization and administration better. Also I spoke French, and Stirling had just got a French detachment of Free French under a marvellous commander, Georges Bergé. Very soon I found myself on operations. Much more fun than administration.

My first op with Stirling was June 1942 on German airfields on Crete and North Africa. There were about five attacks on airfields in North Africa in which the French were involved as well as the rest of the SAS. These were to coincide with the passage of two convoys to Malta, which was extremely hard pressed. One convoy from the east and one from the west. David asked me to go with Georges Bergé

33

and three of his men, and a Greek officer, to attack one of the airfields on Crete at Heraklion.

We took passage in a Greek submarine, the *Triton*, a bit long in the tooth. I wouldn't recommend a voyage in an old French-built Greek submarine. The submarine surfaced at night, we had two rubber boats and paddled in. There was no one on the beach. After landing, two of us swam out with the rubber boats, filled them with shingle and deflated them so they sank and there was no trace of them. Then we had aimed to get into position from where we could observe the airfield that night, but we were further away than we planned because of the wind, which had resulted in our being launched from the submarine further out than expected. The going was very rough and we had far more equipment than we could carry. So we disembarrassed ourselves of some of it. We lay up that day, but not where we could see the airfield. We tried to get in that night, but not having observed it before, we ran into a German patrol, who fired on us. So surprise was lost. So we moved to a position from which we could observe the airfield properly. We did this the next day, and moved to a place where we thought we could get through. The wire round this airfield was pretty deep, about twenty feet. As we were cutting our way through, we were challenged by a German patrol. I didn't know what to do. If we had fired all surprise would have been lost. But the French Sergeant was inspired. He lay on his back and started to snore. The patrol moved on. We later learned from a captured document that they had taken us for drunken Cretan peasants. Then two Blenheims [bombers] came over to bomb the airfield. It had been arranged that they would bomb it if we hadn't got on to it the first night. That also helped us, and in the resulting confusion, we cut ourselves through and placed our charges. We destroyed a Feisler Storch and about 23 JU 88s. We marched out in what we thought was good German formation. We had the pleasure of hearing the explosions going up as we moved off.

It was less pleasant in the morning when we were lying up not having navigated very well. We were quickly discovered by Cretans, who told us that about 80 hostages had been shot as a reprisal, including the Greek governor of Crete. We later learned that when Paddy Leigh Fermor captured the German General Kreipe in Crete he was at pains to leave messages that this had been carried out by the British. We had a long walk back across the island. It took us three nights. That went fine. We kept ourselves to ourselves. We crossed the Masara Plain east of Tymbaki. As usual a Cretan found us. Georges Bergé was suspicious of him. But our Greek guide said he was okay. Shortly after that Georges asked me to go off with Petrakis our guide to meet the agent where we would re-embark. So I went off with Petrakis and made the contact. Petrakis's feet had given out, so I returned alone by night to the valley where I thought I had left my French friends and could not find them. After a great deal of searching and by daylight I found the right place. I was immediately suspicious, because some of their belongings were neatly laid out. I thought this is not how my French friends behave, there is something wrong. At that moment three boys ran up shouting, and I gathered something had gone wrong. What had happened was that by sheer misfortune we had met one of the few quislings in Crete. He had sent one of his boys running into Timbaki to tell the Germans that there were British troops there.

As Bergé was getting ready to move, he found himself surrounded by two companies of Germans. They tried to shoot their way out. One Frenchman was killed, one wounded and Bergé decided to surrender. Georges finished up in Colditz with David Stirling. Georges Bergé was a great loss. I was evacuated three nights later, and joined up with two

35

other parties, SBS. They had not been so lucky. One airfield, Timbaki, had no aircraft on it, one by Maleme was so heavily defended that they couldn't get on to it. We were taken off from the south coast by boat commanded by a marvellous man called John Campbell RNVR. As we went out in a rubber boat, another boat came in and we were hailed, and a voice said, 'I am Paddy Leigh Fermor, who are you?' I shouted back, 'I am George Jellicoe. Good luck to you.' That's the first time I have ever met him. We got back to Mersa Matruh one day before the Germans took Mersa Matruh [28 June 1942].

Following the June raids on the airfields, the SAS underwent a change in its raiding style. Essentially, the SAS's modus operandi had been – despite its insistence on parachute training – to hitch a ride on moonless nights with the LRDG and attack airfields, before scuttling back to base. With Rommel's dramatic offensive during May and June 1942, which rolled up the 8th Army to the outskirts of El Alamein, a new and tempting target presented itself: the Afrika Korps' communication lines, which were at their all-time longest. In order to wreak as much havoc as possible on these over-extended lines of communication as well as the old target of airfields, Stirling determined that the whole of the SAS – some 100 men – should set up a temporary base in the forward area, from which they could raid when they wished, nightly if possible. It followed that the SAS needed its own transport. Employing his customary silver tongue and light fingers, Stirling secured twenty three-ton Ford trucks and fifteen American 'Willy's Bantams', as jeeps were initially known. Stirling had each of them fitted with a pair of Vickers K guns, fore and aft, the suspension was strengthened and an extra fuel tank added. He also secured the services of a very human attribute, Corporal Mike Sadler, the LRDG's master navigator. Sadler's old unit would provide an escort to the forward base, as well as wireless communications.

On 3 July an SAS convoy of thirty-five vehicles left Kabrit, and days later slipped unnoticed through the German lines to rendezvous with Lieutenant Timpson of the LRDG north of Qattara. Timpson penned a memorable portrait of his meeting with the SAS band:

In the afternoon a great cloud of dust could be seen approaching from the east. The country here is full of escarpments and clefts, and one could see the dust and hear the sound of vehicles long before they hove [sic] into view. Robin [Gurdon, LRDG] was in the lead with his patrol. We directed them to a hideout next to our own. Then came truck after truck of SAS, first swarms of jeeps, then three-tonners, and David in his famous staff car, known as his 'blitz-wagon', Corporal Cooper, his inseparable gunner, beside him and Corporal Seekings behind. Mayne, Fraser, Jellicoe, Mather and Scratchley were all there; Rawnsley was wearing a virgin-blue veil and azure pyjamas. Here was the counterpart of Glubb's Arab Legion in the west. Trucks raced to and fro churning up the powdery ground, until most of them came to roost after a while in a hollow half a mile away which we had recommended to them. As aircraft had been flying about we did not quite approve of this crowded activity, yet they had gone through the Alamein Line undetected – an ME 110 which now flew over took no notice – and the reckless cheerfulness of our companions was at least stimulating.

Having to rely chiefly on LRDG wireless communications – and on our navigators – David kept our operators busy sending and receiving messages for the whole party. We had a conference that evening and again the next morning, in which he revealed his plans and gave his orders.

Stirling's plan was for six raids to take place on the next night, which would support the 8th Army's counter-offensive. Two patrols would head for Sidi Barrani and El Daba, while four patrols would attack airfields in the Bagush-Fuka area.

The Bagush raid, led by Stirling and Mayne, was conspicuously successful and led to the birth of a new attacking technique. After planting charges on forty aircraft, Mayne was furious when only twenty-two explosions lit up the skyline. The dissatisfaction was caused by damp primers. Waiting nearby at a roadside ambush, Stirling hit upon a solution to the failed cull. They would all drive on to the airfield in their vehicles – a truck, the Blitz Buggy and a jeep – and shoot up the remaining aircraft with the Vickers machine guns. As with Stirling's best ideas, it combined speed, audacity and simplicity in equal measure. Five minutes later, a further twelve aircraft were destroyed. The only SAS casualty was the Blitz Buggy, destroyed by an Italian CR42 aircraft when the party was on its way back to the rendezvous.

Impressed by the reliability and manoeuvrability of the jeeps, Stirling wired the deputy director of operations from his desert base on 10 July:

Experience in present operations shows potentialities of twin-mounted Bantams at night to be so tremendous to justify immediate allocation of minimum fifty Bantams to L, repeat L, Detachment for modification to be effected immediately on my return. Fear owing to miscarriage of plan, only forty aircraft and some transport destroyed to date.

The 'miscarriage' Stirling referred to was the almost across-the-board failure of the other parties, frustrated by poor maps, imperfect intelligence and heightened perimeter security at Luftwaffe airfields. Nevertheless, forty aircraft was, Stirling's modesty notwithstanding, a decent 'bag', and took the SAS's total so far to 180 enemy aircraft destroyed. Perhaps the greatest proof of Stirling's successes by mid-1942 was that the Germans garlanded him with the accolade 'the Phantom Major'; he even became an item in Rommel's diaries, where Stirling's exploits were noted as having 'caused considerable havoc and seriously disquieted the Italians.'

Stirling's new method of drive-by shootings would also seriously disquiet the Germans. Amassing no less than eighteen jeeps, Stirling set off for Landing Ground 126 at Sidi Haneish, with Sadler's navigation getting them all to within a mile of the target in the moonlight of the evening of 26 July. Sergeant Johnny Cooper recalled:

I walked quietly over to the two column commanders and gave them David's orders, which were to form into their lines as we moved off. The engines roared and we drove on to the perfect surface of the airfield. David took a line straight down the runway with aircraft parked on either side. The blasting began.

It was not long before the whole aerodrome was ablaze. The ground defences had obviously been alerted but they had difficulty as they were using the low-firing Breda, an Italian 15mm machine gun. With the obstruction of so many parked aircraft they were only able to fire at us in fleeting bursts. At the top end of the runway we turned left and right in a complete wheel and came back down again on another track, still firing. We were almost back at the edge of the field when our jeep came to a shuddering halt. David shouted, 'What the hell's wrong?' I leapt out and threw open the bonnet, only to discover that a 15mm shell had gone through the cylinder head and had then passed only inches away from David's knee in the driving position. As if by magic, Captain Sandy Scratchley's jeep came alongside and he shouted, 'Come along, we'll give you a lift.' I jumped into the back, where Sandy's rear gunner was slumped with a bullet through the head. I eased him out of the way and grabbed the machine gun as David piled into the front beside the forward gunner. We roared off the airfield in pursuit of the two columns that were rapidly disappearing in the smoke haze caused by the havoc we had unleashed. The scene of devastation was fantastic. Aircraft exploded all around us, and as we left the perimeter our own jeep went up in a ball of flame – the only vehicle casualty of the raid.

Flushed with success, Stirling planned another mass jeep operation, but his entire command was instead ordered back to Kabrit. Middle East Headquarters had determined that Stirling should be brought under tighter control. There was a new broom at the head of the 8th Army, Bernard Montgomery, and his maxim was 'No more maneuver – fight a battle.' The sort of battle Montgomery had in mind was a battle of attrition, and the entire Allied effort in North Africa was to be subordinated to it. Stirling's part in Montgomery's scheme was to interfere with Rommel's supply depots and harbour facilities at Benghazi and Tobruk. More precisely, Stirling was to attack Benghazi harbour with forty lorries, forty jeeps and 220 men, while Lieutenant Colonel Haselden was to lead a combined SAS and Royal Marines force against Tobruk. Meanwhile, Jalo was to be taken for use as a future forward base for SAS operations.

Stirling loudly objected to his part in the operation. 'The whole plan,' he later wrote, 'sinned against every principle on which the SAS was founded.' The force was too large and unwieldy to achieve the necessary element of surprise; besides, many of the men involved had no special SAS training. But Stirling allowed himself to be 'bribed' into participation in the Benghazi attack, after Middle East Headquarters promised him that his reward would be an enlarged command afterwards.

The Benghazi raid proved to be the disaster Stirling feared. The approach in early September was across the Great Sand Sea. Fitzroy Maclean, now recovered from his injuries, was in the advance party, and described the frustrations of travelling across an expanse of deep, soft sand the size of Ireland:

Our crossing of the Sand Sea was something of an ordeal. With increasing frequency the leading truck would suddenly plunge and flounder and then come to an ominous standstill, sinking up to its axles in the soft white sand. Once you were stuck it was no good racing the engine. The wheels only spun round aimlessly and buried themselves deeper than ever. There was nothing for it but to dig yourself out with a spade and then, with the help of sand mats – long strips of canvas with wooden stiffening – back precariously on to the firm ground you had so unwisely left. Then the whole convoy would wait while someone went cautiously on ahead to prospect for a safe way out of our difficulties.

Or else we would find our way barred by a sand dune, or succession of sand dunes. These were best negotiated by rush tactics. If you could only keep moving you were less likely to stick. The jeeps, making full use of their extra range of gears, would lead the way, with the three-tonners thundering along after them like stampeding elephants. Very rarely we all got through safely. Generally someone hesitated halfway up and immediately went in up to the running-boards in sand. Then out came the spades, sand mats and towing ropes, and the whole dreary business of 'un-sticking' would start again.

But too much dash had its penalties. Many of the sand dunes fell away sharply on the far side, and if you arrived at the top at full speed you were likely to plunge headlong over the precipice on the far side before you could stop yourself, and end up with your truck upside down on top of you forty or fifty feet below.

The tracks we left gave a vivid picture of our progress. Sometimes, when the going was good, they ran straight and even like railway lines; at others, when things were going less well, they wavered and branched off; where disaster had overtaken us, they ended in a confused tangle of footprints, tire-marks and holes in the sand.

41

But ours were not the only tracks which scarred the face of the desert and, fortunately, from the air fresh tracks are not easily distinguishable from old ones. Otherwise it would not have been difficult for enemy aircraft to track us down from the air. Even so, a party as large as ours, trundling across the open desert in broad daylight and throwing up a great cloud of dust, could not hope to be as unobtrusive as a single patrol, and we knew that, once spotted, we should offer a splendid target. Above all, it was important that we should not attract the attention of the Italian garrison while passing Jalo, for they were known to be in wireless touch with Benghazi, and a message from them at this stage of the proceedings announcing our approach would have deprived us of any hope of success.

Accordingly we timed our journey so as to pass the Jalo gap at midday, when the heat haze made visibility poor. When the navigators reckoned we were abreast of the oasis, we halted and I climbed to the top of a little conical hill to have a look round. There was nothing to be seen except a few depressed-looking camels chewing at the almost non-existent scrub, and westwards on the horizon, some black specks, jumping up and down in the haze, which, by a stretch of imagination, might have been the palm trees of Jalo. On the top of my hill I found a chianti flask. I wished that it had been full. Then we had a hurried meal of tinned salmon and biscuits, washed down with half a mug of tepid water, and hurried on.

Now that we were nearing the coast, where we were more likely to encounter patrolling aircraft, we only moved by night, lying up by day and camouflaging the trucks. Once again we picked our way cautiously across the Trigh-el-Abd, keeping a sharp look out for thermos bombs.

But not sharp enough. As we were halfway across, I heard an explosion immediately behind me, and looking round, saw that the three-tonner which had been following in my tracks had had a wheel blown off by a thermos bomb, which my own jeep had gone over but had been too light to explode. Fortunately the height of the three-tonner from the ground had protected the occupants and no one was hurt. The three-tonner's load was distributed among the other trucks and we continued on our way.

Two or three days later we reached the welcome cover of the Gebel. So far as we could tell, our convoy had completed its journey across 800 miles of open desert, to a destination 600 miles behind the enemy's front line, without being spotted either from the air or from the ground. This was encouraging.

On the Jebel, Mayne and Maclean got in touch with Bob Melot, a Belgian cotton merchant who operated as a behind-the-lines spy for the British. Melot was not encouraging; the enemy had reinforced the Benghazi garrison and the date of the impending SAS attack, 14 September, was known even to the local bazaar. However, Middle East Headquarters was firm that the attack should proceed as planned. The attack went ahead – and turned into a military shambles. By the time the main SAS party was approaching Benghazi, the cover raid by the RAF was almost over. James Sherwood of the Special Boat Section, who had been seconded to the SAS for the raid, recalled:

We had a guide with us, some Arab who was supposed to know the way. He didn't know where he was, neither did anyone else. We went down the escarpment with headlights full on – Stirling hoped to bluff his way, that nobody would be stupid enough to come down with their headlights on.

We came to a proper road. Ahead you could see a striped pole. David Stirling got out and walked up to this pole just to see what was going on. All the headlights beamed away behind him. He was a very brave bloke. He quickly found out that instead of Italians being there, the Germans were waiting for us. They knew all about it. They opened up with everything they'd got. The extraordinary thing was that they scored very few hits. Just as well because, sitting on our explosives, we would have disappeared in a big bang.

We were told to get out of it, every man for himself, in jeep and truck as best we could. There was a great deal of confusion, backing and filling of trucks trying to turn round. Shot and stuff was flying all over the place without anybody being hit in the petrol tanks except one jeep which went up in flames, adding to the already illuminated scene. We headed out of it, having achieved nothing at all. A complete fiasco, the whole operation.

At break of day we were all haring hell-for-leather across this big gravelly plain, trying to get to the Gebel area where there were ravines for concealment before the [enemy] planes got up to look for us. We weren't in time. They got the fighters up, strafing and bombing. I can remember trucks with great clouds of dust driving faster than they'd ever driven in their lives before, all trying to reach cover before the worst happened. None of us were hit. Some of us would bale out of the trucks when we thought a plane was diving on us and run like hell. But the plane wasn't diving on us, it was after another truck which it didn't catch. The driver of our truck would slow up so we could catch him, and we all jumped aboard, and off again. Eventually we gained the shelter of the Gebel, the planes having turned presumably to rearm and come after us again.

The first sight that greeted us when we got to a particularly deep ravine was a group of SAS blokes with a fire going, cooking breakfast as though on a picnic. We didn't stop there. It was a daft place to be. We'd two officers with us, and we went up the ravine as far as we could. For the whole of the day we lay up under camouflage netting. Nothing spotted us. The rest of the force had a fearful dusting about a mile or two west of us which went on all day, machine-gunning and bombing. How many were lost then I don't know; very few at the encounter at the border post, but a lot altogether.

We lay up all day. We'd received a message from Stirling: 'The operation all off. Head for Kufra as best you can.'

Kufra was some 500 miles away.

Malcolm Pleydell was L Detachment's doctor, and he gave a vivid account of the carnage sustained in the Benghazi raid in a letter home:

I started off with a fractured femur, which I had to carry on with on the back of a truck, and I had to keep the injured soldiers well under with morphine. Then I had two men wounded through driving over a thermos bomb – one with extensive second-degree burns over chest, abdomen, arms and legs, and one who died quietly during the night. The other man with the amputation I gave two pints of plasma, and he lived. Not bad, amputating with an officer to help me and the dust blowing. We had to hurry up to catch up with the others, and driving behind the truck it was hell to watch the legs and one stump being flung up in the air and falling back each time the truck hit a bump, so in the end we had to tie the legs down with a rope. And the dust was thrown up and fell all over them so they quickly became yellow, and we had to stop now and then to bathe their faces and let them breathe. Later on I had a case of multiple wounds, though not too bad: one shot through the lung, for which there was little to do: one with a compound fracture of the humerus, radius and ulna, with the arm shattered in two places. I left the arm on. All the bad injuries had two pints of blood plasma and I waited until they were stronger before operating. As a last case I had a retention of urine due to the perineal urethra being shot away. I had to do a supra-pubic cystomy eventually, being unable to find the proximal end of the urethra. It was the devil. I was wondering if I would open the peritoneum or what. Again, I was alone and had two spacer wells, two scalpels and one forceps. With nobody retracting and no retractors it's damned difficult to see what you are doing. I dare not risk any bleeding and I could hardly have reached the bleeding point and tied it off. I did muscle splitting with blunt dissection and got down to the bladder with no bleeding. When I got back to the others I found we had no room for stretcher cases as we had lost a good bit of our transport, so I had to leave them with an Italian orderly who had given himself up. I offered to stay but I knew it wasn't really my job. It was a strange scene that night by the fitful light of the burning trucks, and I tossing a one-piastre piece and the two medical orderlies solemnly calling heads and tails. And so home again. I brought back two major wounded and all the minor cases. One was the chap with a shattered arm and the other with multiple wounds. They both made the long trek home ok. I should have like [sic] to have brought the man with the femur, but there was no room for a stretcher.

Reaching Kufra, a dismayed Stirling found that the raid on Tobruk had also failed. In one of the few after-action reports to have survived the SAS's campaign in North Africa, Lieutenant Tom Langton, formerly of the Irish Guards and No. 8 Commando, wrote about the Tobruk attack:

The intention was to drive into Tobruk in three of the 3-ton lorries disguised as British prisoners-of-war, with a guard made up of the SIG party in German uniform (increased in number by Lt Macdonald, Lt Harrison and myself).

The trucks were to turn along the south side of the harbor

and drive to the wadi near Marsa Umm Es Sclau. Here troops were to de-bus, and divide into two parties. Lt Col Haselden with the SIG, RA detachments, Lt Taylor's section, Lt Sillito's section and Lt Macdonald's section were to take the small house and gun positions on the west side of the bay. The remainder of the squadron, under Major Campbell was to take the positions on the east side. Success signals were to be fired by each party on completion of task, and then Major Campbell's party was to proceed two miles east to find out if there were any guns there and to deal with them. Unless it proved to be extremely simple for Lt Col Haselden's party to push on eastwards and take the AA positions there, they were to hold until the Coy of A & S Highlanders and 1 Platoon RNF were landed from MTBs [Motor Torpedo Boats] in the bay.

I was responsible for 'signalling in' the MTBs and meeting the party when they came ashore. The signalling was to take the form of three 'Ts' flashed every two minutes in red from a point on the west shore of the bay and also from a point just outside the bay to the east.

On the journey up, Major Campbell developed dysentery badly, and, although he insisted on seeing the job through, Lt Col Haselden told me to accompany him as Second-in-Command as far as the first objective. My own plan was to station two of the RE [Royal Engineers] party at the eastern signalling point, with a torch and instructions as to how to signal in case I couldn't get back to them. I was then going back to the small house on the west side (which was to be Col Haselden's HQ) to report and to collect F/O Scott and his two Aldis lamps. I would substitute F/O Scott for the two REs and return myself to signal from the western point. Signalling was not due to start until 0130 hours, so there should have been plenty of time.

The rest of the plan does not affect the remainder of the report.

Entrance

Owing to a slight miscalculation the party was late getting on to the El Adem road and it was dark soon after we had turned on to the main road towards Tobruk. However, the entrance went smoothly and no check posts were encountered. Further delay was caused by the fact that, apparently considerable alterations (wire fences, etc.) had been made where the track along the southern bank of the harbour joined the main road. We were still some way off our debussing point when the bombing started.

After debussing, sorting stores, hiding German uniforms, etc, the two parties set out.

Action

Immediately on leaving the trucks, Major Campbell's party had to negotiate a small minefield. This was done by an RE party with a detector, and caused considerable delay and necessitated the party walking in a long single file. In the middle of this operation a rifle was fired from the other side of the wadi. This caused further delay. Eventually one section was sent forward (under Lt Roberts) to investigate and I asked permission to reconnoitre the sandy beach. I walked right across the beach without encountering anything, and directed Lt Roberts to take his party up on the high ground to get round the back of whoever had fired the rifle. I then went back to Major Campbell and guided one section across the beach, the rest following at intervals. Lt Roberts in the meanwhile engaged and put out of action a section of enemy who were manning a Spandau.

We had taken almost an hour to get across the wadi. The same procedure of advance was adopted up the wadi-side and on. I waited on top to guide Lt Roberts and the REs who were labouring under heavy burdens of explosives, etc., and it took some time to catch up with the rest, who I eventually found had struck eastwards away from the bay. Soon after that I met Lt Duffy who said that all the positions near the bay were empty and unused.

By this time the success signal from Lt Col Haselden's party had been fired.

We proceeded to catch up to Major Campbell and soon afterwards came on a small wireless station which was put out of action with its personnel – mainly by Lt Roberts.

In climbing out of that wadi I discovered it was already 0130 hours. I urged Major Campbell to fire the success signal, which was done. I then returned alone and as fast as I could towards the bay. This journey was made more difficult by the fact that I had to skirt a small enemy camp in a wadi which we had missed on the way out. I found the eastern signalling point and was relieved to see that F/O Scott was signalling from the west side, although he was far too high up. The REs had disappeared by this time, and I presume that they returned to HQ on finding no guns to destroy. I had no watch and only an inadequate torch. I tried to time my signalling with F/O Scott's.

After a short while I saw two MTBs come in. After that, however, no more appeared. My problem now was whether to stay signalling or to go to meet the landing troops and conduct them to HQ as I was supposed to be doing. I decided to try a compromise by wedging my torch in a rock and leaving it alight. I did this and started back but, before I had gone 200 yards I saw a light flashing out to sea and it appeared to be on an MTB proceeding *away* again. I rushed back to the torch and started to signal again. But nothing materialised. After another half hour I left signalling and started back towards the landing point. On the way back I found that my haversack and Tommy gun had been taken from the Sangar, where I had left them before climbing down to the rocks. I later ran into two enemy, one of whom I hit with my revolver.

On reaching the landing point I found the two MTBs unloading. Lt Macdonald appeared to be organizing the landing, so I took one man with me with a Tommy gun and returned at once to continue signalling. During all this time F/O Scott was still signalling from the west side.

By the time we got back to the eastern signalling point the searchlights were sweeping the entrance to the harbour and our own shore. However, I resumed signalling. Heavy fire was coming from the opposite shore of the harbour out to sea. Once the MTBs got caught in the searchlights and I could see their wake, and tracer bouncing off one of them. They were well to the east of us, however, and it was obvious that there wasn't much chance of them getting in. One of the two MTBs slipped out past me during a slight lull, and appeared to get away safely. At 'first light' I decided to abandon signalling and I returned to the landing point. By the time I got there dawn was breaking and I saw one MTB apparently aground. Sounds of rifle and LMG [Light Machine Gun] fire was coming from just over the west ridge of the wadi, near where we had left the trucks. I hailed the MTB, but getting no answer, I walked around the bay and up the small wadi to the house which was Lt Col Haselden's HQ. Rifle fire was coming down the wadi. I got to the house to find it deserted and I saw the heads of about a platoon of enemy lying covering the house from about 300 yards away. I walked back down the small wadi, and thinking I heard a shout aboard the MTB, I boarded her, but found no one. I filled my water bottle and took what food I could find. Lt Russell, Lt Sillito, Pte Hillman and Pte Watler then came aboard. Lt Russell opened up with the twin Lewis guns forward on troops on top of the hill. I went to the engines to see if there was any hope of getting them started, but not even Pte Watler – a mechanic – could help there. We then took all we could in the way of food and water and boarded one of the assault craft lying alongside. We paddled out into the bay but were forced to go ashore by being fired on from the rocks on the west side. We saw some of our own men dodging along the west side of the bay and there were large explosions coming from behind them. It was impossible to tell who they were, but I think they may have been the REs dealing with the guns on the point. We climbed through a minefield and into a wadi. Here we were joined by Sgt Evans. We made for the hills, having to hide frequently from low-flying aircraft. I looked back from the higher ground and saw what I now know to have been *HMS Zulu* with *HMS Sikh* in tow. The latter appeared to be burning and shells were bursting round. We were fired on heavily, going over a ridge, from the direction of *Brighton*, but got safely into a large wadi where we found about 15–20 others waiting. These included 2/Lt Macdonald and Lt Barlow, also those of the RNF who had been landed from the MTBs. We decided it was now useless to resist. No one knew what had become of Major Campbell's party. It seemed clear that Col Haselden had been killed. We decided to take to the hills and make for Wadi Shagra north of Bardia, where we had been told we would be picked up five days later.

Escape

We did not stop long in the big wadi. Lts Sillito and Macdonald took their respective sections. I believe their intention was to make towards the coast further east and try to get taken off by the MTBs the same day. I have not heard of any of them since.

Lt Barlow, Lt Russell and myself went off up the wadi with eight men. We found a small wadi and lay up all that day among the bushes. At dusk we disposed of everything we did not require, divided what food we had into three and

51

ourselves into three parties. We split up and made for the perimeter that night. Later in the night – after avoiding two enemy posts – I joined up again with Lt Barlow's party. Soon after we met, we 'bumped' another enemy post and had to head hurriedly to the nearest wadi. When we regathered Lt Barlow was nowhere to be found, and I have not seen or heard of him since. After 'bumping' several more posts we eventually got through the perimeter wire and lay up the next day in a cave in a wadi.

We had two nights of dodging camps, etc., during part of which we walked on the road. We hid up every day in caves in the wadis. On the fifth night, just as we were desperate for food and water, we found the first Arab village, where we were taken in, fed and given water. Pte Hillman acted as interpreter. The Arabs knew all about the Tobruk raid. They also said they could not understand how the English managed to come all the way from Kufra.

Going from village to village, we eventually reached the wadi Am Reisa. There was a large Carabinieri post at the shore end of this wadi, the strength of which had recently been doubled, according to the Arabs. They also told us of boats cruising up and down at night – they said they thought they were British. One had landed a party one night and someone had shouted 'Any British here?'

The Arabs then showed us to the wadi Kattara about five miles north of Bardia. Here we found an Indian soldier of the 3/18th Garwhal Rifles who had escaped three times from Tobruk and had been living there for two months.

We also found Pte Watler. His story is as follows

On leaving us on the night of the fourteenth, Lt Russell, Pte Watler and one member of the SIG got through the perimeter and walked 'all out' towards Bardia along the road. They arrived at Mersa Shagra one day late. That night they ran into the enemy post in wadi Am Reisa and were fired on. In making their getaway Pte Watler got left behind because of bad boots. Nothing further is known of the other two. The man with Lt Russell spoke only German.

We lived in the wadi Kattara for four weeks, being fed by the Arabs as best they could. We tried making fires by night to attract the attention of aircraft, but only got a stick of bombs extremely close. The only news or information we got was obtained from Italian or German soldiers via the Arabs who sold eggs, etc., on the road and engaged the soldiers in conversation. It was apparent that the enemy was very low in morale and very short of food. We had to take great care not to get caught because the Italians would undoubtedly have 'wiped out' the village. As it was, we saw no one during our four weeks there.

After three weeks, Sgt Evans unfortunately got dysentery and later we had to help him to the road by night and leave him to be picked up the next morning. The same happened a few days later to one of the Leslie twins and his brother went with him. The rains had come heavily and it was very cold and damp. I decided to move. The Indian stayed behind, and so the party consisted of Cpl Wilson, Pte Watler, Pte Hillman and myself. I was lucky to have a German compass and a small German map, though the latter was not much use being 1:5,000,000. We had some tins of bully-beef, some goat meat and bread and ten water-bottles. We started on 26 October.

Apart from getting fired on on the second night, our journey was uneventful. We did not see anyone from the day after we climbed through the frontier wire until we were picked up at Himeimat on Friday 18 November, with the exception of one convoy which looked very like an SAS patrol – near the Siwa-Mersa Matruh track on 5 November. We walked south of the Qattara depression for the last four days and thereby missed the 'retreat'.

The Benghazi and Tobruk raids were the first major failures by the SAS since its maiden outing, a mere ten months before. Stirling arrived at Middle East Headquarters expecting censure but, ironically, found smiling faces and plaudits. He was even promoted to lieutenant colonel, while the SAS was to be expanded into a full regiment – an emphatic acknowledgement that Stirling's style of guerrilla warfare was now an accepted part of the British military effort. (Almost certainly the hand of Winston Churchill was behind the SAS's elevation to regimental status; not only had the Prime Minister received glowing reports of the SAS from Randolph, but he had twice dined with the persuasive, charismatic Stirling in Cairo.) In order to make up the SAS to regimental strength, Stirling went to see Montgomery with a view to recruiting officers and non-commissioned officers from the 8th Army.

Montgomery, never a fan of 'mobs for the jobs', flatly refused. He had a point: Montgomery needed his best men – the same men Stirling wanted – for his offensive beginning in just a fortnight. In the event, Stirling was left to pick the best men he could from the Base Depot, the Palestine–Iraq force, the disbanded 1 Special Service Regiment, the remnants of the Commandos and the Greek Sacred Regiment. For a while a shotgun marriage resulted in the Special Boat Section being part of 1 SAS, but by mutual agreement the SAS and SBS divorced the following year.

While Stirling busied himself with raising and training 1 SAS, he placed the regiment's most seasoned men in a squadron under the command of Paddy Mayne, who was charged with establishing a base in the Great Sand Sea. From there Mayne and his A Squadron were to mount sorties against the coastal railway, with a view to frustrating the retreat of the Afrika Korps following Montgomery's victory at El Alamein. In mid-November, Mayne's A Squadron was joined by B Squadron, and together they attacked not just the railway but the coastal road along a front of several hundred miles. Mayne's merry band of veterans proved conspicuously successful at sabotage, but most of B Squadron's patrols (which suffered both from inexperience and the presence of unfriendly Arabs in the Bir Fascia area) were either killed or captured within days. Among those who escaped the Afrika Korps' net were the veteran Reg Seekings and the newly recruited Wilfred Thesiger, later to earn an illustrious reputation as an explorer. Thesiger's patrol, in the circumstances, did remarkably well:

Our target was the road to the west of Bouerat. We decided to lie up in daytime at El Fascia: there were bushes along the various wadis where we could camouflage our jeeps against air observation, and water in the cistern, but with no evidence that it was being used by others. We should be within striking distance of the road at night but far enough from it, we hoped, not to be stumbled on inadvertently.

Stirling was determined to have another go at the Germans before he went back to Egypt, so he and his driver, Sergeant Cooper, went with us on our first raid. We left the two signallers and their jeep at El Fascia and set off as it grew dark, separating when we reached the road, Stirling to shoot up a camp, while Alston and I waited for a convoy.

Shortly afterwards, with Alston driving, we saw the lights of a large convoy coming from the direction of Agheila. We waited until it was close, when I enfiladed it with a pair of our machine guns, emptying both drums into it. We then drove off down the road, blew up some telegraph poles, cut the wires and laid some mines.

Further on we came to a large tented camp where cars were driving about with their lights on. We switched on our own lights and motored into the camp, raked a line of tents and drove out on the far side. Again, no one fired at us, but almost as soon as we left the camp, one of our tires went flat. We stopped and tried to get the wheel off, but the nuts would not move. We hammered away, unable to make any impression on the nuts and very conscious of the proximity of the camp we had just shot up. Eventually we drove back to El Fascia on a flat tire. In the morning Cooper pointed out that we had been tightening instead of undoing the nuts. I had never changed a wheel before.

As it got dark Stirling set off with Cooper on his long journey back to Egypt, and Alston and I went back to the road, again leaving our signals' jeep at El Fascia.

Each night we found more parked vehicles and more tents, but now less and less traffic on the road. On one occasion I saw a large tanker driving towards us, and at the same moment a Staff car coming from the opposite direction. I decided to take the tanker; as it blew up the Staff car skidded to a halt and its occupants scrambled for cover. During these nights we shot up camps over a wide area, including one which turned out later to be a Divisional Headquarters. We would drive into a camp and stop to select a target. We often heard men talking in their tents, and sometimes saw people moving about in the moonlight, but I had a comforting delusion that we were invisible, for we were never challenged or shot at. Once we drove up to a group of tents and found ourselves among a number of tanks; we were evidently in a tank repair workshop. When I tried to open fire on the tents the guns jammed. I changed the drums as quietly as possible, conscious even so of the rattle, but the guns still refused to fire, so we drove into the desert, put them right and found another target. One night we motored up to a canteen with a dozen trucks parked outside the large tent; inside men were talking, laughing and singing. I fired a long burst into the tent, and short bursts into the engines of the trucks as we drove off.

During these operations we must have killed and wounded many people, but as I never saw the casualties we inflicted my feelings remained impersonal. I did, however, begin to feel that our luck could not last much longer. It seemed inevitable that sooner or later a sentry would identify us and fire a burst into our car. Even if he missed Alston and myself the land mines in the car would probably go up.

Several times while lying up at El Fascia, we heard the sound of engines and suspected that patrols were hunting for us.

One morning Alston took the two signallers in our jeep to fetch water. Shortly after he had left I noticed a small reconnaissance plane flying towards the cistern; it circled and went off. A little later I heard the sound of several heavy vehicles coming along the wadi towards me. We had carefully hidden the wireless jeep under a camouflage net among some bushes. I took a blanket, went some distance away into the open, where there was no apparent cover, and lay down in a small hollow, covering myself with the blanket on which I scattered earth and bits of vegetation. Peeping out from under it, I saw two armored cars; I thought I heard others on the far side of the wadi.

The cars nosed about but failed to find the jeep. One of them passed within a couple of hundred yards of where I lay. I heard it stop; my head was under the blanket and I wondered if they had seen me and were about to open fire; then it went on. It seemed ages before they finally drove off. Soon after they had gone I heard several bursts of machine-gun fire. I felt certain they had either killed or captured the others, and that I was now on my own.

Thinking things over under my blanket, I decided the best thing would be to remain at El Fascia and hope the Eighth Army would eventually turn up; there was water in the cistern, food in the wireless jeep and some petrol, but I had no idea how to work the wireless. I felt that the Germans, having searched the place once, would probably not come back another day; meanwhile I stayed under the blanket in case they came back now. I had Doughty's *Arabia Deserta* in my haversack but felt little inclination to read.

Some hours later I spotted Alston moving about cautiously among the bushes and startled him by calling from cover, 'Hello, Gordon. I thought they'd got you.'

'I thought they'd got *you* when I heard the firing. I just hoped they hadn't found the wireless jeep. I came back to look for it. The plane came right over our heads. Luckily our jeep was in some bushes and they didn't spot it. The armored cars never came very close.'

'Well, they came damned close to me!'

Alston went off and fetched the jeep and the other two. Later that afternoon Lieutenant Martin and his driver, both of them Free French, turned up in their jeep. They had been with one of the patrols in B Squadron and had been surprised by the Germans, but had managed to escape. When they got near El Fascia they had again been chased and shot at by armoured cars. This accounted for the firing we had heard.

We now decided that after dark we would move to another wadi some distance from the well, and lie up there to await the arrival of the 8th Army. Our petrol was very low; we had not enough left to go on raiding the road. Martin was also short of petrol and decided to remain with us. In the late evening several armored cars arrived and laagered nearby. They must have heard us when we eventually motored off; it looked as if, having found our tracks, they intended to deny us the cistern, and go on searching for us.

Our new hiding place was in a delightful wadi full of trees and carpeted with green grass and flowers. Some Arabs turned up in the morning. Like all these tribal Arabs, they wore white blankets wrapped round their clothes. They were very friendly and I found their Arabic comparatively easy to understand. We made them tea and later they fetched us a goat and spent the night with us. They hated the Italians, who during the pacification of Libya had treated the inhabitants with incredible brutality. I was confident that as the Germans were helping the Italians these Arabs would not betray us. On Christmas Day, two days after we had left El Fascia, we again heard armored cars; they sounded fairly close but did not enter our wadi. I was certain that they would not be able to follow our tracks over the rocky ground we had crossed to get there.

Stirling had given El Fascia as the rendezvous for B Squadron, and we expected some of the other patrols to arrive shortly in our neighborhood. We had no idea that all the others had actually been killed or captured; but we were aware that our combined raids had brought night traffic more or less to a halt during the critical days of Montgomery's offensive.

Rommel had been very concerned by these SAS raids on his communications. He wrote in his diary, later edited in English by B. H. Liddell Hart:

They succeeded again and again in shooting up supply lorries behind our lines, laying mines, cutting down telegraph poles and similar nefarious activities . . .

On 23 December we set off on a beautiful sunny morning to inspect the country south of our front. First we drove along the Via Balbia and then, with two Italian armored cars as escort, through the fantastically fissured wadi Zem-Zem towards El Fascia. Soon we began to find tracks of British vehicles, probably made by some of Stirling's people who had been round here on the job of harassing our supply lines. The tracks were comparatively new and we kept a sharp look out to see if we could catch a 'Tommy'. Near to El Fascia I suddenly spotted a lone vehicle. We gave chase but found its crew were Italian. Troops from my Kampfstaffel were also in

59

the area. They had surprised some British commandos the day before and captured maps marked with British store dumps and strong points. Now they were combing the district, also hoping to stumble on a 'Tommy'.

When I read this after the war I realized that Rommel himself must have been with the armored cars that I had seen searching for us at El Fascia.

Stirling arrived back from Cairo, and Alston, Martin and I joined him near our hideout, which was still some forty miles behind the German lines.

In what was destined to be the last phase of the SAS's war in the Western Desert, the SAS were charged with four tasks, all of which were intended to aid and abet Montgomery's offensive against Tripoli in January 1943. One party was to operate west of Tripoli to facilitate the 8th Army's advance; another was to reconnoitre the defensive Mareth Line with a view to discovering a way around it; a third operation consisted of raiding the enemy's supply lines between Gabes and Sfax; lastly, Colonel Stirling would lead a patrol as far north as northern Tunisia, where it would cut the Sousse railway line. Stirling also intended to link up with his brother, Bill, who had formed the 2nd SAS Regiment, which was advancing eastwards as part of the 1st Army, following the Torch landings in Algeria in November. The link-up with Bill Stirling had more than fraternal importance: David Stirling intended to build the SAS (which some wags now said stood for 'Stirling and Stirling') up to Brigade strength:

My plan was to bring in my brother Bill's 2nd SAS Regiment, and to divide my own regiment, which had grown beyond the official establishment of a full regiment, into the nucleus of a third one. This would enable me to keep one regiment in each of the three main theatres – the eastern

Mediterranean, the central Mediterranean–Italy, and the future Second Front. I felt it was vital to get intervention and support from a more important formation than Middle East Headquarters. The first step in this plan seemed to be to acquire the sympathy of the 1st Army's top brass, and to consult my brother Bill, who had recently arrived on the 1st Army front, as to the state of the game at the War Office. I was conscious that the reputation of the SAS would be greatly enhanced if it could claim to be the first fighting unit to establish contact between 8th and 1st Armies.

David Stirling set out for northern Tunisia on 10 January. After successfully completing his reconnaissance of the Mareth flank, he sped towards Sousse. Rommel's position was deteriorating, and haste in knocking out his communication lines seemed sensible. Instead of taking the slower, safer route south of Chott Djerid salt marsh, Stirling, with five jeeps and fourteen men, headed for the Gabes gap. Another SAS party, led by the Frenchman Captain Jordan, had already been through the gap. Accordingly, the Germans were on the alert. As Stirling's convoy passed through the gap it was spotted by a Luftwaffe reconnaissance aircraft. The SAS patrol hid in a wadi near the Gabes-Gafsa road.

And it was here that a German paratroop battalion found them. Unaccountably, Stirling failed to post sentries. Cooper and Sadler, kicked awake by a German who then rushed off to get reinforcements, ran up the wadi to warn the rest. Shouting that it was every man for himself, Stirling, along with MacDermott, was trapped in a shallow cave. In the confusion, Cooper, Sadler and Freddie Taxis dived into a shallow depression covered by camel scrub and, by lying inert, marvellously managed to evade capture.

The seizing of Stirling was enough of an event for Field Marshal Rommel to write an entry in his diary:

During January, a number of our AA gunners succeeded in

surprising a British column . . . in Tunisia and captured the commander of the 1st SAS Regiment, Lieut. Col. David Stirling. Insufficiently guarded, he managed to escape and made his way back to some Arabs, to whom he offered a reward if they would get him back to the British lines. But his bid must have been too small, for the Arabs, with their usual eye to business, offered him to us for eleven pounds of tea – a bargain which we soon clinched. Thus the British lost the very able and adaptable commander of the desert group which had caused us more damage than any other British unit of equal strength.

Rommel was being slightly loose in his use of the words 'to us'; it was the Italians who recaptured Stirling, and highly delighted they were at their success compared to the butter-fingered clumsiness of the Germans. Eventually, Stirling was sent to the prisoner-of-war camp for bad boys: Schloss Colditz. For the founder of the SAS, the war was over. Yet his many desires for the SAS would be realized, even that it would be the first unit to link up with the 1st Army. After several adventures, including an encounter with a gang of Arab robbers, Cooper, Sadler and Taxis reached the Free French Legion at Tozeur. The French then handed them over to the Americans – who promptly arrested the trio as spies. Cooper wrote later:

. . . during the late afternoon an American armored patrol arrived to collect us. We must have looked a motley crew; my head was swathed in bandages and all our feet had been similarly treated as we were covered in blisters from our march across the desert. The Americans were most uncivil while trying to handcuff us, and bundled us into an armored car with soldiers guarding us. Without any nourishment whatsoever we were driven through the mountains to Tebessa.

Eventually, after an exchange of signals Cooper, Sadler and Taxis were cleared. 'Cairo,' wrote Cooper, 'had confirmed our names and numbers, and somewhat reluctantly our American captors began to fête us with canned substances of all types. To our chagrin, though, there was only Coca-Cola to drink and no beer!'

Soon afterwards, Mike Sadler was flown back to the 8th Army and asked to retrace his steps, this time as 'honorary guide' to General Freyberg's New Zealand Division as they outflanked the Mareth Line:

> Thus I passed for a second time over the same territory that I had reconnoitred with David, but in far more comfortable conditions. It was good to know that the original journey had not been in vain.

Little, indeed, of the SAS's life under Stirling's leadership had been in vain. As Malcolm Pleydell, the SAS's first doctor, noted in his memoir, *Born in the Desert*, about the Regiment's days in North Africa:

> To those who love statistics, I can only quote the following figures: we destroyed a total of approximately four hundred enemy aircraft in the desert; A Squadron, during the autumn of 1942, demolished the enemy railway line on seven occasions; while between September 1942 and February 1943, forty-seven successful attacks were made against German key positions and communications. Our raids then were more than mere pin-pricks, and there were occasions when we must have diverted enemy forces and upset their road convoy system considerably, while the steady drain on aircraft probably exercised an influence on the desert war.

Paddy Mayne's personal 'kills' were more than twice that of any British or American fighter ace. As a return on investment, which is the only true measure of the worth of a unit, the SAS gave high dividends for a very small outlay.

One important testament to the viability of the SAS was that it survived the removal of its leader. It wasn't a one-man show. Nonetheless, Stirling's capture left both his subordinates and Middle East Headquarters with headaches, because only Stirling knew who was where and for what reason in 1 SAS. When Harry Poat's patrol returned from raiding Tripoli, nobody else in 1 SAS had any idea that they had been sent on the mission. Confusion was only added to by the geographical scattering of the regiment in early 1943, with sections as far flung as Tunisia and Lebanon. In the latter location, detachments of A Squadron had been sent on ski-training courses, a proof in itself that Stirling had been carefully planning a future for the regiment in the European theatre, when it finally opened. Captain Derrick Harrison was among the ski novices at the Cedars of Lebanon ski school:

> After lunch Major Riddell, the chief instructor, offered to take a few of us out and show us around. His eyes glinted keenly from a lean, weather-beaten face as he explained: 'Of course, work does not really start until tomorrow, but if you would like to go out on one of the slopes . . .?'
>
> We had drawn skis and clothing from the store and been shown how to put them on. Now, sweating profusely and slipping and sliding all over the place, we made our way painstakingly up the road to the top of Chapel Hill – a hundred and fifty yards of sheer agony. By the time I reached the top the lesson had started.
>
> 'Now when doing the kick turn,' Major Riddell was saying, 'you kick one ski up, like this.' He demonstrated, digging the back of one of his skis into the snow, tip pointing to the sky.

'We'll take it stage by stage. Now all do just as I have done. Ready? All together. Up!'

I gritted my teeth, steadied myself on my sticks, took a deep breath, then – up! I swung the ski skywards, followed it, describing a far from graceful arc through the air, and a thud was down, snow in my eyes, my ears, everywhere. All around me was a struggling mass of bodies, sticks and skis. We struggled to our feet and started again, practising it again and again until we could do it and still stand up.

'All right now. We'll just have a shot at going down this slope.'

During the next six weeks we were to go down that slope many times, in gentle traverses from side to side. Now Major Riddell pointed his skis straight at the bottom and pushed off. In a flurry of snow he arrived safely in the valley below. Grinning broadly, he called up to us. 'Come along. Nothing to be frightened of.'

Somewhat dubiously we pointed our skis, and pushed off. Immediately the chapel vanished, the trees in the valley vanished. Everything vanished in a mad swirl of white.

Next morning the course started in earnest. We learned to walk and turn. Like pompous penguins we 'herring-boned' up hills. We learned the easy way of traversing up hills, and still lost pints of good honest sweat. Back in the hotel we had to wear greatcoats and mufflers to keep warm. In the mornings we woke to find our wet ski clothes, even our boots, frozen stiff.

With snow all round us we soon began to forget the desert with its heat, dust and flies. And sometimes as we sat in our rooms huddled round the cold radiators we wondered why we were there. The official story was that it was a reward for good work done in the desert, but as the days passed, there came a spate of rumours.

The Germans were pressing hard through the Caucasus

towards the Russian oilfields at Baku. We, so the rumour had it, were to be taken through the Black Sea by submarine and landed behind the German lines, here to carry on our work of harassing their communications. Sweeping down from above the snow-line we were to ambush his troops, blow up his supplies and report on his movements. We could get no confirmation of this, but neither were there any denials. From then on there was an edge to our training.

After two and a half weeks we could climb a hill with moderate ease, and glide down again with a fair measure of confidence. For six and a half days a week we slaved at it, gliding, falling, picking ourselves up again. Cursing and sweating up the hills – an hour to get up and five minutes to come down. There were no cable railways. It was hard, uphill work with an occasional brief but exhilarating dash across the snow into the peace of the valley. For six and a half days, for on Wednesday afternoons we were free. And on Wednesday afternoons, immediately after lunch, in twos and threes we drifted down to the locker rooms. For a while bedlam reigned and the rooms echoed and re-echoed to the sounds of laughter: strong, hearty, good-natured laughter, the chatter of small talk and the shouts of men in high spirits. Gradually silence came again as, still in our twos and threes, we glided away to spend the afternoon on the nursery slopes, or to attempt that run we had noticed the other day but had not been allowed to try. The snow was in our blood.

On the third Wednesday after our arrival I found myself trudging along by Alec Muirhead's side, rucksack on my back and a good deal of foreboding in my heart. Behind and below us lay the water tower that served the school and the village, looking for all the world like a small pebble. To the right, a small dark smudge – the sacred cedars of Lebanon. Immediately behind us our zigzag tracks showed black where they had trapped the only shadows among the vast expanse of white.

Ahead of us the edge of the snow seemed to cut a black line across the sky. It had been aptly named False Crest. From where we stood it seemed we could go no further. It was the edge of the world. For another five minutes we trudged on in silence. At the crest we would rest.

Standing squarely across the slope we removed our skis. Many a man has come to grief by neglecting that precaution; has slipped his foot from the trap, only to see his ski go hurtling away by itself down the slippery mountainside.

'How far now?' I was sweating freely.

'We've come about a thousand. That leaves us something over two thousand feet to go.' Alec looked towards the far ridge. 'A bit windy up there, by the looks of it.'

'Yes, and cold,' I added bitterly, 'with the last five hundred feet sheer ice. And what do we get when we get there?'

'The view, old boy, the view from ten thousand feet.'

Two days later we had to pass the elementary test. The sun shone vividly from an ice-blue sky. Three thousand feet above us, wisps of white cloud trailed across the surrounding peaks. Wearing goggles to protect our eyes from the dangerous glare, we winged our way down Chapel Hill, through the clump of sturdy cedars towards the examination ground. All morning we climbed, executed kick turns, snow-plough turns. We glided, halted, ran along balancing first on one ski then on the other, till we were passed okay. Now I was lined up with about twenty others for the climax of the test – a three-hundred-foot climb followed by a speed descent.

A whistle shrilled and we were off. Some took it the hard way, by direct ascent. Most, like myself, preferred the long easy traverses across the slope. Ten minutes later I was at the top, breathless but happy to know I had done it under time. Only the descent remained. I had studied that run down. I could go at it like a bull at a gate. That did not appeal. The alternative was a wide sweep round the hill, coming in to the finishing line almost at right angles to the course. But it meant steady judgement round the curves.

The whistle shrilled again. The starter's thumb jabbed at his stopwatch. Away we went. Gently, gently. Round the first curve all right. It was too easy. In front someone stumbled. Too late I swerved. I was over. Head first I ploughed into the soft snow, rolling over and over. One ski was wrenched from my foot and I had a brief glimpse of it careering down to the bottom, skimming lightly round the second curve. Sliding, rolling, I followed it at great speed, up the banking of the curve, and over the top.

That evening a short note was posted up to say that those who had failed in either the ascent or descent would be re-examined the following day. I breathed again.

At length, order came to the chaos caused by Stirling's capture; 1 SAS, placed under the command of Major Paddy Mayne, was renamed the Special Raiding Squadron (SRS), while 2 SAS continued to be commanded by Lieutenant Colonel Bill Stirling. Both units functioned independently of each other. Meanwhile, the SBS was unshackled from its marriage to the SAS and rebranded the Special Boat Squadron and placed in care of Major, the Earl, Jellicoe.

Reorganization was all well and good, but what was the British Army to do with the abundance of special forces at its disposal now the war in North Africa was all but over? In truth, there was no place else for the SAS but the Mediterranean. Direct cross-channel attack on Nazi-occupied France was more than a year away, and the Far East campaign had its own special forces in Orde Wingate's 'Chindits'. Accordingly, the SRS and 2 SAS were warned for action in the forthcoming invasion of Sicily.

As a preliminary to the invasion, Major Geoffrey Appleyard of

2 SAS was requested by General Alexander to survey Pantelleria, an Italian-held island midway between Tunisia and Sicily, in May 1943. Accompanying Appleyard on his 'excursion', codenamed *Snapdragon*, was Lieutenant John Cochrane:

Our party consisted of Geoffrey, two sergeants, six men and myself. We left the submarine base, at Malta, in (if I remember correctly) His Majesty's submarine *Unshaken*, under the command of Lieutenant Jack Whitton, RN.

After an uneventful trip we arrived off the coast of Mussolini's secret island fortress and for the next twenty-four hours Apple and Jack made a periscope reconnaissance of the fortifications in order to decide on the best place to make a landing.

At last, after an intensive study of both air photographs and the beach defences, Geoff finally decided on a very high and particularly inaccessible cliff as the best landing place – naturally the success of the operation depended upon taking the enemy by surprise and off their guard, and the harder the climb the greater the surprise.

The raid had a two-fold purpose: to spy out the best landing places for the Allied assault troops, and secondly to try and find out the enemy's strength – the latter being very important as our own intelligence did not have much information on the subject.

In order to gain the necessary information, Geoff had been told to try and capture a sentry and bring him back with us in the hope that he would be able to supply us with the enemy's strength.

As in all his operations, Geoffrey had to have the moon in his favour (that is, to land under the cover of darkness and work in the light of a rising moon). The whole plan was calculated to a split second – so many minutes to get ashore, so many minutes for the raid and so many minutes for the return to the submarine; all this was vitally important otherwise both the submarine and our party might have been discovered in an early dawn.

During exhaustive tests Apple had decided that RAF rescue dinghies were more suitable than canvas boats and these we blew up as the submarine surfaced half a mile off the coast and launched them over the side.

Leaving the submarine was a matter of minutes and I soon found myself following Geoff's dinghy ashore, each boat holding five men.

Our landing was uneventful, and after posting one sentry on the two dinghies Geoff started off in search of the way up that he had already seen from the submarine – no mean feat in the pitch blackness. We had one false start and then began the hardest climb any of us had ever experienced – we pulled ourselves up completely by instinct and every foothold was an insecure one, the rock being volcanic and very porous, crumbling away under our hands and feet.

By what seemed to be a miracle, Geoff finally got us safely to the top, covered in scratches, for we had decided to wear shorts so that in an emergency swimming would be easier.

We were nearly discovered as we reached the top of the cliff, which was about a hundred feet high at this point. Geoff and the others were crawling away from the edge towards a path that they could dimly see, and I was just pulling myself up over the edge when we heard men approaching. We all froze where we were and then, to my horror, I felt the edge of the cliff on which I was lying begin to crumble.

The sounds of marching feet and voices were coming much nearer and it became obvious that the Italian patrol was going to pass along the very path by the side of which Geoff was now lying, and there was I slipping slowly back over the edge and not daring to move a muscle for fear of dislodging some of the loose rocks.

Just as the patrol came level with Geoffrey, who was lying in the gorse not three feet from their feet, the worst happened. A large stone slipped out from beneath me and I waited tensely for the crash as it hit the rocks a hundred feet below me.

The crash came and Apple and the others prepared to let the patrol have it at short range. But the Italians, chattering to each other, apparently didn't hear a sound and passed by, little knowing how near to death they had been. We breathed again and prepared to start the work we had been sent to do.

Of course, the capturing of a prisoner in our case depended upon silencing him in the quickest way possible, and Apple had decided that the best plan was to crack our particular man on the head with a leaded hosepipe and then lower him down the cliff and away.

Because of the stiff climb we had encountered, Geoff changed the plan on the spur of the moment – it being impossible to lower or carry an insensible man down the route we had followed. He decided to jump on a sentry, half throttle him and, when he had calmed him down, force him to make his own descent.

Apple therefore detailed me with two men to guard the route down and under no circumstances to give our position away unless directly attacked. He then crept away with the others to find a sentry.

Hardly had we settled ourselves into our position when the whole guard passed by on their relieving rounds – so close that we could have touched them had we stretched out our hands.

Geoff and his party also had to lie in the gorse further down the path as the guard passed them and then wait for things to settle down again.

Very close by they could hear an Italian sentry singing 'O sole mio' and decided that he was their man. They crept

71

silently up to him and then Geoff sprang for his throat. In the uncertain light he missed his hold and the sentry let out a scream of fear. Needless to say it was the only sound he made, because by this time four desperate men were sitting all over him and Geoff's fist was literally jammed down his throat – all to no avail, even though Geoff was whispering '*Amico! Amico!*' in his ear. The Italian reciprocated by getting his teeth well into Geoffrey's wrist.

The next sentry, about fifty yards away, heard the scream and came running through the gorse towards them. Herstall was nearest to this new danger and although armed only with a rubber truncheon gallantly rushed forward in an attempt to silence him. He was met by a burst of fire in the abdomen, and above the sound of firing I heard him call out to Geoff that he had been hit. That was the last anyone saw or heard of Herstall, because by now the whole guard was aroused and Apple and the other two survivors of his party were desperately fighting them on the cliff edge. Geoff accounted for at least three with his automatic and Sgt Leigh got one and possibly two.

By this time things had got so hot that just as my small party had decided to join in the fray Apple shouted, 'Every man for himself,' and as we turned to go back down the cliff I saw him, outlined against the gun flashes and tracer, dive over the edge along with Leigh and the other trooper.

I thought, as I scrambled madly down the cliff, that I'd seen the last of Apple, but when I reached the bottom he was already there with his two men. How they got down is a mystery because the piece of cliff where they went over was quite strange to them, they were being shot at the whole of the way down, and all the rock was loose and crumbling away. It had taken us nearly three-quarters of an hour to climb the cliff and they got down in about a minute and a half – Sgt Leigh put his knee out falling part of the way.

Somehow or other we all managed to find the boats and started to paddle like mad for the rendezvous with *Unshaken*, which was lying submerged offshore.

By this time considerable activity had begun from the shore – Very lights and machine guns were going off in all directions. Luckily they had no searchlights and we were soon out of Very light range.

We had arranged an emergency signal with Jack Whitton just in case of a hurried withdrawal – two grenades to be thrown into the sea, the explosions bringing Whitton to the surface in a hurry.

Geoff let the grenades off and *Unshaken* broke surface very close by. What a relief it was to see her! We clambered on board and down the conning tower in double-quick time, while hefty sailors slit the rubber boats in little pieces and sank them.

Unshaken immediately submerged and set course for Malta. I'd like to say that the officers and crew couldn't have treated us with more consideration or kindness – they bound up our considerable cuts and bruises and insisted upon giving up their own comfortable bunks to those of us who had been more severely cut.

One last tribute I want to pay to our naval hosts. Jack's orders had been quite implicit: rather than endanger his submarine he was to abandon us to our fate. But luckily for us he had waited around, although we had been ashore longer than expected, and was prepared to cover our retreat with his 3-inch gun if necessary.

Pantelleria was captured shortly afterwards, an important stepping-stone in the taking of Sicily.

While it was a feather in the SAS's cap that Alexander had asked Appleyard personally to perform the Pantelleria job, the Army continued to show little real appreciation of what the SAS could do in a strategic sense. What the SAS should have been doing was dropping deep behind enemy lines; the Army instead began a habit of using the SAS as assault troops.

A case in point was the invasion of Sicily itself, where the SRS arrived in landing craft as part of the invasion fleet, and was tasked with the seizure of a lighthouse suspected of housing machine guns. Captain Roy Farran recalled:

We embarked on the *Royal Scotsman* in Sousse the night before the party. We were housed in all the luxury of a modern Irish Channel packet and the food was better than anything I had experienced since South Africa. The few remaining men were in good heart, quite confident of success in spite of their reduced numbers, and spent most of the next day in cleaning their weapons for the fight.

It was a brave display of strength. All around, as far as the eye could see, ships of all sizes were tossing up and down on the waves; rakish LCIs rolling sideways, waves washing over their bows, clumsy tank-landing craft, gunboats, motor torpedo boats and the larger hulls of the mother ships (all converted Channel packets). On the horizon were the watchful shadows of lean, wolfish destroyers and to the south-west we could see the comforting silhouettes of the big ships of the Fleet. Although the weather was fine and the sun set in a crimson glow behind the masts, the sea was so rough as to cause us to be anxious that the operation might be cancelled.

In the afternoon I developed a serious headache and began to sweat on my bunk. Boris Samarine, my Russian second-in-command, who was one of the many foreigners in the SAS, borrowed a thermometer which showed that I had a temperature of 102°F. It seemed clear that I also was in for a bout of malaria. Boris scrounged a quantity of quinine from the doctor and I took about four times the normal dose – so much that I fell back into a deep sleep from which I was not roused for eleven hours.

At three o'clock in the morning Boris shook me and told me that the boys were already in the boat. I buckled on my equipment and staggered out of the cabin. The ship was at rest, tossing silently on the waves, and round about I could just see the shadows of other vessels through the darkness. Over on the shore, which was a thick black smudge at the foot of the dark-blue sky, a searchlight was probing the water. The barge was lowered down the last few feet to land with a bump in the sea. And then we were being thrown about in confusion in the bottom as we were caught up in the angry turmoil of the waves. It was rough – too rough for a landing. Flynn, our Naval lieutenant, put her blunt nose into the rollers, which crashed over the end to swamp everybody sitting forward. The men crouched under the sides, bent over their weapons to keep them dry, while the spray dashed against their faces. They were just black huddled shapes, immobile and silent in the dark.

I reeled over the metal deckboards, trying to recapture my footing, to where Flynn was sitting, face into the wind, dressed in black shiny oilskins. I saw that he was trying to follow a small launch with a red tail-light. And then he shut off the engine and we wallowed for a little, being tossed about at will by the waves. Behind were the bobbing shapes of the first flight, who would idle there at the rendezvous until they had given us our proper start. He glanced at his watch, and looking up, gazed once behind and once at the shore before giving the signal to restart the motor. Our bows began to carve into the white, splashing crests once more. The searchlight momentarily lit up the faces of the men, but passed on mercifully without pausing. Overhead the drone of hundreds of aircraft became louder. I could see by their black silhouettes that they were Dakotas, heavily laden birds of the night bound for the bridges at Syracuse. Then red tracers shot up dotted lines into the sky as the anti-aircraft guns opened fire from Pachino.

We were getting in closer to the shore now and we could see the color of the sand sloping up from the water's edge. There were little white houses and fields of cabbages beyond the beaches. Everything was ominously quiet. The landing craft swung into calmer water north of the island and then she turned to approach the place where our objective was joined by a sandbar to the shore. Still there were no signs of hostility. She ground to a standstill some five yards from land, her hull stuck hard on the bottom. I told Flynn to lower the ramp. Dropping myself into the sea, holding my carbine above my head, I found myself in water to my waist. I waded steadily ashore and the others followed behind, breaths bated. One fool slipped on a rock and dropped his Bren gun into the water. Then we were wriggling on our bellies up the slope towards the lighthouse, white and gleaming now in the moonlight. I saw three shadowy figures come out of the front door and disappear round the back. We took the last few yards in a rush, fingers on our Tommy guns ready to fire. I kicked open the front door to find the house deserted, although the uneaten meal on the table showed that the occupants had only recently left.

While we were searching the rooms and the outhouses, firing started from the Argylls' beach on the left. The first flight was ashore. Odd tracer bullets zipped into the lighthouse, shattering the glass. I walked out of the front door and fired our success signal into the sky. There were lights going up on both sides now and further back there were the occasional flashes of mortars fired by the enemy. Tracers were criss-crossing into the dunes. I walked back into the building and sat down, decided to change my socks. Boris came in after a few moments to report that a further search of the island had revealed three terrified little Italians, crouching in holes in the ground, and an abandoned machine gun. I directed a party to take up fire positions on the neck connecting us with the shore, while we resumed our search of the lighthouse. Suddenly there was a tremendous roar, which shook the broken glass out of the tower and sent us diving under the tables, thinking that the end of the world had come. It was some time before I realized that it was not the biggest bomb in the world, but that the new rocket barges were firing their first salvoes at the shore. One cannot wonder that the Italians put up so little resistance.

Soon afterwards Randolph Churchill, now a liaison officer between the SAS and the Highlanders, appeared and told Farran to take his men to Bizerta and reinforce other SAS operations on Sicily, including an attack on the four-gun coastal battery at Capo Murro di Porco. The raid on Capo Murro di Porco may not have been the stuff for which the SAS was intended, but the task was executed in superlative fashion. Among those taking part was Derrick Harrison of 1 SRS, who with his men was taken to the foot of the cliffs at the cape by an LCA (Landing Craft Assault):

We clambered ashore, slipping and sliding in our rubber-soled boots on the spray-drenched boulders. I tried to recall the photos of the area. There seemed little doubt that this was the right place.

In single file we began to scale the cliff. I could see neither foothold nor handhold. I felt for them instinctively, hauling myself up inch by inch. My dread of heights had gone. Only once during the climb did it threaten to return. We had been edging our way along a ledge of rock for some minutes when . . . the ledge was not there any more. I remember thinking only that I must try another way. I could see nothing. It was as if someone else were guiding my hands and feet. I stretched up above me. The rock was broken but firm. I scrambled up.

How long that climb took I do not know. It could have been ten minutes or ten years. At the top I lay down among the rocks and boulders strewn around, and took out my .45 revolver. I had brought that and twelve hand grenades with me.

A moment later I was joined by my signaller with his small .38 set. 'Any news of the others?' I asked.

He shook his head. 'There's some dame singing on my frequency,' he whispered.

We lay there watching and listening while the rest of the section clambered up over the cliff top and took up their positions one by one among the rocks on either side.

So far there had been neither sight nor sound of the enemy. The unexpected silence was unnerving. My imagination began to run riot. Somewhere above us, and unseen, they were preparing to open fire. A stone rattled loose and clattered down to the cliff edge. From in front came the sudden, excited shouts of Italians. My finger tightened on the trigger. Then the shouts died away into the distance.

'Half right till we meet the wall . . .'

As we rose from the cover of the rocks and moved forward in open formation, I ran over in my mind the route we were to take. Soon we should reach the junction and . . . There was a sharp swishing sound through the air. As one man we fell flat. Above us and not more than thirty yards away there came a blinding flash and a deafening roar. Mortars! A bright red glow stained the night and I tried to sink into the flickering uncertain shadows that darted among the rocks. I felt as naked as a floodlit monument.

Cautiously I raised my head. Where the bomb had fallen a shed was burning. In the flare of the flames I could see, only a few feet away, a tangle of wire and beyond that the menacing muzzle of a big gun. We had been advancing right into the enemy battery, and into our own mortar fire. For a moment I was tempted to rush the battery from where we were. The defenders were obviously unaware of our presence but, if we attacked frontally, we would meet Tony and Peter with their sections coming in from the opposite direction. And my job was to get the Engineers safely on to the gun positions.

There was only one thing to be done: retrace our steps and carry on with the original plan.

It was obvious now that we had not landed at the right place but had scaled the cliff almost beneath the battery. We had lost a good deal of time so set off at a good pace, dropping to the ground every so often to avoid being spotted in the flash of bursting mortar bombs.

From somewhere on the right a light machine gun opened up on us as we scurried across the open ground between the battery and the farm. Bending low, we made for the wall ahead as fast as we could. Once on the other side we were safe for the time being.

We were behind the battery now. Most of the buildings appeared to be blazing, and in the light of the flames we could see the guns. So far there had been no sign of the other two sections, so I guessed they must already have reached the gun positions. I had to get those Engineers there, fast.

From behind came a sharp rattle of machine-gun fire. Streams of green tracer cut through our ranks. As we dived for cover our two Bren gunners swung round, firing from the hip in the direction from which the tracer had come. No more firing came from the mystery gunner. His one burst had mercifully done no damage.

We were about to step over the one remaining wall between ourselves and our objective when, from our right front, came a stream of red tracer. Lying full length in the nettles behind the wall – it was no more than a foot high – I yelled the challenge at the top of my voice: 'Desert Rats!'

Back came the answer: 'Kill the Italians.' We breathed again. Tony and Peter. Somewhere we must have passed them in the dark. We scrambled to our feet. At once there came another burst of fire from their direction, and once more we fell flat. This time we lay there hugging the earth as bullets chipped the top of the wall. It was good shooting but we did not appreciate it.

I shouted again. Once more came the reply: 'Kill the Italians.' The firing continued. I crawled to the end of the section to have a look from higher ground. The last man peered through the darkness.

'Mr Harrison? They're our chaps. They keep shouting the challenge and I've answered right each time but I don't think they can hear me.'

I stared back, beginning to understand. 'That was me challenging. We've been shouting to each other. Come on, let's all shout together. Pass the word down.' We yelled at the top of our voices. Faintly came the answer. Tony stepped forward out of the night.

Together now, Tony leading, we stormed into the gun positions. The noise of battle was already dying down. Here and there an occasional shot was fired but, in the main, the fight was over. Then, out of the corner of my eye, I caught a slight movement three or four yards away, at ground level. Something froze inside me as the light gleamed on the barrel of a machine gun pointing straight at us. They could not miss.

I was too close to use a grenade and could pick off only one man at a time with my revolver. If only I could attract the attention of one of the Tommy-gunners. All these thoughts passed through my mind in the fraction of a second before three very frightened Italians crawled out of their hole, hands high in the air. Taking them with us we crossed the wire and headed for the first gun.

While the engineers prepared the guns for the big bang we started to round up the prisoners and wounded. If they could walk we herded them over against one of the huts where they stood dejectedly, a dazed look on their faces. They were dirty and unshaven, and had that unkempt look about them that men who have fought long and hard in impossible conditions might have – but without that excuse. A little way off, under separate guard, was a second group of prisoners, about twenty women and children. They had fled to the safety of the shelters on the battery position thinking it was yet another RAF raid. They were numb with fear. Italian home propaganda was nothing if not thorough.

On the whole battery position we found only one officer, and he claimed to be a doctor. He was lying in one of the gun pits, his legs lacerated by mortar fragments that had embedded themselves deeply. As we carried him across the battery to the rest of the prisoners he waved his arms wildly, insisting loudly, '*Dottore, dottore, dottore!*' He calmed down a bit when we started to dress his legs, and watched our efforts with professional interest. Among his papers were visiting cards describing him as 'obstetrician and gynaecologist'.

He confirmed that he was the only officer but that he was the doctor. There had been some German officers, however. He waved his hand vaguely in the direction of the high ground. He had sent them word that the British were landing but they would not believe him. No one, they told him, could land on a night like this. They would not come. Now, no doubt, they had fled.

By this time the Engineers had laid all their charges. From the pits came the warning, 'Stand clear.' The guns were ready to blow. Prisoners were shepherded to safety behind a rise in the ground. The wounded were carried there. We lay down and waited. There was a sharp concussion and flying pieces of metal whined eerily above our heads. As the sound of the explosion rolled away, from the signaller's wireless set came the strains of 'Land of Hope and Glory', as a broadcasting station crashed in on our frequency.

When a previously unknown battery began firing at the Allied invasion fleet, Paddy Mayne, with his usual contempt for his own safety, led the attack in person, brandishing nothing more dangerous than his favourite Colt .45 automatic. Next day Mayne marched his men into Syracuse, with nearly 500 Italian POWs in tow. For his leadership at Cape Murro di Porco Mayne received a well-earned bar to his DSO.

A proper, strategic use of the Regiment came in early September 1943, with Operation *Speedwell*, which was designed to stop the flow of German troops down Italy following Mussolini's surrender. 'Tanky' Challenor took part in the operation:

We were to parachute in to two areas of Italy and derail trains in tunnels by explosives . . . It was to be no picnic. We were to be dropped by night on a tricky operation deep behind enemy lines in hostile mountain country. Nobody had any information as to conditions we were likely to encounter. The actual purpose of the raid was straightforward, but afterwards it was to be the age-old method of Shanks' pony, the hard footslog through enemy-held country towards advancing Allied armies which had landed at Reggio, on the toe of Italy, three days before the launch of *Speedwell* . . . The sun was dipping low over the horizon as we took off from Kairouan. There was a great deal of aimless chatter about the respective merits of Italian wine and women. At least they could not be any worse than the North African variety, particularly the wine . . . By 11.30 p.m. we were nearly there. We met some flak in the Genoa/La Spezia area, which ceased as we flew inland. I was No. 6 in the dropping order and last out. I saw that we were a nice tight stick. In the direction of Spezia we clearly heard the wail of an air-raid siren. Down below the Appenines looked like hillocks. It had been a high drop, 7,000 feet, the highest I had been on.

Finally I plunged into a small tree and spent a frustrating time tearing the chute from the branches and then scraping a hole in the ground with my knife to bury the damn thing. I had landed in a small wooded copse on a scrub-filled mountainside. I began to walk on my line to link up with Mr Wedderburn, using a low whistling sound as a pre-arranged means of identification. Within an hour we had all linked up.

After checking their bearings and agreeing a rendezvous for a week later, the SAS parachutists split up. After several days scrambling around the mountains, Challenor and Wedderburn found the ideal railway tunnel to blow. At midnight they entered the unguarded tunnel, and placed two charges:

We were making our way back to the entrance when we heard a train coming. It was travelling on the down-line where we had placed the first set of charges. Running and falling, we just cleared the tunnel mouth as the train thundered in. With a rumbling 'BOOM' the explosion echoed down the tunnel. There followed a crashing, smashing, banging, screeching sound of metal piling up. As we left the scene we both heard it – a train on the up-line. We listened in awe. BOOM! Again, more crashing noises and then an eerie, awful silence. We had claimed two trains and undoubtedly blocked the La Spezia–Bologna line as ordered.

Challenor and Wedderburn reached the rendezvous, but when no one else turned up after three days, they left on 'Shanks' pony' for the Allied lines. After numerous adventures, including the demolition of another railway tunnel, generous hospitality from Italian farmers and debilitating bouts of malaria, the two men split up on Christmas Day 1943. Both were captured shortly afterwards, but Challenor succeeded in escaping dressed as an Italian woman. Seven long months after the start of *Speedwell*, Challenor made it back to British lines. All he could say, over and over again, was, 'I've done it, you bastards.'

For the size of the force dropped – 13 men – the *Speedwell* operation achieved a significant result, and Bill Stirling pressed Supreme Allied headquarters in Italy to action more such deep-behind-the-lines sabotage by SAS units. For the most part, Bill Stirling's pleadings fell on deaf ears, beginning a disillusionment with the top brass that would see his eventual resignation as 2 SAS's commanding officer.

Even if not deployed to its best advantage, the SAS contributed substantially to the campaign in Italy. In September 1942 detachments of 2 SAS landed with the 1st Airborne Division at Taranto, to operate on the enemy's flanks and frustrate counterattacks. An ambush of a German column outside Ginosa by Roy Farran's D Squadron was just one of the spectacular actions that followed.

I led the column in line-ahead for about eight miles beyond Pogiano until we came to an Italian policeman on a crossroads. He told me that German vehicles were passing all the time and usually turned left towards a village called Ginosa. I waved the jeeps into ambush positions and the last vehicle was still backing into the trees when I saw the head of a large column approaching from the west. I threw myself into the ditch, pointing my Tommy gun up the road. I half-suspected that they were Italians and the first vehicle was nearly on top of us before I noticed the German cockade on the front of the driver's cap. The squeezing of my Tommy gun trigger was the signal for the whole weight of our fire-power to cut into the trucks at practically 'nil' range. Having once started such a colossal barrage of fire, it was very difficult to stop it in spite of the fact that the Germans were waving pathetic white flags from their bonnets. I remember screaming at a Frenchman called Durban to cease fire and making no impression on his tense, excited face until the whole of his Browning belt was finished. At last the racket stopped and I walked down the road towards a tiny knot of Germans waving white flags from behind the last vehicle. All those in the front trucks were dead. Still panting from the excitement of the ambush, we screamed at them to come forward with their hands up. A totally demoralised group of Germans was led up the column by an officer, bleeding profusely from a wound in his arm and still shouting for mercy. It was plain that there would be no question of further resistance from any of them. In all we took about forty prisoners and four trucks. Eight other vehicles were destroyed and about ten Germans were killed.

My greatest fear was that the Germans would retaliate from Ginosa or at least investigate the cause of the shooting. We had not sufficient strength for a pitched battle so that, after sending back the prizes with the prisoners, we sabotaged the remaining vehicles and withdraw a short way down the road.

The Germans sent down a number of infantry in armored troop-carriers within an hour of our attack. They halted at the crossroads and began to salvage the remnants of the vehicles and to bury their dead. I sent up two men hidden in the back of an Italian hay cart to get a better view of their activities and they returned later to say that the enemy had withdrawn to Ginosa.

Like other SAS officers, Farran revelled in the opportunity to 'twist the tails of the Germans', which of course made it easier for uncomprehending generals to use the SAS as a 'fire brigade'. These were men who were never averse to a spot of action against the enemy, no matter what it was. A month later Farran was busy behind the lines escorting escaped POWs to embarkation points on the coast, when he was ordered to proceed to Termoli and requisition a house to use as a billet. The town had just been liberated by the SRS, No. 3 Commando and 40 Marine Commando. In the event, Farran was in the nick of time to participate in one of the SAS's most brutal engagements of the war, a straightforward soldiers' battle with the German Parachute Division as it attempted to retake Termoli on 5 October. Roy Farran takes up the story:

We were engaged in settling into our new billet while the first parties were landed up the coast, and one night we were entertained to dinner by our comrades in the 1st SAS Regiment. There was nothing to indicate an impending enemy attack.

By the next morning the whole situation had been transformed. Reports came in about an enemy counterattack developing and shells began to crash all over the village. Several landed in the street outside our billet, wounding a number of civilians. As the day went on the weight of the bombardment increased.

All I did was to improve the safety of our billet with sacks of corn as protection against blast. As far as we were concerned the battle was somebody else's affair. The regular infantry with several tanks had arrived in Termoli and I could not see where we could fit in with our twenty-odd men. It may have been a weak view but we had had a good run from Taranto and were supposed to be resting.

Several times during the day a pair of Focke-Wulfs swooped in at ground level to bomb the shipping in the harbour. They landed one small stick astride the jetty, sinking one of our fishing boats with a direct hit. I dived into the water to rescue a wounded man but neglected to remove my German jackboots. In consequence they filled with water to weigh me down so much that I also had to be rescued.

The bombardment had become, if anything, more intensive by the next morning. It was impossible to get a proper perspective on the situation from behind our corn sacks, so I sent off Peter Jackson to see if he could find some news at Brigade. He came back at about midday, after an adventurous drive through bursting shells, to tell a comic story of his encounter with the Infantry Brigadier. Apparently a rather pompous man, he had said, 'Don't worry, old boy! Nothing at all. Everything perfectly under control.' At that moment a spandau had begun to fire into the Brigade Headquarters at close range, forcing the Brigadier to cut short his interview by diving under an armored car. Peter did not seem at all sure that the situation was under control. He said that 78th Division was fighting off fierce counterattacks between the bridge and the brickworks, that whole units were fleeing in panic from the village and that the Commandos had been called back into the line to hold Termoli itself.

In the afternoon when the bombardment was at its height, Sandy Scratchley arrived in the billet, having recently come out to Italy from North Africa. He quite rightly reprimanded me for sitting idle like a rat in a hole while Termoli was in acute danger of falling to the enemy. I sheepishly collected twenty men with six Bren guns and followed him down to the Commando Headquarters. Even the short walk down to their billet was extremely perilous. I got in a burst with my Tommy gun at a Focke-Wulf diving low over the houses and shells were bursting everywhere.

The first hour was spent in the cellar beneath Brigade Headquarters, where we found some delicious apples. The building had been hit only a few minutes before by a shell which killed the Staff Captain. Brigadier Durnford-Slater, and especially the Brigade Major, Brian Franks, struck me as being incredibly cool amongst it all. German tanks had approached the edge of the railway line, overrunning the Commandos, who nevertheless stuck to their ground although hemmed in on three sides. It appeared that the counterattack was being made by a Panzer and an infantry division – a formidable force in view of the fact that 78 Division had not got all its heavy equipment across the river. I am sure that if the enemy had been less half-hearted, he would have taken Termoli.

When we were led out to a position in the windows of the hotel, it was humiliating that I felt forced to duck at every shell, whereas Sandy only half-ducked and Brian Franks walked on as though nothing had happened.

We chose positions on the second-floor balconies, but it was fortunate from our point of view that in less than an hour Sandy arrived with fresh orders for us to hold the railway goods yard. When the battle was over I noticed that not a single balcony remained intact.

Our first position was on a crest at right angles to the coast, perhaps a mile north of the village. We had not been there long when the Germans advanced on our left to seize the cemetery, which forced us to fall back on the last ridge before the goods yard.

Although we only had a strength of twenty men, our fire power was quite abnormally strong. In all there were six Brens and a two-inch mortar. I covered our thousand-yard front between the 1st SAS and the sea by putting ten men with three Brens on each side of the railway line. Our main trouble was that we had no tools with which to dig weapon pits.

In spite of the fact that heavy fire was directed on us from the cemetery and that constant attempts were made to advance down the line of the railway, we held our positions for three days. Mortar bombs swished down all the time but most of them crashed harmlessly in the engine sheds behind. Only one man was wounded although I am sure we inflicted heavy casualties on the enemy. The range was so short that we could not fail to hit a man advancing in an upright position.

Crossing the railway from one side of the position to the other was a most perilous venture. A sniper cracked bullets dangerously close to our heads as we raced across the open track. We had been in our position for nearly a day before we discovered that the railway engine and truck in the middle of our front was loaded with high explosive, ready to be detonated. I was terrified during the entire battle that it would be hit by a mortar bomb.

We were short of rations and the nights were bitterly cold. It was the only pure infantry battle I fought in the war and I never want to fight another.

Finally, on 6 October, the SAS units disengaged, licked their wounds and buried their dead. Termoli had not fallen.

The SRS was withdrawn from Italy shortly afterwards, but detachments of 2 SAS continued to operate in Italy until the end of the war in Europe. The Regiment's most effective actions in the twilight of the Italian campaign tended to be those jointly undertaken with the partisans, as with 3 Squadron's *Tombola* operation. Newly raised, mainly from volunteers from the 1st and 6th Airborne Divisions, 3 Squadron was commanded by Roy Farran, now promoted to major. The idea behind *Tombola* was to insert a well-equipped SAS party into the enemy-held province of Emilia-Romagna, where it would cooperate with partisan brigades ('Commando Unico') in operations against the German defensive position to the south known as the Gothic Line. The centrepiece of *Tombola* was an attack on the German corps headquarters at

Albinea in the Po Valley. Farran – going under the *nom de guerre* of Major McGinty – was specifically ordered not to accompany 3 Squadron's drop into Emilia-Romagna, but 'accidentally' parachuted down with the advance party on 4 March 1945. Meeting the party was Mike Lees, the British SOE liaison officer who subsequently helped Farran birth the 'Battaglione Alleata', a mixed partisan and SAS combat group comprising 25 SAS, 30 Russian POWs and 40 largely Communist partisans under Farran's command. Few of the partisans had any military experience, but two weeks of intensive training by the SAS welded them into a decently effective force. Shrewdly, Farran gave the partisans a distinctive green and yellow feather hackle to wear in their beret, and allowed them to embroider the SAS motto 'Who Dares Wins' on their pockets in Italian. (Farran wrote later, 'I regret to say that the British often parodied this motto ['*Chi osera ci vincera*'] to read, 'Who cares who wins'.)

On the approach to corps headquarters, Farran received a wireless message telling him to call off the attack. He decided to ignore the order, on the basis that the SAS contingent would lose all credibility with the partisans if the attack was cancelled. After lying up at a farm about ten miles from the objective, Farran led the 'Battaglione Alleato' towards the corps headquarters, which consisted of the Villa Rossi, the commander's house, and the Villa Calvi, the chief of staff's house, and a number of billets:

> The moon glowed palely through the banks of mist. I had not realized we were so close to the limit of the mountains and it was with something of a shock that, at the top of a grassy rise, I suddenly saw the Lombardy plain laid out beneath us. The hills ended so abruptly, and beyond all was dark and flat except for the silver Po that shone in the moon and the pinpoint dots of light that marked farms and villages below. It all seemed so close, and only Albinea, presumably at our very feet, showed no lights. All around us the night was silent.

It seemed so improbable that soon we were to break it with the din of battle. As I slid softly down the hill into the black abyss I looked back once. The long file was silhouetted on the skyline against the background of mist and moon, and their figures were elongated like distant bushes in a desert heat.

My Italian guide whispered goodbye and crept off into the night. The main road, he pointed, lay only a few yards ahead. The columns stayed motionless in the wet grass while our scouts went ahead to find it. They tiptoed back, crouching despite the cover of darkness. It was twenty yards in front and there were no signs of the enemy. We moved slowly forward into the ditch and lay still again. I told the columns to fan out on either side of me, but to be careful not to get mixed in their ranks. We would re-form on the other side. Then we scurried across the exposed hardtop and crawled under a thick hedge on the north side, scratching our faces and rattling our weapons alarmingly as we wriggled through.

I lay in the grass beside Kirkpatrick, the piper, Morbin and my faithful Bruno, awaiting the message that all our hundred men were safely over the road. In an amazingly short time the word came back. All were with me, even the Russians, ready in their columns to move forward again. A small Italian farmhouse gleamed white in the moon and I recognized it from the air photograph. Now the responsibility for navigation was mine alone and a single mistake might lead us to disaster. I took a north bearing on my compass and began to count my steps. The columns closed up tight behind me, each man less than an arm's length from the next, and we crept stealthily forward. I tested almost every footstep before putting down my weight and paused frequently to listen for danger. A dog barked in the farm and my heart leapt. We made a detour to avoid two more buildings, neither of which I remembered from the photographs. I heard a truck pass along the road we had crossed and I threw myself flat. The

91

others dropped to the ground behind me and we lay still for several minutes before daring to move again.

We came to a ploughed field where the going was heavy and I was terrified the sentries would hear the rattle of our equipment. Twice I stumbled into a wet ditch, stepping into it unawares in the dark. And once I heard a German shout. Then, as my count of paces told me that the time had come to swing east, I caught my parachute jacket in some barbed wire and shook the whole fence as I broke free. Still no sound, and the men were incredibly quiet behind me. It had taken more than an hour to cover a few hundred yards.

We were on the objective before I was ready. Suddenly I found myself on the edge of the crescent-shaped wood that lay at the foot of Villa Calvi – the villa which contained the staff-officers and their operations room. I had not expected it so soon, but my navigation was accurate. Our force of a hundred men had penetrated the German headquarters undetected.

The time for action had come, but, since my excitement had been gradually mounting to a crescendo ever since we crossed the road, words seemed to stick in my throat. My mouth was dry and when I did manage to speak the words came in whispered gushes. I sent a runner back to find the Russians, to tell Modena to form his protective screen to the south. Above the half-moon wood I could see the white walls of Villa Calvi on the top of a small hill. No lights were showing and I vaguely wondered whether we had been misled, whether the villas were really occupied by Germans. The British columns stood around me in the dark, but somehow the Russians had become separated. The air was heavy and still. Not a single sound disturbed the night – no dogs barked now, no wind disturbed the trees in the woods, and the men held themselves tense, ready for my word to advance.

The runner came back. He was so quiet that he was by my side before I knew he had returned. He had failed to find Modena and the Russians. I could only assume that without waiting for orders Modena had already led his men into position. He must have branched off from the moment I changed direction to the east. We could delay no longer. At any time now the Russians might alert the sentries and surprise would be lost.

I called for Riccomini and told him to start. I would allow him only three minutes before I let Harvey attack Villa Calvi in front of us, so it was important that he move fast. He was to remember that the main German strength lay to the south. That was the direction from which enemy machine guns would probably fire. After twenty minutes, whether his attack was successful or not, he was to withdraw back to the mountains. If I fired a red Very light before that, he was to withdraw anyway.

I watched him go, hoping as I did so that he was not infected by my obvious fear, by the difficulty I had in speaking. Lees lumbered by his side, a big hulk of a man in the darkness. Behind him came the ten British and the Goufa Nera led by Bruno and they disappeared into the darkness towards Villa Rossi, their weapons carried at the ready.

The black silence was almost forbidding and I shivered from both cold and excitement as I cocked my carbine. I led Harvey to the edge of the wood, below the hill that led up to Villa Calvi. One of the Garibaldini pointed to the wire fence that surrounded the trees and crossed a narrow path leading up the bank to the lawns around the villa. Nailed to a tree behind it was a sign in red letters – 'Achtung – Minen.'

There was no time to make a detour. The three minutes was up. But Ken Harvey did not falter. He swung through the fence and the British swarmed up the path behind him. Yani and his Garibaldini hesitated, but I pushed them from behind, forcing them to follow the British up the bank to the villa. The minefield was obviously non-existent, a bluff.

I began to move over to my allotted position on the road. The others had lost me somehow in the darkness, but Kirkpatrick, the Highland Light Infantry piper, was still by my side. I walked into a slit-trench and lost my carbine, but Kirkpatrick retrieved it. Then, as I was still recovering from the shock of my fall, the fighting began.

The silence was broken by a tremendous burst of fire from Villa Calvi above. It sounded like a whole Bren magazine fired without pause and, as much as if it were a signal for which both Germans and ourselves had been waiting, it triggered automatic fire from every direction – from the enemy billets to the south, from Villa Rossi and from Villa Calvi. The night was shattered by the rattle of machine guns. I heard the harsh rasp of a spandau and knew the Germans were firing back. Bullets whistled over our heads as if the Germans could see us, which was impossible. All along the line to the south Modena's men maintained continuous fire and I saw tracers bouncing off the white walls of the guardhouse. A siren wailed from the direction of Villa Rossi. That was unfortunate because it meant the alarm had been sounded there before Riccomini entered his target. Even mortars added their thuds to the general racket and, between the rattle of small-arms fire at Villa Calvi above, I heard the thump of a bazooka.

Having loosed off the attack, I had no more control and I could only sit with Kirkpatrick and wait. I told him to play 'Highland Laddie', just to let the enemy know they had more than a mere partisan attack with which to contend. The British at Calvi cheered when they heard the defiant skirl of the pipes. Our job was to cause panic and confusion and, even if we failed to clinch our attack, this had already been achieved. An enemy spandau singled us out and the bullets whizzed uncomfortably close. I pushed Kirkpatrick into a convenient slit-trench and he continued to play from a sitting position. I wondered whether I should join Harvey at Villa Calvi, but decided against it. Someone had to stay in the middle to fire the signal for withdrawal. So, while Kirkpatrick played his pipes, I sat beside him amidst the bullets, cursing myself for not having restrained Harvey a few minutes longer.

Only later, when we were on our way back to the mountains, did I piece together what had happened.

The British at Calvi crept up the bank to the edge of the lawn. Four German sentries were standing on a gravel drive in front of the villa. There was no time for finesse, so Harvey shot them down with his Bren and that initial burst of machine-gun fire which awakened the whole headquarters carried death to these sentries. Then the British charged across the lawns to the house, covered by the Garibaldini who fired into the windows. The front door was locked and several minutes elapsed before the British shot it in with a bazooka. By then Harvey and Sergeant Godwin had entered through ground-floor windows and were fighting Germans in the operations room. Bursting into one ground-floor room, Harvey was confronted by a German with a Schmeisser sub-machine gun. He ducked but forgot to extinguish his flashlight. Fortunately, Sergeant Godwin, who was close on his heels, fired over his shoulder and killed the German in time. Four other Germans, including the staff colonel, were killed on the ground floor, as were two other sentries in the outhouses. But the remainder fought back down a spiral staircase that led to the upper story. Several unsuccessful attempts were made to climb this stairway but failed in the face of intense enemy fire. The Germans were able to cover the first landing from behind balustrades and could not be seen from below. In one of these attempts Parachutist Mulvey was wounded in the knee. Then the Germans began to roll grenades down the stairs, one of them wounding Corporal Layburn. Harvey decided to raze the villa. It was impossible to take the house in the twenty minutes allowed. Working frantically against time, the British piled maps, papers, files and office furniture into a heap in the middle of the operations room. Then, with the assistance of a little explosive and some petrol found in one of the outhouses, they started the fire. Our men kept the Germans confined to the top floor, shooting up the stairs and through the windows outside, until the flames had taken good hold. After firing the rest of their bazooka bombs and most of their ammunition through the windows, they withdrew from the grounds, carrying their wounded with them.

The story at Villa Rossi was similar except that there, because firing broke out at Villa Calvi first, our raiders did not have full advantage of surprise. Riccomini's men were still in the ditch beside the road when the fighting began at Villa Calvi. They had used more caution in their approach than time allowed and were still outside the grounds when sirens sounded from the roof of their villa. Realizing that surprise was lost, the British shot the three sentries in the grounds, firing through iron railings that surrounded the lawn. Then they charged the house, cheering as they heard Kirkpatrick's pipes. Several more Germans were killed in outlying buildings and most of the thirty raiders – British and Goufa Nera – crashed through the windows into the house. In the ground-floor rooms, more Germans were encountered, two of whom surrendered. These two prisoners were locked in an outhouse and presumably lived to tell the tale.

As at Villa Calvi, a furious battle took place for the upper floor. The British led attack after attack up the spiral stairway, but were always repulsed when they ran into merciless fire on the landing. Mike Lees led one attack and was severely wounded, as was Bruno, the Goufa Nera leader. Riccomini and Sergeant Guscott tried again and almost reached the top, but, there on the second landing, Riccomini met his death. He was shot through the head and died instantly. Sergeant Guscott dragged his body down. Then, angry at the loss of his leader, Sergeant Guscott led another attempt. While shouting from the landing, urging the others to follow him, he too was mortally wounded and died there on the staircase. Both had volunteered for Operation *Tombola* although entitled to a rest after the operations north of Spezia. Both met their end at Villa Rossi.

Then the Germans, heartened by their success, attempted to come down the stairs. A hail of fire greeted them at the bottom and three more Germans died with Riccomini and Guscott on the staircase. Kershaw, Green and Taylor decided to light a fire in the kitchen. They poured petrol on the walls, heaped up curtains and bedding from the other rooms and started the blaze. Sergeant Hughes and Ramos, one of our Spaniards, carried the wounded outside.

Meanwhile I waited nervously, wondering whether to fire the signal for withdrawal. The planned twenty minutes had long expired and I saw flames licking around the roofs of both villas, especially at Villa Calvi. German return fire was becoming more intense and mortar bombs crashed into the trees of the half-moon wood at the foot of Villa Calvi. A few Italian and Russian stragglers had already joined me, and I knew that soon trucked reinforcements would be arriving in Albinea from other German-occupied villages nearby. The time had come for retreat if we were ever to return safely to our mountain base. I pointed my Very pistol at the sky and fired three red signal flares. Immediately the alert spandau to the south sprayed bullets all around me, sending the Italians scuttling for cover.

I waited until all the British, at least, had rallied around me. They came down from Calvi in twos and threes, jubilant at their success. Corporal Layburn and Mulvey, the two wounded, hopped between them, supported by a man on each side. Those from Villa Rossi were less triumphant. They told me how Riccomini and Guscott had died and that Mike Lees was being carried on a ladder to safety by Burke and Ramos. And the Goufa Nera, they said, were also carrying Bruno, their leader.

I waited as long as I dared, but Burke, a red-headed Irishman, and Ramos never arrived with Lees. In fact, they carried him on a ladder for four days and, by some miracle, escaped capture by the hundreds of Germans who scoured the area after our raid. Considering that Lees, who was seriously wounded, weighed at least two hundred and fifty pounds, it was a tremendous feat. Both were awarded the Military Medal after they carried him to a safe hiding-place in the mountains. Bruno also evaded capture, and a few days later I arranged for a light aircraft to evacuate him and Lees to Florence. Burke and Ramos later rejoined us at Tapignola.

The sky was red from the blazing villas as we straggled west to the River Crostollo. We glanced occasionally over our shoulders at the burning headquarters and at the star shells now being fired over the area by the guns from Pianello. It was a satisfying sight. If only we could regain the safety of the mountain, the raid could be marked up as at least a partial success.

Though our withdrawal was far from organized, by astonishing good fortune most of the scattered parties managed to link together on the banks of the Crostollo. Our progress was slow, since neither Layburn nor Mulvey were capable of walking, and I was desperately anxious to cross the main road before dawn. I led them across the river and then cut south towards the hills. We were extremely tired, but there was no hope of rest for many hours. It was already getting lighter. German trucks drove helter-skelter along the road and once we hid for several minutes when we heard the rumble of tank tracks. Only Green's alertness in spotting a German unit sign saved us from walking into an anti-aircraft battery. Wearily we made yet another detour. Sounds of firing still came from Albinea and I could only guess that either some of the Russians were still in action or the Germans were shooting at themselves.

At last we crossed the road safely and began to climb into the hills. Obviously something had to be done about the wounded. Mulvey was in great pain and could go no farther, even with the help of the others. I took him into a farmhouse and, after laying him on the kitchen table, did my best to bandage up his shattered knee. The peasants promised to hide him until the fuss died down and then to bring him up in an ox-cart to our mountain base. I did not like leaving him, but there was no alternative. And Mulvey himself, well aware that he risked capture, begged me to hurry away while there was still time. I gave the Italians some money and promised more after safe delivery of our comrade. Layburn could limp along with the help of two others and, with some misgivings, I allowed him to accompany us as long as he could. In the event, the Italian peasants were as good as their word and delivered Mulvey safely to the mountains. The farm was searched, but the Germans did not find him.

It was broad daylight by the time we reached Casa Del Lupo. The poor *padrone* was very frightened after the excitement of the night and at last seemed to realize that we were not Germans. He begged us to go away as soon as possible. We did not need urging. After tying Corporal Layburn's wounds with a field dressing, I lashed him to an ancient horse we commandeered from the farmer. The horse was extremely decrepit and blind in both eyes, but it served the purpose. Layburn was much more badly hit than I had imagined. He had multiple grenade wounds in both legs and it was remarkable how he had managed to struggle along so far. I tied him tightly to the saddle with his wounded legs hanging limply by the horse's side. Though those dangling legs, dripping blood most of the way, must have been extremely painful, he never once complained.

There could be no more halts now. According to peasants we met on the track, the countryside buzzed with Germans and we frequently skirted round danger areas. At first the mist was still thick, aiding our escape, but a light rain made the muddy path slippery underfoot. This time I did not doubt peasant rumours. We had to believe all reports of enemy patrols for it was illogical to assume they were not looking for us. We were too short of ammunition and our weapons had fallen too often in the mud for us to look for a fight.

The men were exhausted, but their morale was high. Only the loss of Ricky Riccomini and Guscott marred their good spirits. Incessantly, as we plodded through the mud, they recounted stories of their experiences during the raid. The best anecdote had it that one German officer at Villa Rossi was chased on to the lawn in his pyjamas. But as the day dragged on and I kept them marching without pause, fatigue began to tell and they trudged silently behind me, straggling raggedly down the track. I was probably more tired than most, for the old wounds in my legs ached and I doubt if I was in as good condition as the men. But I was more alive to danger than they were and knew that only a forced march across the Secchia would save us from capture.

The old horse frequently stumbled in the mud, throwing Layburn to the ground. Even on the best of going it was inclined to trip over the slightest obstacle, causing him to slip sideways in the saddle. When it finally collapsed, crushing Layburn beneath, we decided to abandon it. We made a rough stretcher from saplings and parachute blouses and four of us carried Layburn up and down the hills. I took my turn with the rest at this gruelling chore and soon we were all so tired that we could only reel blindly forward. Often, with the poles across our shoulders, we slipped to our knees in the mud. Layburn volunteered to stay behind, but the men would not hear of it. Actually I thought I made better progress when I took my turn at the stretcher, for then the weight on my shoulders made me forget the aching in my legs. We marched mechanically now, tramping wearily in step with our heads down. If we had encountered any Germans, resistance would have been impossible. Our weapons were caked with mud and we were so tired that we were incapable of anything more than this monotonous trudging along the track. We marched without scouts, for no one had enough energy to climb to higher ground. Soon I even abandoned my earlier practice of skirting around danger points and we crossed the north-south highway without any attempt at concealment. We walked openly through a village, to the amazement of the inhabitants, and were still lucky enough not to meet any Germans.

I remembered that Mark Antony made his soldierly reputation not so much from feats of arms as from his endurance while retreating from Modena through this very country. But our own endurance was close to an end. Without bothering to discover if the German drive was still in process around Baiso, I followed the route by which we had come, up the steep slope to Vallestra. Still we were lucky, although homesteads on the way were strangely silent. I gathered later that the Germans passed through this area and aimed along a Baiso-Carpineti axis, by-passing Vallestra.

We managed to conjure up enough energy to stage a little show for the villagers of Vallestra. Forming columns of threes outside this village from which we had launched our raid, with Layburn leading the way on his stretcher, we marched through the streets to the music of Kirkpatrick's pipes. Women came to doorways and cheered us and little children ran beside the parade, but no men were to be seen. I hoped that the Germans in Baiso would hear the pipes and take them for defiance, for proof that we were safely beyond their reach. The men tried to pick up their sore feet and to straighten their shoulders as if they, too, realized that more by luck than good judgement we had successfully passed through the German lines without making contact.

After Vallestra, where my immediate fears were at an end, my legs refused to respond to the demands I made on them. I lagged farther and farther behind the rest, even though it was now easy going downhill to the Secchia. Some of the men took mercy on me and found a horse on which I finished the last four miles to Cavola. I was so completely exhausted that I could not appreciate the tumultuous welcome given us by the Green Flames, who carried the men off to celebrate in various houses in the village. I know the mayor made some sort of speech, but I was more grateful for the bed of the local schoolmistress. She, of course, was not there, but even if she had been she would have been safe. I did not awaken for another fourteen hours. We had marched for twenty-two hours without pause and, excluding the eight-hour halt at Casa Del Lupo had been awake for more than two days.

When all was reckoned, our raid cost us three British dead and three wounded, three Italian wounded, two Russians wounded and six Russians captured. At first we thought we had killed the German general at Villa Rossi, but apparently this was not so. However, we did kill Colonel Lemelsen, the chief of staff, and many other Germans. We destroyed the two main buildings in the headquarters together with many maps and papers. Above all, we made the enemy realize that he was not safe anywhere, no matter how far behind the front.

A court-martial of Farran, for twice disobeying orders during *Tombola*, failed after an intervention from Colonel Riepe, the US officer in command of clandestine operations in the 15th Army

Group's bailiwick. Riepe signalled SAS Brigade: 'Farran's gallant actions . . . have completely sold to American part this HQ the tremendous value of SAS operations.' In fact, *Tombola* and the SAS campaign in Italy 'sold' the SAS to many, since it proved that the Regiment could operate in any theatre, even the populated confines of Italy. One notable feature of *Tombola* and similar operations in Italy, was that junior non-commissioned officers and private soldiers were put in charge of partisan teams. 'It was extraordinary,' Farran wrote, 'how successful the British common soldiers were as detachment commanders.' In this respect *Tombola* and its counterparts anticipated 22 SAS operations in Oman in the 1960s, when the Regiment fought alongside tribal levies.

Tombola aside, Italy was a minor theatre for the 2 SAS from mid-1944, since it, alongside the SRS, was preparing for the main invasion of Europe: the D-Day landings. Both 2 SAS and SRS became part of SAS Brigade commanded by Brigadier R.W. McLeod, under Lieutenant General Frederick Browning's 1st Airborne Corps. To the undisguised irritation of the SAS, 'Boy' Browning made them exchange their sand-colored berets for the red ones of Airborne. There were other changes. The SRS reverted to its former name of 1 SAS, and expanded to regimental strength. Paddy Mayne remained as commanding officer. The remainder of the Brigade comprised two French parachute battalions, 3 and 4 SAS (also known as *2eme* and *3eme Regiment de Chausseurs Parachutistes*), a Belgian squadron, and F Squadron GHQ Liaison Regiment (Phantom). Almost inevitably, there was an argument as to how the SAS Brigade, of some 2,500 troops, should be used. Despite two full years of SAS activity, most 'top brass' continued to be blind to the proper employment of the SAS as saboteurs behind the main battle area. It was at this juncture that the exasperated Bill Stirling resigned his command. He was replaced by Lieutenant Colonel Brian Franks, a founder member of No. 8 Commando. Eventually, there was an outbreak of wisdom and Bill Stirling's concepts were adopted. In brief, it was decided that the

SAS Brigade would carry out three types of operation during the invasion of France. First, the SAS would identify targets for the RAF, as well as sabotaging such targets themselves. Second, the SAS would train the French Resistance, to enable the Resistance to help delay the flow of German reinforcements to the front. Third, the SAS would undertake offensive patrols deep behind the lines in armored jeeps. Any SAS men caught would be likely executed: Hitler had decreed that 'these men are dangerous' and needed to be 'ruthlessly exterminated'. Hitler's notorious 'Commando Order', however, did little to put off recruits to the expanding SAS.

Roy Close, a lieutenant in the Parachute Regiment, was among the many action-seekers who transferred to the SAS in the build-up to D-Day. The training at 1st SAS camp at Darvel in Scotland was rigorous; a police officer impersonating the enemy brought an unexpected and authentic degree of violence to one of Close's exercises.

I remember vividly the one-set for my section. Our objective was the police station in the centre of Kilmarnock which, for the purpose of the exercise, was an enemy-occupied town with a radio transmitter in the police station that had to be put out of action. The rules of the exercise allowed for the killing of protagonists on either side by pointing a weapon (unloaded, of course) and saying something like (I forget the exact mantra) 'exercise blankety blank; you're dead.' As usual we were taken out early in the morning in covered trucks and dropped we knew not where, with maps and compass. We had to attack our target that night, so we needed plenty of time to 'recce' our route into the town. Fortunately it did not take long to discover where we were. Having taken a good look at the topography to assure ourselves that our approach, if we were careful, would be concealed from the 'enemy', we set off.

It took several hours of cautious approach work before we found in the late afternoon a spot from which we could observe the entries to the town and the coming and goings. From my point of view there was a downside: the midges. I was, and still am, very susceptible to insect bites. By the time nightfall came, all exposed parts were their feeding ground. The irritation was maddening. As we got ready to move in, having identified a road that would lead to the police station, but which we could access by a roundabout route, my sergeant looked at me and exclaimed, 'My god, sir. Your face is awful!'

'I think I could put you on a fizzer for that, sergeant,' I replied, trying to smile.

'Yes, sir,' he replied, grinning.

Moving slowly and quietly, we went down from our position and entered the town as it got dark. We took a circuitous route of back streets that we knew from our observations would take us close to our target. There was no opposition. Perhaps the 'enemy' had not sufficiently studied, if at all, SAS methods. Or they had decided to let us get to the point where we would have to make our final 'attack'. Certainly we knew we would have to get into the main road to force an entry into the police station and then we would be vulnerable. But so far all was well, and as we approached the main road from the last side street before the police station we hid in someone's front garden to see if we could identify where their guards were positioned. Wait and watch is a good maxim. It is very difficult for a guard to keep quite still for a long time, sooner or later he must scratch his nose, ease a cramp, look round, or something. After several minutes our patience was rewarded. We detected a movement under a hedge in the police station's own front area. Was there another? We waited. Yes there was, on one side of the main entrance.

Now we knew how to make our final assault. We would have to rush the building; there was no way we could sneak in. My sergeant, with two men, would concentrate on 'eliminating' the two guards while I, with the others, carrying parcels of plastic explosive without detonators, would charge through them to the inside office, wherever that would be, and simulate the destruction of the alleged transmitter and anyone else who was around. Simple plans are the best, we thought.

After taking another careful look, as well as we could in the dark, to check where we had seen the hidden guards, I looked round to see if everyone was ready, tapped my sergeant on the shoulder, crept out of our front garden 'observation post' and moved, crouching, alongside the low wall towards the entrance to the police station about twenty yards away. I raised my arm, instantly we stood and rushed the target brandishing our Colt .45s, unloaded of course. I saw my sergeant and two men make for the guards shouting the exercise 'mantra', proving they were no longer operative. I headed straight into the station, past a reception desk, disposing in the same way of the officer behind it, and headed down a corridor towards what I guessed would be an inner office. Suddenly, in front of me there loomed a huge figure in police-blue uniform. I pointed my .45 at him; 'Blankety blank exercise, you're dead.'

'Och no I'm not, laddie. You're for the lock up,' he said and swung a large-fisted right hook in my direction. I managed to turn my head from the blow, but it caught me on the shoulder and bowled me over. As I scrambled to my feet I quickly changed my hold on my .45, held it by the barrel and, lifting my arm, threatened the zealous sergeant with the butt end as two of my men rushed forward and pinned him against the wall.

'You don't want to play by the rules of the exercise? That's okay by us. Now take me to the officer in charge of the station or I'll use this on you. The rest of you go through the building and deal with anyone else under the rules.' My own sergeant, having 'killed' the two guards, arrived by this time and said, 'Okay, sir, let me deal with him.' The police sergeant looked at him, then at the men holding him and then at my raised automatic. 'All right. This way.'

He led us down the corridor to an office where two of my men were already pointing .45s at the officer behind the desk.

'What's all this?'

'I assume you know the rules of the exercise?' He nodded.

'Your sergeant ignored them.' I went on to explain what had happened and pointed out that, whereas we would have dealt with his men, planted our 'explosive charge' and begun our withdrawal, now we could not. 'We must ring the Referee and get a ruling. It's important for my men. I have his number and so do you.' After some argument he agreed, picked up the telephone and dialled the number. As the one who had a complaint I insisted on speaking first. I explained the situation from my perspective, then handed the phone to the Inspector and heard a few reluctant confirmations. The phone came back and the ruling was that our assault on our target had been successful and we should have begun withdrawing without opposition, so we were to be given ten minutes to withdraw before the police notified the defending forces of our whereabouts.

Given their performance so far, I did not trust the police, but agreed. We shook hands and I walked out of the station with my section quite openly and down the road. Bearing in mind that this elaborate excuse was meant to indicate how good we were at our job, I paused to reassure my comrades that the 'cock up' was not their fault. They had done everything required of them skilfully and properly.

'We'll walk to the end of the road, then we have to find a

107

hidden way out. We're supposed to get back to base safely, but after what happened, they'll soon be after us.' I was walking beside one of my corporals. 'Very unfair all that, sir. Still, I hope the inspector doesn't put his hat on too soon.' I was another few paces on before I realized there could be trouble in what he had said.

'What the hell do you mean?'

'Just a plastic visiting card, sir.'

It was a moment or two before I realized what he meant. 'Get into a garden and wait,' I said as I turned and ran back to the Station and, passing a couple of policemen, straight into the Inspector's office. Not surprisingly he was and looked astonished. 'What the hell? You're supposed to be on your way.'

'It's just that I've been talking to my troops and, although we were very angry, we want you to know there's no ill feeling. Oh, sorry!' As I stretched forward to offer my hand I knocked his hat on to the floor. Picking it up to replace it, I kept the small ball of plastic explosive, unprimed, in my hand. It would not have hurt him, but he would have had cause for a very serious complaint.

We shook hands and parted, him still surprised, me relieved. I was not pleased with the turn of events and the corporal soon knew very well that I was not. At first I wondered about his future, but then reflected that we might benefit later from his type of cunning and initiative. I did not regret the second thought. He was a good and reliable corporal. All in all it was a very satisfactory exercise. By taking a very circuitous route, we returned to 'base' undetected. We had shown endurance. We had worked as a team and we now had confidence in each other, a vital ingredient for our future work behind enemy lines.

But it wasn't all work. 'One of the key tasks at Darvel,' Close recalled, 'was to turn this larger, reinforced unit into an integrated regiment, the members of which respected each other and shared the very special SAS *esprit de corps.*' Bonding was only helped by the easy, social informality of the Regiment. The Reverend J. Fraser McLuskey, like many another newcomer to the SAS, was struck by the warmth of his welcome. After being appointed the Regiment's padre, McLuskey travelled overnight to meet the 'hush-hush' unit for the first time.

In the cold, grey dawn of the following day the night train drew into Kilmarnock Station and a very sleepy padre stepped out. Point number one in favour of this mystery unit – they had remembered to meet me! I made my way over to the little utility that stood outside the station. I assumed the emblem on the wings must be the Brigade sign. It was striking enough, anyway: a dagger with wings, and underneath the motto, 'Who dares wins'. It all seemed very impressive; if, indeed, anything could be impressive after a cold night journey north.

The driver was a friendly chap, and we chatted away as we drove through the sleeping streets of Kilmarnock. He wasn't quite sure where he was expected to take me, but he thought I was meant to go to the 1st SAS Regiment. I had no alternative scheme to offer, so there we went. It was pleasant to be back in Ayrshire again and to see all the old familiar names: Kilmarnock, Hurlford, Galston, Newmilns, Darvel. The 1st SAS Regiment was stationed in Darvel. The officers' mess, as is the habit of such institutions, lay at the end of one of the bumpiest and longest drives I have ever encountered – and encounter it certainly was, as one jolted and banged one's way from pothole to pothole. But at last we were at the top, and the house came into view: a very pleasant house set in thickly wooded grounds. I appeared to have struck a good billet.

I levered myself up from the utility and straightened myself out. The front door was open, and I wondered if I were too early for breakfast. Hoping for the best, I advanced into the hall, where a strange and somewhat confused sight met my eye. Officers were passing through the hall into the dining room to the strains of a small and exceedingly wheezy gramophone playing, 'Mush, Mush, sing Tooral-aye-ary.' Round the fireplace and the ashes of a dead fire, and oblivious both of the breakfast procession and the orchestral accompaniment, sat several officers, in varying attitudes of repose. From this somnolent party a large man – a very large man – detached himself on my entry and heaved himself in my direction. If he didn't actually ask who the devil I was and what the devil I was doing there, I gathered at least that that was at the back of his mind. He seemed to be someone in authority, for I observed, even in my own bleary-eyed and breakfastless condition, that he was a Lieutenant Colonel. I announced that I was the new padre, and waited in vain for any light to break upon his countenance. I gathered that the 1st Special Air Service Regiment had not expected a padre, that the Brigade authorities had not informed them of a padre's coming, that this was what one would expect of Brigade, and that the whole business was obviously most irregular. However, this particular Lieutenant Colonel, who with every passing minute was making me feel that when last I was weighed and measured a mistake must have been made somewhere, was obviously a fair-minded man. Rightly or wrongly, and more probably wrongly than rightly, I had come, and I must have breakfast. I was reminded that I was in the mess, that I should remove my hat, and go in for breakfast. My inquisitor rejoined the bodies, whether alive or dead, I could not have told, around the fireplace, and I gladly accepted the invitation.

It does not take long to sense the atmosphere of a strange

mess. In some, the stranger is simply frozen. In this particular mess I had hardly sat down before I felt completely at home; and before I had finished the meal I had made up my mind that if this particular unit would have me, this was where I would stay. I found myself sitting between two young officers, both of whom I quickly came to know well. One was a fellow Scot, Leslie Cairns, and the other a Devon man, Roy Bradford. Before many weeks had passed we were to lose them both: Leslie when the plane that was taking him with his section to France went missing, and Roy when his jeep came under German fire on one of the roads of France.

The others at the table were equally friendly. I had eaten in many messes in the course of my district travels, but never in one like this. What struck me just as forcibly as the friendliness of the officers, even at the breakfast table, was their extreme youth. That major at the table in the corner, for example, with the fair hair and the strikingly handsome features, couldn't be more than twenty-three or twenty-four, and yet he was in command of C Squadron, it appeared, and wore the ribbon of the DSO. They all looked ridiculously young.

Fraser McLuskey was destined to become one of the Regiment's best-loved characters, and given the special accolade of 'Honorary Original'. He was a regular fixture in mess parties at Darvel. Roy Close recalled:

As the beer flowed the songs got louder, while our Church of Scotland padre, the Reverend J. Fraser McLuskey, serenely played the piano, occasionally wiping spilled beer from the keys with his handkerchief. It was a bit of a shock to the 'newcomers' to discover that the Regiment's favourite song was 'Lili Marlene', so loved by the Germans but now 'legitimized' with the Regiment's own words. When loud songs turned to lewd songs, the padre would just stand up

111

from the piano and turn to the Colonel: 'Permission to withdraw, sir?' To which the answer was always, 'Certainly, padre. Good night.' And to a resounding chorus of 'Goodnight padre' from the momentarily sobered members of the mess, he went up to bed.

The SAS version of 'Lili Marlene', composed by a member of L Detachment, went so:

Out in the desert in 1941 L Detachment SAS was formed to fight the Hun,
We used to hear a soft refrain,
A lilting strain each night again,
Of poor Marlene, of poor Lili Marlene.

Then back to Cairo we would steer, and drink our beer with ne'er a care,
And poor Marlene's boyfriend will never see Marlene.

Check your ammunition, see your guns are right,
Wait until a convoy comes creeping through the night,
Then you have some fun, my son,
And blow the Hun to Kingdom come,
And poor Marlene's boyfriend will never see Marlene.

Then back to Cairo we would steer and drink our beer with ne'er a care,
And poor Marlene's boyfriend will never see Marlene.

Driving into Fuka, thirty planes ahead, belching ammunition
And filling them with lead,
A flamer for you, a grave for Fritz,
Just like his plane he's shot to bits,
And poor Marlene's boyfriend will never see Marlene.

Then back to Cairo we would steer and drink our beer with
ne'er a care,
And poor Marlene's boyfriend will never see Marlene.

Afrika Korps has sunk into dust, gone are his Stukas, his
tanks have turned to rust,
No more will we hear that soft refrain,
I heard this strain each night again,
And poor Marlene's boyfriend will never see Marlene.

On 5 June 1945, the eve of D-Day, the first SAS patrols were
dropped into France. By the time of the German surrender eleven
months later, SAS Brigade had completed more than fifty operations in north-west Europe. The omnipresent Fraser McLuskey
dropped with A Squadron on 21 June, southwest of Dijon. His
descent was a vivid illustration of the dangers of insertion by
parachute at night:

We stood bunched up together doing our best to keep our
balance, while the dispatcher, with the exit hole uncovered,
counted out the minutes: 'Ten minutes to go . . . nine . . .
eight . . .' A hurried conversation with the pilot intervened.
Conditions would be all right for jumping, but enemy fighters
were around. He could only make one run over the target,
and we would have to jump as one stick. Well, that suited us;
the sooner we were out the better! We moved closer together
and shuffled nearer the hole. 'No need to push,' protested
Hamish. 'Who do you think you're shoving?' 'Four minutes
to go . . . three minutes . . . two . . . one minute . . .' Would
our reception committee be there? If they were, and if our
navigation were correct, the pilot should be seeing the lights
on the dropping zone now. He was. The light flashed red, and
then green. Almost before it changed Roy Bradford was out,
and No. 2 followed. One by one we shuffled up to the patch

113

of grey that was the exit hole. I must be near it now, I thought, and at that moment Hamish hurtled down at my feet. Heaving my kitbag up, I jumped. I was vaguely conscious of a form beneath me and of the smack of his static line against the hole. But by that time I was out, falling, falling, whipped by the wind and hanging on like grim death to the kitbag on my leg. With a jerk, I found myself twisting and turning, with my 'chute spread wide above me. Below me I could see only a blurred blackness. I grabbed for the quick release, and as carefully as I could paid out the rope attached to the kitbag. I mustn't lose that, anyway. And then I looked down again. I was coming down over a thick forest, and wherever I landed I should almost certainly hit a tree. I wasn't far off them now, by the look of things. I braced myself for hitting something, and gave my head and face all the protection I could. The kitbag swinging beneath me went crashing through thick branches, and almost simultaneously I followed suit. I was down – or was I? All I knew was that I felt acutely uncomfortable. I discovered that I was hanging upside down – suspended by one leg from the branch of a tree – whether large or small I could not say. All I could say was that the leg by which I was suspended was hurting like blazes. It was caught up in some tangled fashion in my parachute harness. I remembered my knife, shoved into my smock at the last moment, and easily accessible. I got it out with no difficulty, and started hacking at the harness. And there I ceased to take any further interest in events. What happened exactly I shall never know. Either I cut away the only strap which attached me to the branch, or else my not inconsiderable weight brought the branch down with me. But whatever happened, I fell, and fell to some purpose. My last recollection is of crashing head first through innumerable branches. I knew no more until I wakened up on a soft, grassy bank at the foot of the tree being violently and noisily sick.

Memory slowly returned – the flight, the jump, the crash-landing, the suspension on the branch, the fall. I saw from my watch I had been unconscious for about forty minutes. I was in France, then, and my landing on French soil might have been heard fifty kilometres away! I was lucky not to have broken my neck, although how far I had fallen it was too dark to see. One good thing: my precious kitbag lay at my side, smothered in some of the branches that had accompanied my descent. I couldn't find the knife anywhere. That was a perfectly good jack-knife, as well as a kid glove, to the bad. This wasn't my lucky night – or perhaps it was! I was still in one piece, anyway. Meantime, it was black as pitch, and I appeared to be in the densest concentration of trees on the Continent. It was nearly 3 a.m., and all was quiet. I decided I had done enough damage for one night, and, propping myself up against my precious kitbag, I dozed off to sleep.

McLuskey woke an hour and a half later and was violently sick from concussion throughout the morning. He had fallen forty feet.

Major Bill Fraser, A Squadron's commanding officer, also became tangled in branches during his night drop into the Morvan hills where the squadron was establishing its operating base. Deciding that discretion in this instance was the better part of valour, he waited for morning to cut himself free. With the break of dawn, Fraser realized that he was swinging no more than three inches above the ground.

Operation *Houndsworth*, on which both McLuskey and Fraser were engaged, was typical of the offensive patrols of the early SAS mission in France. Over three months, 153 jeep-raiding troops from A 1 SAS Squadron (with some 2 SAS and Maquis) made twenty-two railcuts on the Dijon–Paris line, derailed six trains, destroyed seventy vehicles and caused more than 200 enemy casualties.

As with nearly all the SAS missions in France, supplies for

Houndsworth were parachuted in. The parachutage was a nerve-wracking affair; the wait, when short of supplies, was interminable. And when supplies were dropped, there was much that could go wrong. Fraser McLuskey remembered:

Every night we expected a drop, but night after night passed and no planes appeared. The weather, which had greeted us so kindly on our arrival at our new post, proceeded to behave abominably. Day after day we had a series of thunder showers which did their best to wash our little camp away. We had lost the parachute tents with our first camp, and sleeping out of doors with only the trees for shelter became less and less comfortable. As often as a roaring camp fire dried out our sleeping bags, the heavens opened and they were drenched again. In addition to being most unpleasant, the weather conditions made flying in our area impossible, and we waited in vain for the planes to appear. As our second week began in the new base, the food situation grew really critical. We all had the usual emergency pack containing chocolate, biscuits, tablets, etc., but by this time most of these packs had been consumed. We rationed ourselves severely, and the most-felt want was lack of tea. That was the biggest threat to morale, lack of tea and lack of cigarettes. I think what made us realize most of all that we were not getting enough to eat was our reaction to the usual trek to the old camp to collect what was left there in the way of stores. The journey began to take us a good deal longer and loads dropped in size. Every night we expected the planes to come. The final cancellation only came over our wireless in the late evening. All day long the topic of conversation would be the likelihood of the planes coming that night, and when the last news came through of their failure to leave England it took the heart out of everyone. At the end of our third week in France with continuous bad weather and very scanty nourishment, we were all beginning to feel the strain. We were not in a good area for getting food. Strong German forces had dispersed the Maquis units in our area, and there were not many farmhouses within reach. We were almost entirely dependent on the diminishing contents of our own food-containers. I remember the excitement when a British agent, acting as liaison officer with the Maquis, appeared one afternoon leading a young white goat. It seemed such a shame to have to kill the animal – a very attractive creature; but killed it had to be! One of our Signals Section had been a butcher in civilian life, and soon the job was done. I doubt if our brief friendship with the animal in question greatly lessened our enjoyment of the resulting stew!

We knew, of course, the planes would come eventually, and come they did. The weather improved, and the evening arrived when there was no cancellation. Three planes were on their way, and each plane carried, in addition to supplies of food, one jeep. Excitement ran high in camp that night as we set out for the dropping zone, which was a small valley running at right angles to the main valley adjacent to our camp. Contact by this time had been resumed with the Maquis, and they were sending helpers to gather in the results of the drop. About midnight we started to assemble. The planes were due overhead at 2 a.m., and we proposed to try out a kind of 'walkie-talkie' apparatus whereby we hoped to be able to speak to the occupants of the planes. In spite of much feverish hand-winding of the machine, this did not prove possible. But in the general excitement of the occasion it was soon forgotten. Well on time, the first plane appeared and dropped its load. And there, sure enough, was the jeep with parachutes attached to each corner, drifting down among hampers and containers.

The first jeep fell conveniently in a field. The second jeep fell not so conveniently among trees. The third jeep fell most

117

inconveniently on a wooded bank by the roadside, and hung upside down, suspended from the trees which it brought down with it. The other two jeeps were quickly extricated from the crates in which they were packed. With a little persuasion, both engines started up, and soon they were running between the dropping zone and the camp with the eagerly awaited stores as their load. The third jeep required our undivided attention for the rest of the night. We had to have it extricated before morning, as the destruction wrought by its arrival was clearly visible from the road, and its presence could not be concealed from any passing German patrols. I don't know how many trees we had to cut down before we had it on its four wheels, but somehow or other we righted it. And then, after we had it right side up, there was the business of driving down the slope on to the road without clearing too obvious a track. There must be a special providence superintending the operations of all concerned with the extrication of jeeps from such positions, and somehow or other we did get the jeep on to the road before the valley woke up. It was remarkably little damaged after its rough reception, and proceeded to camp under its own power.

Among the supplies dropped for *Houndsworth* was McLuskey's pannier containing an altar cloth, an oak cross, a set of Airborne Communion vessels, hymn books, some copies of the New Testament (service edition) and a Day Book of Prayer. The following Sunday, the Reverend Fraser McLuskey held his first communion service in occupied France.

With the help of two tables, and when the cloth and cross were added, it focused worship quite effectively. In the clearing near the camp fire we met for our first act of worship. Everybody came, and everybody seemed glad to come. There were few of the usual accompaniments of worship. We were

118

our own organ and choir. The men gathered round in a half-circle in shirt sleeves or jumping smocks. They squatted on the ground for the lesson and the address. They stood for the hymns and for the prayers. Few of these men, I knew, were regular churchgoers. Few of them, in different circumstances, would have gone of their own accord to worship God. All that was undeniably true. It was just as true that in this forest glade they were finding the activity of worship the most natural thing in the world. In varying degree, we were all homesick and sometimes afraid: but these men were not cowards. It was not simply to curry favour that they stood before God. The life we had begun to lead together tested our sense of values. The ambitions and worries that loom so large in more normal conditions shrank out of all recognition, and the deep, basic needs of man, no longer overlaid by social custom and convention, stood revealed. Because one of these needs is the need of God, there was no feeling of strangeness as we stood together and said together Our Lord's Prayer. The sense of oneness our outlaw state had given us was a sense of oneness too with our common Father. As men draw closer, one to another, they draw closer to Him. We acknowledged His love and power in the works of nature, in the green earth that was our couch each night, in the tall trees that lifted our eyes to the heavens, in the clear water that supplied our needs, in the skies through which we had travelled safely, in the loyalty of the good friends we had found. We commended our enterprise, and our comrades, to His keeping; our loved ones to His care. We asked forgiveness and the skill and courage we should need. The forest was very still, and green and fresh after the night's rain. The smell of pinewood, and logs burning slowly on the camp fire, was the incense that rose with our prayers. No man-made house of God could compare with the tracery of the leaves above us, the boughs and branches that walled us round, the heavens that were our canopy. The benediction was pronounced, and echoed in the works of God's hands. The hymn books were collected and carefully packed in the hamper with the altar cloth and the oak cross. Men drifted off to clean their weapons or prepare the lunch. We had waited on God. We had renewed our strength.

Our peace that Sunday evening was rudely and abruptly shattered. ('This is what comes of having a service, padre!') As we were sitting round finishing off supper, we heard the noise of firing in an adjacent part of the wood. I have never seen supper cleared so quickly! The noise was coming our way, and it was clear that some force or other had decided to attack the Maquis with which we shared the wood: it was also pretty clear that unless we did something about it, we should soon find them attacking us. There had been a rumour the day before of an impending German attack, and most of the day a 'flap' had been on. But the Maquis intelligence service was apparently one day out in its reckoning, and the attack came when we had ceased to expect it. For the first time I saw my friends in action. The MO and I had our own duty station – a clearing a few hundred yards off, selected when first we pitched camp, as the Regimental Aid Post. As rapidly as possible, we collected our stretchers and our first-aid kit and moved to the appointed place.

During the engagement which followed a German patrol was beaten off on the approaches to the wood, and we suffered only one casualty. That was, unfortunately, our very remarkable sergeant major, Reg Seekings. When they brought him back later in the evening it appeared he had been hit rather badly in the head. It was fortunate that we had the doctor with us, and for the first time in my life I assisted at a surgical examination. We laid him under the tarpaulin, and with the somewhat uncertain light of a torch we found that a bullet had entered the back of his neck and lodged itself

120

deeply near the base of the skull. Probe as he might, the doctor could not get hold of it, and so he decided to leave whatever it was where it was. Reg was decidedly uncomfortable, and we hoped he would feel more like himself in the morning.

The bullet was finally removed in Chelmsford hospital several months later.

Inevitably, months of work behind the lines took their toll. Throughout *Houndsworth*, Roy Close never got a decent night's sleep, worried that the Germans might discover the squadron's forest camp at any time. The wise decision was made to withdraw A Squadron – their triumphal column of jeeps, stolen German trucks and cars, and a Maquis escort, was seen off by the cheering villagers of Mazingem – and replace it with Major Tony Marsh's C Squadron, who were to extend the area of operations to the west of Auxerre in Operation *Kipling*. After establishing a base, with Maquis help, in the Forêt de Merrivaux, the squadron's advance party, commanded by Captain Derrick Harrison, began road recces. The Germans appeared to be thin on the ground; a much greater danger seemed to be an ambush by excitable, itchy-fingered Resistance fighters, so Harrison attached Union Jacks to the party's jeeps. One fine day, when Lieutenant Richardson declared he was going to drive over to the Maquis workshop in Aillant to get his gun-mountings fixed, Harrison decided on a whim to accompany him. What followed was one of the SAS's most dramatic engagements of the Second World War. The event is vividly recorded in Harrison's memoir, *These Men Are Dangerous*:

We were about to turn into the road when I caught sight of a curl of thick smoke above the trees over to the right. I stopped the jeeps and Stewart came running forward. I pointed. 'See that? What do you make of it?'

121

'Looks as though it's over towards Les Ormes – something big on fire. What are we going to do?'

'Carry on and keep our eyes open. It may be further than we think.'

At top speed we raced away along the bumpy, dusty road towards the ever-growing column of smoke. Breasting the top of the hill outside Les Ormes I signalled the jeep behind to stop. Together we screamed to a halt. Ahead of us the road forked.

From the left came the crackle of firing. A number of buildings were ablaze. The crossroads on which we had halted was not more than a hundred yards from the village, but all the noise seemed to be coming from the far end. While I debated what to do, a woman on a bicycle came pedalling for dear life down the left-hand fork towards us. Head down, she came quickly on with her grey hair blowing in the wind. Tears streamed down her lined face. With surprising agility she leapt from her bike.

'Quick, messieurs,' she called out, 'save yourselves . . . the Boches . . . there.' She pointed to the burning buildings. 'Now I go to bring the Maquis back.'

'Just a moment.' She hesitated as she made to remount her bicycle. 'Quickly, how many Boches are there?'

She shrugged her shoulders. 'Two hundred . . . three hundred,' she hazarded. 'Who knows? A lot. Yes, a lot. Too many for you, monsieur. Now I must go.'

'Wait a minute. We'll go. With our jeeps it will be quicker.' I had made a quick decision. 'Leave it to us.'

Astonishment showed in her face. 'Thank you, monsieur. Thank you, thank you.' She climbed back on to her bike and cycled slowly back into the burning village. The rest of the patrol gathered round.

'Well,' I asked, 'what do you think? Go for the Maquis or attack the village ourselves?' It was a hard decision. In my own mind I had made it already, but I wanted the reactions of the others.

We were five in all. Fauchois was the first to speak. 'I say attack.' Fauchois had been sent to us from the French SAS. He carried false papers showing him to be a Canadian to ensure that, should he be captured, his family would not suffer. He was keen, dependable, and ever anxious to get at the '*sales Boches*'.

I turned to ask Curly Hall.

'If we go to Aillant for the Maquis I think it will be too late when we get them here.'

'Brearton?'

Brearton was Stewart's driver, and like Stewart, an ex-tank man. His reply was short and to the point. 'Let's have a crack at them.'

'And you, Stewart?'

'I feel like Hall. We haven't time to go for the Maquis.'

'Good. That's just what I feel. But we can't make an open attack. I suggest we take this right-hand fork into the part of the village that is quiet. Once in, we can drive through the village at speed with our guns going. We'll have the element of surprise and should be able to shoot our way out of anything we meet. The odds are something like fifty to one, but I hope they'll get such a shock that we'll pull it off.'

Union Jacks fluttering in the wind, we tore down the road, round the bend and into the village. Even as we came into the square I saw him. He was dressed in SS uniform, walking towards us, pistol in hand. He looked up in surprise – and died.

I took in the scene in an instant. The church in the middle of the square . . . a large truck . . . two German staff cars . . . the crowd of SS men in front of the church . . .

The staff cars and the truck burst into flames as, standing in my seat, I raked the square with fire from my twin machine guns. The crowd of SS men stampeded for cover. Many of them died in those first few seconds in front of the church, lit by the flickering flames of the burning vehicles.

Even as I fired I shouted to Hall to reverse. The jeep jerked to a halt about thirty yards from the church. The Germans who had escaped the first fury of our assault were now returning our fire. I turned to see why Hall had not got the jeep moving back. He lay slumped over the wheel. The tell-tale gouts of blood told their own story. Curly Hall was dead.

Still firing, I pressed the starter with my foot. The engine was still, hit by the burst of fire that had got Hall. Then my guns jammed. No time to try and put them right. I dashed round to use the rear gun. It fired one burst and stopped.

There was now only the single gun by the driver's seat. I got round to it, managed to fire a couple of short bursts before that, too, jammed. A dud jeep and three jammed guns. Hell, what a mess!

I had forgotten all about the second jeep. Now I could hear its guns hammering away over my shoulder. It was drawn up against the wall of the road leading into the square. There were Germans at the upper windows of the building immediately overlooking us. Stewart's Colt cracked again and again as they tried to fire down on us.

All this I took in in a flash. My own plight was too desperate, standing as I was in the middle of the crossroads. I reached over and snatched up my carbine. Thank heavens it was semi-automatic. I fired off the fifteen rounds in the magazine . . . changed the magazine. Blast this broken finger. The damned splint gets in the way. Another magazine . . .

I fired wherever I saw movement. A German made a dash for safety. I fired from the hip and he pitched forward on to his face. Now I grabbed Hall, lifting him from the jeep. A sniper stepped from a doorway on my right. I took a quick pot-shot and dropped him. Aim was instinctive.

I managed to get Hall to the centre of the crossroads. The

124

Germans redoubled their fire. I started shooting again. I could see tracer streaming towards me. I weaved backwards and forwards like a boxer as if to dodge the flying bullets. There came a shout behind me.

'Look out! The orchard on your left!'

There was a low stone wall to the left. I ran to it. On the other side was the orchard. Germans were advancing through it at the double. I fired as fast as I could pull the trigger. They disappeared.

Back to the jeep. Fauchois had run forward and was trying to drag Hall back to the second jeep. 'Get back, you fool! Get back!' I yelled. The Germans were concentrating their fire on him now. No sense in having another man killed.

Standing by the disabled jeep I kept up a rapid rate of fire. How many magazines left? I didn't know. Suddenly I remembered it was my wedding anniversary. With complete inconsequence I found myself thinking: Lord, my wife will be furious if I get myself killed, today of all days.

My right hand jerked and went numb. I looked down. It was smothered in blood. With my fingertips I fished out another magazine from the pocket of my smock and after much fumbling managed to clip it into the carbine.

With both hands partly out of commission now, my aim was getting erratic. The Germans, who had seen me jump when hit, increased their fire. The sound of firing from the second jeep had stopped. I dared not look round. Keep on firing, keep on firing . . . the words went round and round in my head.

A German stepped from behind one of the trees to take a more careful aim. I raised my carbine, now slippery with blood, and squeezed the trigger. Nothing happened. I lowered the carbine. My hand jerked again as the marksman's bullet snicked across my knuckles.

I looked down. Two rounds were jammed in the breach.

No time to put it right now. I grabbed for my Colt. The holster was empty. I swore. The damn thing must have jerked loose in the fight. Nothing for it but to get that jammed magazine out. Resting one foot on the jeep I wrestled with it as best I could with my gammy hands. The Germans were still firing, but there was nothing I could do about it until I got that carbine firing again.

The new magazine was in. Miraculously I was still alive. I raised the carbine. From behind came a shout: 'Dash for it!'

I heard the wild revving of an engine. The second jeep had been turned round. Stewart, Brearton and Fauchois were already in it. They shouted again. Firing as I ran, I dashed crabwise towards them. The jeep moved forward even as I leapt for it. Fauchois seized the rear guns and poured a last, long burst into the square. In a cloud of dust we disappeared down the road.

Harrison and his men had interrupted an SS execution party who were intending to shoot twenty French hostages. Two had been shot when the SAS arrived, but in the subsequent *mêlée* the other eighteen escaped. German casualties were sixty killed and wounded. Curly Hall lies buried in the village cemetery. He was much mourned by Harrison, who had been his friend as well as his officer since the desert. For his gallantry at Les Ormes, Harrison was awarded a well-deserved Military Cross. The SAS had many fine hours during the Second World War, but none finer than Harrison's attack on the SS at Les Ormes.

Another dramatic prover of the validity of the Regiment's motto, 'Who dares wins', was Major Roy Farran. His squadron of sixty men and twenty-three jeeps was loaded on to Dakota airfield on 19 August 1944 and flown to Rennes airfield, from where they slipped through the frontline. So began Farran's remarkable jeep Operation *Wallace*, which covered more distance behind the lines than any other 2 SAS mission of the war. The party drove 350 miles eastwards to join up with Captain Hibbert's Operation *Hardy* in the Chatillon forest. From there Farran began offensive patrolling. The local Maquis were active and well organized under the proud Colonel Claude, and Farran realized that they could not be subsumed under his command; 'a loose liaison, only combining together for certain joint operations' was the only way to proceed. Not that Colonel Claude was unfriendly; on the contrary, in the pursuance of the *entente cordiale* he invited Hibbert and Farran to dinner. Farran recalled:

It was a wonderful dinner, and in spite of our beards and dirty clothes the French treated us with as much courtesy as if we had been important plenipotentiaries. Many toasts were drunk and I partly blame the actions of the next day on the quantity of red wine consumed.

Over the wine-fuelled dinner, Farran hatched a wild scheme to attack the German headquarters at Chatillon château with the Maquis' help.

Thus was the genesis of the Battle of Chatillon. At dawn the next day, 30 August, the combined squadron moved into place. In his war memoir, *Winged Dagger*, Farran wrote:

My plan was to seize the important junction of the Montbard and Dijon roads. From there we would send a foot party with Brens, carried as far as possible by jeep, to attack the north of the château. The signal for the attack to begin would be the firing of the three-inch mortar on the château from the south.

Jim Mackie crossed the aerodrome and occupied the crossroads without incident. I then moved the remaining nine jeeps containing forty men through him into the town. We occupied all the main junctions leading into the market square, while Jaimie Robertson took the foot party round the back. I placed Sergeant Major Mitchell with two jeeps on the Troyes-Chaumont crossroads and Sergeant Young cut all the military telephone wires.

Dayrell began to mortar the château at about seven o'clock. He placed forty-eight bombs on the target in all. Fifteen minutes later a long column of about thirty German trucks, presumably containing the relief, arrived at the river bridge near Mackie's position on the Montbard-Dijon crossroads. The battle was on. Sergeant Vickers, whose jeep was in the middle of the road, allowed them to approach to within twenty yards before he opened fire. The first five trucks, two of which were loaded with ammunition, were brewed up and we were treated to a glorious display of fireworks. A motorcycle combination skidded off the bridge into the river. I thought I noticed a woman in the cab of the leading vehicle, but it was too late to worry. All the sounds of war echoed in the streets – the rattle of the Brens, the rasp of the Vickers, the whine of bullets bouncing off the walls, and in the background the stonk-stonk of the mortars. I got a Bren myself and, balancing it on a wall, hosepiped the German column with red tracers. The Germans had baled out from the back of the convoy and were firing a lot of mortar bombs. Bullets were whistling everywhere and it was good to see our tracers pumping into them. Parachutist Holland was killed by a bullet in the head and a brave French civilian dragged him into a doorway.

I could hear other shooting from the centre of the town as well as firing from behind the château, so it seemed that Mitchell was also engaged, although by far the greatest weight of fire was around our position on the Montbard-Dijon crossroads.

A pretty girl with long black hair and wearing a bright red frock put her head out of a top window to give me the 'V' sign. Her smile ridiculed the bullets.

A runner came up from Mitchell to say that a number of

Germans were fighting their way down the street from the château. The situation was so confused that the enemy was mortaring its own side. I sent Dayrell Morris up to reinforce the position in the centre of the town which was now hard pressed. Jaimie Robertson's Brens were firing briskly from the back of the woods to the north.

At nine o'clock, three hours after the action had begun, I felt that since Mitchell was being subjected to such strong pressure from the houses, although only one jeep had been hit, I had better give the signal for a withdrawal. The Montbard column was becoming more organized and there was still no sign of the promised Maquis reinforcements. I walked into the middle of the road, waving to the girl in the red frock, and fired two Very lights into the air.

Grant brought out Lieutenant Robertson's troop, while I led the remainder back along the Dijon road for breakfast. On his way back with the foot party, Grant met sixty of the promised five hundred Maquis waiting on the aerodrome. He undertook to lead them into the town with a party of seven men, at the same time sending a message to ask me to cooperate in a second attack. He became involved in a street fight in which he knocked out an armored car, but was beaten into a tight corner from which the party only narrowly escaped. A bicycle patrol of thirty Germans trapped them in a garden and, while they were fighting their way out, Corporal Brownlee was hit in the most precious part of his body. When I arrived with the main party I posted jeep ambushes on all the main roads leading out of the town, which destroyed eight German vehicles loaded high with troops. Supported by Jim Mackie in a jeep, I led a foot patrol round the east of Chatillon. It was all very quiet except for occasional firing from the direction of Grant Hibbert. With our heads bowed, we stalked round some Germans on a crest among some beech trees, crossed a canal by a lock and walked along the sides of the towpath. There were several Germans around the hospital on the other side, but they did not see us.

After walking for about an hour we found ourselves in a narrow lane leading down to the Troyes road. Looking around the corner, I was astonished to see a German machine-gun post on each side, facing outwards. They were all in greatcoats and had their backs to us. I could not think what to do, so we sat in a garden and waited. Lieutenant Pinci begged a bottle of wine, bread and cheese from a French cottage, so we had lunch.

I tossed up which German we should shoot in the back and it turned out to be the left-hand one. Sergeant Young took careful aim through his carbine, and when I gave the word he pulled the trigger. At the same moment, Pinci, excitable as ever, shot a German on a bicycle to the right. All hell was then let loose. I do not know from where they were coming, but our little lane was soon singing with schmeisser bullets. It was so high-banked and so open on each side as to make it a death-trap. With angry bullets buzzing round our heads, we burst into the front door of a French house. Running straight through, we scrambled down the bank to the canal.

After we had run along the towpath to the lock, I led the party across country to the east. We had just reached the cover of a thin hedge on a skyline when two machine guns picked us out. I had not realized that we could be seen. We wriggled on our bellies along the furrows in a ploughed field with the bullets kicking up great clots of earth all round. I have never felt so tired. I knew that if we remained on that crest we would be killed and yet I could not force myself to move any faster. Sergeant Robinson, behind me, was hit in the leg and still he moved faster than I. When we had reached a little dead ground I tried to help him, but I was too exhausted. Never have I been so frightened and so incapable of helping myself.

Jim Mackie appeared and we loaded Robinson into his

jeep. At the friendly farmhouse from which we had telephoned the mayor the day before, I dressed his wounds on the kitchen table, while all the women clucked and fussed around with kettles of hot water. After we had dispatched him to the Maquis hospital at Aigny-le-Duc, we motored back slowly through the forest glades to our base. The Battle of Chatillon was over. They say that we killed a hundred Germans, wounded many more and destroyed nine trucks, four cars and a motorcycle.

Operation *Wallace* ended on 7 September 1944, by which time Farran's squadron claimed 500 Germans killed or seriously wounded, twenty-three cars and thirty-six other vehicles brewed up, one train derailed, and 100,000 gallons of enemy petrol blown up. Many important bombing targets were identified and reported. All this was achieved at a cost of seven men killed, seven wounded, two captured and sixteen jeeps lost. Even so Farran, one of the most astute of 2 SAS officers, identified weaknesses as well as strengths in *Wallace* in his official post-operation report. The self-same report, incidentally, gives a valuable overview of the operational conditions in occupied France, and is quoted in full below:

It had been proved again that jeeping is not only possible but easy when the front is unstable. As soon as the front becomes firm, however, jeeping becomes difficult. The concentration of enemy troops on the line of the Moselle made penetration by vehicles very dangerous. It might have been possible with strict control of troops by wireless from a squadron HQ and with a firm line of supply. In this operation lack of previous training made it necessary to move the jeeps from one area to another in large parties under experienced officers. If sufficient troop leaders of high quality, reliability and experience had been available, I believe that more damage

131

could have been inflicted on the enemy by widely dispersed troops, only regrouping periodically for resupply. Three jeeps could have penetrated to areas impossible for nine. A firm base is not necessary for jeeps and it is better to maintain mobility by aiming at complete independence, without being tied to dumps. This of course is contrary to our previous ideas when we thought jeeps should always operate from a fixed base where refitting and refuelling could be carried out. When an enemy is withdrawing our type of troops do the most damage when they are placed directly across his axis of withdrawal. In this operation we were faced with two enemy centre lines, one from the west and one up the valley of the Rhône from the south. It was necessary therefore to move our area of operations about fifty miles south-east at least once a week. It was not always easy to find a forest large enough to conceal a base for nine jeeps. On the other hand there were always plenty of small woods adequate for concealing a troop. A troop could move daily with the greatest ease. Movement of a squadron column was always fraught with grave risk. It is possible to equip a troop to be independent of supply for a period of a week and to have a range of 200 miles. I believe that our operations were most effective during the last two weeks in the area of the Vosges, although during this time the enemy was very sensitive to our attacks and made our life very uncomfortable. I take this as proof that he disliked our presence more there than in other regions. During this period we actually knocked out a smaller number of vehicles but our patrols covered a wide area and knocked out important vehicles from large convoys. Another explanation of the enemy's dislike of our activities, apart from the fact that he was thicker on the ground, was that we had reached the point where the axis of the western and southern armies converged.

The best tactical team is two jeeps, but a troop of three jeeps means that there is always one vehicle in reserve in the event of a breakdown. A trailer carrying a 3-inch mortar is valuable to a squadron but the strain on a jeep's clutch over bad country makes more trailers inadvisable. In any case, in view of the tremendous weights carried on DZ's, spare clutches must be taken. In ambuscades it is better to sacrifice cover to enable the jeep to take on targets at close range. The twin Vickers gun will cut a truck in half at under fifty yards, but at greater ranges is too inaccurate. The principles of a good ambush are as follows: A position where the jeep cannot be seen until the target is within range but where the jeep cannot be seen until the target is within range but where the jeep is certain of getting a long burst into the bonnet of the truck as soon as it appears. A burst in the front part of the vehicle will set it on fire nine times out of ten. A good covered withdrawal. No banks or undergrowth which enemy troops can use for retaliatory fire. As soon as sufficient damage has been done, the jeep must disappear. It is not necessary to stay long enough to count the bodies. We were very pleased indeed that we had decided to take a Bren gun on the rear mounting. It was invaluable for accurate fire and foot parties. Fifty per cent of our bags were obtained by the Bren when the Vickers had failed. If the Bren is fired from a dismounted position, it must not be so far away from the jeep as to prejudice a quick withdrawal. Other jeeping principles remain unaltered. Firing on the move again proved to be a waste of time.

Jeep modifications

Although the modifications were quite sound, the workmanship was so bad that the welding gave way in many places. The following are the chief suggestions. The rear mounting should be on the back of the jeep in the centre. So many airlocks were experienced in the pipes from long-range tanks that it is thought that it would be better to carry three jerricans

133

on each side. This would also eliminate the total wastage of petrol if a tank is hit. The clips for Vickers magazines must be secured more firmly. The spigot swivel on the twin Vickers mounting frequently snapped. This was due to the standard mounting being too heavy. A lighter, strong, firm mounting must be designed immediately. The weight of the mounting also hindered accurate firing, being balanced on such a weak small centre point, it was top-heavy and unwieldy. A big iron rack should be fixed on the back of the jeeps for carrying personal kit. The following modifications were unnecessary – spotlights and smoke dischargers.

Personnel

The men and NCOs were all absolutely first class and their standard of discipline was high. Most of the newly arrived officers require training especially in handling men of this type. I suggest that no officers who have not had previous active service experience in a service unit should be recruited. Extremely young officers are usually an embarrassment in operations of this nature, which call for a great understanding of men and unshakeable self-confidence.

Resupply

On the whole was good. The only criticisms are the delay in sending articles demanded. Essential goods should not be put in one plane, i.e. one plane carrying all petrol, all cigarettes, etc. Too much ammunition and explosive was dropped when not demanded. There has been practically nothing to blow up in France since D+7. The method of dropping panniers, the irregularity of lever messages.

Wireless

Wireless worked perfectly well. The night emergency frequency seemed hopeless. Many encoded fatuous useless messages were sent on the broadcast which used up signallers' time unnecessarily. More use could be made of the broadcast to ease the strain on control by sending messages when reception on the Jedburgh set is bad. The tendency of No. 22 sets to wander off frequency made them useless for jeep intercommunication. I think a No. 19 set would have been better.

Although the lion's share of French duty fell to the larger 1 and 2 SAS Regiments, the French and Belgian units of the SAS were also busy behind the lines. Numerically tiny, about 300 personnel at its greatest strength, the Belgian SAS Regiment was commanded by Captain E. Blondeel and tended to be used for intelligence-gathering operations. In late August 1944, Lieutenant Gilbert Sadi-Kirschen, accompanied by five troopers, dropped near Compiègne to report on enemy dispositions in the area. By now the Allies had broken out of their Normandy beachhead, and northern France became an increasingly important area of SAS activity. Below is Sadi-Kirschen's diary of the operation, which was codenamed *Benson*.

London, 26 August 1944

It was the first day of my leave and I had to go back to Fairford Camp that evening. I didn't like the idea of a long journey by train and truck. Then I thought of ringing up Special Air Service Brigade Headquarters at Moor Park. They were sure to have a jeep doing a shuttle service between London and Fairford.

Captain Blondeel answered the telephone.

'Certainly, my boy. I'm going back to Fairford this evening. Be here by four o'clock.'

Blondeel had hardly set eyes on me when he said:

'Ah, there you are. How would you like to go off on an operation tomorrow evening?'

'Certainly. Where to? Belgium?'

'No, I'm sorry; north of Paris. It's another intelligence mission. SHAEF need to know every movement in that area. You'd have to send reports daily or even twice a day on the volume of traffic on the roads running from Paris to Compiègne, and Paris to Soissons. You may say they ought to be able to find that out with aerial reconnaissance, but the countryside is stiff with anti-aircraft batteries. You're also asked to pinpoint these Ack-Ack batteries, so that the RAF can either avoid them or beat them up, depending on how they feel.

'This time you'll be met on arrival by a reception committee provided by the local resistance, and of course that'll save you a lot of time – Oh, and I forgot to say that the name of your operation is *Benson*.'

'Who's *Benson*?'

'No idea. Look him up in the *Encyclopaedia Britannica*. There'll be six of you altogether – two WTs of course. Who would you like?'

'Moyse and Pietquin – I was very pleased with them last time.'

'Good. As second-in-command I thought Lieutenant Franck might be good. He's a Frenchman, and before the war he had a factory in the area where you're to operate.'

'Excellent. I came across Franck during training last year and we get on well together. For the two others, let's see, what about Flips and Bouillon who were with me in Normandy? They're real toughs. They used to be in the Foreign Legion.'

We were driving fast through the English countryside. It was a wonderful summer evening, and I felt far less nervous than the day before my first operation. Blondeel also was much less strung up. The squadron hadn't had many casualties up to the present in these French operations, and the results had been satisfactory.

'We're in Belgium at last,' he said. 'The office was against parachuting men into Belgium, and I had to drop Paul Renkin's group into the French Ardennes, but they were attacked and crossed over into the Belgian Ardennes, where they were received with open arms by the local Maquis, and I'm hoping to send them some reinforcements very soon.'

He was humming to himself at the wheel, and to my surprise, he suggested stopping and having a drink in a pub on the banks of the Thames.

'You're a lucky devil, Kirschen,' he sighed suddenly, as we raised our glasses. 'When I think that in a day or two you'll be overrun by the Americans and you'll be able to go and enjoy yourself in Paris.'

27 August

Fairford Camp was a foretaste of the Apocalypse: every uniform of the United Nations was to be seen, every language spoken. Scotsmen tested their weapons by firing over your head. Frenchmen checked over their WT sets or tried on their parachute harness. Norwegians, lying flat on their stomachs, studied their maps. There were some on their way to France and others who'd just come back, and who were telling stories of their experiences. And there were a few emaciated airmen who had just been fished out of the Channel after days in the water.

Lorries picked their way carefully between the tents looking for men who were due to leave for somewhere behind the German lines. 'Who's pinched my helmet? Anyone seen my parachute?'

There was a crowd round a jeep which was armed with a machine gun, a bazooka, one or two Brens and fitted with several reserve petrol tanks. Evidently this jeep was to be dropped by parachute. We wondered what sort of state it would be in after landing.

In all this confusion I managed with great difficulty to find Freddy, who was in great spirits. He had just been told that he was to speak daily on the radio in the five o'clock broadcast to the Belgian SAS. The thought of this greatly amused him.

'The broadcast will be preceded by the first notes of "Sur le Pont d'Avignon",' he explained. 'No one could fail to recognize it, even if they were as unmusical as you are. Messages for you will begin with the words, "Hello, Loulou Two".'

'That's charming. And what sort of stories will you tell us?'

'I'll give you the latest news of the various SAS groups, and also what schemes are being hatched in high places. As soon as your mission is over, I'll tell you if you have to come back direct or if you can stop in Paris and come back by easy stages.'

Everyone talked about Paris to me as if I were already there. For this departure I felt as though I were going through an old routine. The number of people who saw me off this time was much less impressive than for my first operation. Freddy was the only one at the take-off, and he gave me a great wink as the door of the plane closed on us.

The operation was to be a short one and I was to be met on landing. I felt that things were going very well.

28 August

Things went far from well.

First, of course, the kitbag went wrong. I remembered to unhitch it as I jumped, but I didn't manage to hold on to it tightly enough as it fell. I tried to slow its fall, but all I did was to rip the skin off my fingers. That damned kitbag. I always knew it would give me trouble before I finished.

Then I saw Moyse limping up to me. He had made a good landing, but had managed to sprain his ankle walking into a rut in a cart track.

138

And Flips had winded himself by falling on to his kitbag and getting the barrel of his carbine stuck into the small of his back.

Franck had injured his foot pretty badly.

Otherwise everyone was all right.

There was a storm somewhere in the distance, and we found each other by the light of lightning flashes.

But what was so comforting was that there wasn't the slightest trace of the famous reception committee who were supposed to meet us. We peered vainly into the darkness. There was no movement, no shouting.

It had hardly been worthwhile the pilot of the Stirling who had dropped us making me spend the last twenty minutes before jumping crouched beside the hole we were to jump through . . . His idea was not to let us drop without being absolutely certain of having found the right ground, and recognizing the signal letter.

'My instructions are quite clear,' he had said, 'if I'm not dead certain of the ground, I take you back to England.'

He was a conscientious man, this Australian pilot, and his conscience was surely quite clear, having persuaded himself that he had seen the lights of the reception committee. And then he came back over the ground. He must have uttered a sigh of relief as he dropped the twenty-four containers to his imaginary reception committee. We heard the aircraft disappearing towards England, the sound of the engines getting softer and softer.

Frank came up and whispered.

'King, what are we going to do with these containers? Where are we? Has anyone found the case with the WT equipment in it?'

'I know no more than you do. It's so dark we'll never find the wretched containers or the cage. Besides, with four out of the six of us injured, how could we carry them? Forget the

139

containers. Let's get out of here double-quick. As soon as it gets light the Germans will realize that parachutists have been dropped. Just a minute. Do you see that red light winking over there? Maybe that's where the reception committee is waiting for us, because the pilot did say he saw lights.'

In the blinding rain we walked as far as the red light. It wasn't the reception committee – it was a light on an abandoned train. Luckily there were no sentries, no Germans. Perhaps we were somewhere in liberated territory.

History repeated itself. As in Normandy, I looked for a signpost and then I studied my map and discovered we were ten kilometres further away from those delights of Paris which I had been promised so consistently.

We set off walking eastwards, and after five kilometres of difficult going, we went through a village, Valescourt. An hour before dawn all we had found in the way of shelter was a miserable clump of about a dozen stunted trees. Otherwise there was nothing but bare plateau and cornfields which had already been cut. Oh, for the deep forests of Normandy.

We woke up from a short sleep, soaked to the skin. Without moving from our clump of trees we looked about us. It was a dull, grey day. We could see German cars moving along the main road about 500 yards away and in the other direction we could hear tanks and carriers clanking along cart tracks.

This place was not too healthy for us. There was no farm to be seen. It wasn't like Normandy – here all the farmers and labourers lived in the villages. Just as Franck and I were wondering how we were going to make contact with the local inhabitants we noticed a peasant on his way to work in a nearby field.

I decided to disregard all the accepted rules. I knew one should not show oneself during the day, especially when wearing uniform. I knew one should not reveal one's hideout to local people. But our wretched little wood gave us such

140

uncertain cover that some relaxation of the rules was justified.

I went out and accosted the peasant. We were lucky. He was the son of a Belgian farmer and he offered to give us all the help he could.

'You've come to the right place,' he said. 'There are Germans in every village and thousands of them pass through here, because the main roads cross at Saint-Just-en-Chaussée, a few kilometres away. Personally, I'm not in the Resistance, but I can get Monsieur Lucien to come along later. He's one of the chiefs I think. Won't you take my sandwiches? You must be hungry and cold under those trees . . .'

In our first message to London I gave our position and asked to be allowed to remain where we were, so as to observe the Paris–Beauvais and Amiens–Montdidier roads. I explained that with things as they were, it would be difficult as well as a waste of time to shift our position.

In the afternoon, Monsieur Lucien of the Resistance came to see us. He was a local farmer, short and thick-set, with bright eyes.

'The first thing to tell you,' he said, 'is that one of my chaps has found all the stuff that was parachuted last night. He and the others made a real good job of it and everything was unpacked and hidden away before the Jerries got up this morning.'

'You didn't by any chance find my cigarettes, did you?' said Moyse.

'No, I don't think so,' said Monsieur Lucien, looking slightly embarrassed. 'I'll bring you some bread and smoked sausage this evening. Is this where you sleep, under the trees? It doesn't look very comfortable.'

'Do you know anywhere else we could go?'

'Why not try Folly Cellar?'

'Did you say Folly?'

'The Folly's what we call the barn over there, the other

side of the hill. It's a very good barn. Loving couples used to use it at one time. The entrance to the cellar is hidden by bushes. I could take you there this evening if you like.'

At five that afternoon we got a message confirming that we could operate in this area. We sent them the position of an anti-aircraft battery Lucien had told us about. I wondered what Blondeel had thought when he heard we had not been met. He'd been so proud of having that reception committee arranged for us.

At nightfall we settled ourselves in the cellar of Folly Barn. The name was ominous and so was the atmosphere of the place.

'The local couples can't have been hard to please,' sighed Franck. We lay on the damp stone floor of the cellar and thought regretfully of the warm sleeping bags we had purposely left in England, to give us less weight to carry about. But at least it wasn't raining directly on us.

29 August

We lay in the cellar till Lucien came and brought us some food and a detailed summary of last night's traffic on the roads.

'I asked Dr Caillard to come and see you,' he said. 'He's a good doctor and a good man. He'll attend to the sprained ankle and to your hand, Captain. He should be here in a minute or two.'

While waiting for the doctor to come, we went into the barn, about twenty yards away from our cellar, to try and get a message through to London.

The doctor, seeing this bunch of crocks, would hardly be impressed by us as professional parachutists, so we would try and put on a clandestine radio exhibition for his benefit.

The doctor arrived on a motorbike and introduced himself.

I've seldom seen a man so calm and methodical as he was.

142

He dealt with Moyse's ankle and Franck's foot and while he was bandaging my hand he suddenly began to talk.

'Maybe this will interest you, Captain. Yesterday, at the crossroads at St-Just-en-Chaussée, there was a German major directing the traffic. He stopped each vehicle to examine the driver's papers and pointed out which road he should take. I was rather intrigued by all this so I stopped and watched him for a few minutes. And suddenly the major wiped his forehead and went off to the café to have a drink. I followed him and noticed he put his map on the table. While he wasn't watching I made a copy of the map.' At this point he carefully unfolded a piece of paper. 'There's my rough sketch. That's the Channel coast and that line there's the Somme.'

'But it's incredible, Doctor. It shows every German division on the Somme. All the division numbers, the ones up in the line, and those in reserve. It even shows the position of Army Headquarters.' We looked at one another astounded.

'I'm very pleased to have been of service to you,' said the doctor quietly. 'Goodbye, and good luck,' and off he went.

We had an hour before our next period of transmission. Franck went into the cellar to shave. The five of us in the barn were sitting bunched up together while the rain rattled on the roof and swept in through the door which wouldn't shut.

I began to dictate. Never had a message been composed with such fervour or coded with such care.

'Following enemy divisions on Somme. Between Abbeville-Amiens . . . Between Amiens-Peronne . . . south of Doullens . . .'

'Can you hear that noise?' whispered Pietquin.

We listened. Yes. There was a strange noise – it sounded like a carrier clanking along a muddy lane.

The noise got nearer. We grabbed our arms. The noise ceased and three yards in front of us a German self-propelled

143

gun came to a standstill. The five or six soldiers riding on the gun carriage stared at us stupefied.

Flips and Bouillon opened fire at once. The Germans replied, firing incendiary bullets. The firing quickly became intense and then one side of the barn caught fire. Suddenly the gun carriage went into reverse and took up a position on the other side of the barn. Flips and Bouillon seized their chance, rushed outside and disappeared.

The firing started up again.

'Destroy the set, Moyse, quick.' But Moyse preferred to take it to pieces. He was very expert and he only took thirty seconds to do it. Moyse was very attached to his wireless set.

I stuffed the doctor's plan into my pocket. The smoke was getting very thick and at any moment the straw would catch fire. We ran out, screened by the smoke. We threw the parts of the set into a bush and ran towards the only thing which offered any cover at all – a row of trees.

We threw ourselves down in the wet grass under the trees.

'I don't think they've seen us,' said Pietquin.

For a minute or two there was silence, then the firing started up again more violently than ever. We saw two men running towards us, bullets whistling round them. Flips arrived first and threw himself down, he was followed by Franck who still had his face covered in shaving soap. He murmured: 'They've got me in the arm, but it's nothing much.'

'Where's Bouillon?'

'No idea.'

For a moment there was a lull. The Jerries had probably gone off to get some reinforcements, so we decided the best thing to do was to get away. But there was no cover, nothing but a field of stubble.

'We could hide under the cornstacks,' Flips suggested. 'They're damned small but it's better than nothing at all.'

Each of us crept under one of those miserable cornstacks.

The straw had gone brown with all the rain there'd been.

Franck kept a bit apart from the rest of us. I went over and gave him some sulphonamide tablets. 'Don't worry about me,' he said, 'I can manage all right.'

We waited all through that long afternoon. Between the sheaves I could see Folly Barn burning. A wave of depression swept over me. There I was, soaked to the skin, bent double, wretched, not able to move one yard and knowing that in my pocket was a document of the most vital importance which was quite valueless if I didn't succeed in getting away.

I was hungry.

And what had happened to Bouillon? I'd been so proud of coming back from Normandy with all my men.

And this was the operation which was to have gone so well, so smoothly and was to take me, after a few days, to Paris. And now it was raining torrents and I had cramp. Here and there I could see cornstacks moving a little and I guessed my men were as impatient as I was. But there was no question of leaving our hiding places before it got dark.

By nightfall we were all ravenously hungry, all of us that is except Franck who had gone off on his own with a peasant.

'We may find something to eat in a village,' said Moyse. 'Perhaps the Germans have left by now.'

He was indulging in a little wishful thinking. We tried approaching several villages but we heard nothing but shouts and orders in German. We would have to last out until the following day.

Luckily we found a few bales of straw and made ourselves a kind of roofless hut. Compared with our cornstacks of the afternoon, it was wonderfully comfortable.

We hardly slept that night and everyone woke up about four, in a very bad temper.

'Of course it's raining,' groaned Flips.

'And no smokes,' added Moyse.

145

I had one idea only and that was to transmit the message at all costs. I had to go back to the barn.

We moved off in single file and arrived safely at the row of trees where we had hidden the previous day. I told the men to wait there, and taking my carbine, I set off towards the barn. I crawled slowly forwards stopping every two or three yards to look around me in the half light of dawn. I saw no Germans near, only a column of smoke from the barn rising slowly into the air.

I went back to the trees to fetch Moyse. I wanted him to collect the parts of his set from the bush where he had hidden them.

I decided to go down to the cellar in the hope of rescuing some chocolate I had left in my haversack. As I entered, I heard a strangled voice say in French: 'Who goes there?' It was Bouillon's voice. 'Oh, it's you, sir. That's wonderful. I thought you were all roasted alive in the barn. I've been hiding here since yesterday. How are all the others?'

A few minutes later we were all five of us together behind the line of trees which had become our new base. But I'd learnt my lesson and I got Flips and Bouillon to keep a lookout, while Moyse and Pietquin fixed up the radio.

Making contact wasn't easy. London could hardly hear us. Pietquin put all he'd got into turning that generator handle while Moyse, swearing and groaning, adjusted the dials and knobs on the set. At last they could start sending. We held our breath.

Q.S.P. (I have an important message for you). Q.S.P. It was a long message: 125 words, each word repeated for safety and several times London stopped to ask for extra repeats.

Pietquin and fat old Flips took turns at the handle, smiling and sweating. Five hundred yards away we could see German cars going along the road. I wondered if we'd ever come to the end of the message.

We had been on the air for more than an hour when Moyse said:

'At last. They've received all of it, and I'd give a lot to see their faces when they start decoding that.'

We all relaxed. Our one problem now was food. We waited for Lucien as if he had been the Messiah. Late in the afternoon he appeared. He had expected to find our remains in the smouldering ruins of Folly Barn, and he was quite surprised to find us full of life and very hungry. He went off at once in search of provisions.

While we were eating, a German battery came and took up its position between our line of trees and the barn. We felt they might have had the decency to choose somewhere else. Luckily it was very dark and yet another thunderstorm came and broke over our heads. We retired discreetly from the tactless battery and slept in our shelter of the night before. We woke to a sunny day at last. We dried our uniforms and watched the German convoys go past, thinking each one would be the last one. We went on sending reports of enemy traffic.

At midday, London had a message for us. As Moyse decoded it, he beamed all over.

'A personal message from the General, sir,' he said, trying to seem unconcerned.

It was Brigadier McLeod who sent us his personal congratulations and thanked us for the information transmitted, which was of the greatest value.

'Very good of him,' said Flips, 'but we were damned nearly roasted.'

We listened at five o'clock. Freddy's voice was jubilant.

'Good work, Kiki. You should have seen the excitement here when your message arrived. Everyone rushed to telephone SHAEF. You never heard such a noise.'

'You might almost think that message had given them

more trouble than it gave us,' said Flips, taking a large bite at a sausage.

For the last few minutes an artillery duel had been raging just over our heads. From our observation post we could see the road clearly and we followed the battle with great interest, but without understanding very much about it.

More German cars came along the road. We counted them almost mechanically. Then they got fewer and fewer. We talked in whispers, watching the road. A Jerry motor cyclist scorched past, and as the noise of his engine died away, a silence seemed to settle down on the whole countryside. The sun began to set. And then, as we were sitting there, a little surprised at this strange lack of noise, suddenly all the bells of St Just pealed out together.

1 September

Liberation was followed by a kind of explosion of joy. We were invited everywhere, fêted, gorged, kissed. We went to St Just to fetch Franck, who had been put up by the mayor and whose wound in the arm was recovering.

Toasts, ceremonies, speeches. I managed to repeat the talk I had given at Longny a fortnight before, which still suited the occasion.

In a German truck and with American patrol, we bowled along towards Paris.

2 September

At Paris.

3 September

'Hello, Loulou two. Hello, Loulou two.' Freddy's voice was calm and cheerful as ever. His first message was for Eddy. He promised him some food in the near future.

Eddy? So Eddy Blondeel had gone into action. I wondered

where he was. Probably in the Ardennes; that was always his great ambition.

Then there were a number of short messages for Paul, Jean, John, Jean-Claude Pilou. Each name made me jump – all my friends were 'in the field'.

At last he got to me. 'Hurry up and come home, my boy, I'm off myself this evening. So long.'

We set off once more. We crossed Normandy, going via Longny to collect Regner, who had spent a pleasant convalescence at Monsieur Bignon's house.

As for good old Bignon, he'd progressed a long way since we'd last seen him. He talked about jeeps and MP's and doughnuts as if he'd lived for years on the banks of the Missouri.

6 September

Our arrival in England marked the happy ending of Operation *Benson*. And to this day I don't know who Benson was.

While Sadi-Kirschen was engaged in Operation *Benson*, 2 SAS was running its largest operation of the French campaign, *Loyton*, which took place slap up against the French–German border in the Vosges mountains. Strategically, 2 SAS was in the right area, since a retreating German army would be forced along a relatively small number of east–west roads and railways through the chain of hills. Consequently, ambushes on, and demolitions of, the communication lines could seriously disrupt a German withdrawal. Tasked by Operation Instruction No. 38 to gather intelligence and attack enemy installation in cooperation with the Resistance, an advance SAS party, accompanied by a Phantom patrol and 'Jedburgh' team (guides provided by Headquarters Special Forces), parachuted in on 13 August. John Hislop, who dropped with the advance, was the officer in charge of the Phantom party:

Our plane was one in which the parachutists' exit was through a large coffin-shape hole in the floor; so that the jumper had only to put forward the leg to which his kitbag was attached to be whipped down and through it by the weight, with no danger of 'ringing the bell' and without option of any last-second change of mind about jumping.

The first stick was made up of the SAS personnel, less David Dill, who led our stick.

The plane had been coming down gradually as we approached the DZ, till it was at a height of about 800 to 1,000 feet, when the pilot began his run-in. The men stood poised, taut, yet cool, like swimmers awaiting the start of a race.

As we neared the DZ, a clearing in a valley bounded by wooded hills, the blaze of the guiding fires on the ground came into view. I remember wondering whether the local Maquis hadn't overdone the illuminations a bit – they looked like bonfires in celebration of Guy Fawkes night – and speculating on the possibility of the Germans seeing and investigating it, though there were supposed to be only a few troops in the area, and those of indifferent calibre.

The plane sank lower, the noise of its engine changed in tone and lessened, and the pilot began his final approach. The red light went on, changed to green, the dispatcher shouted 'Go', and like pins in a bowling alley the first stick vanished through the floor. To the crescendo of its engine, the plane at once started to climb again before swinging round for the second run-in.

We took up our positions and waited. By this time I was trembling with excitement and tension, my heart pounding like a mechanical hammer, as I stood jammed between the man in front and behind – the tighter a stick is packed, the quicker it gets out, thus lessening the chance of dropping outside the area of the DZ. I felt a sense of claustrophobia blended with suspense and discomfort which, though it cannot have lasted more than two or three minutes, seemed interminable.

Just as it became almost unbearable, the green light went on and in an instant I was out.

The plunge into the night air and the brief, soothing caress of the slipstream as it twirled me about before my parachute opened, was as refreshing as diving into a cool stream on a stiflingly hot day.

This sybaritic illusion was dispelled immediately by the opening of my parachute and the start of my descent, hastened beyond normal speed by the weight of the kitbag. As soon as the opening of my parachute put me on an even keel I pulled the cord to release the kitbag from my leg, but only one strap became undone and the kitbag remained attached by the other, swinging about like a dog who has taken hold of a trouser-leg and will not let go. This was not a particularly happy situation. With some 50 lb heaving to and fro on my leg there was a sporting chance that if I landed awkwardly it would be broken, which rather disturbing thought at once occurred to me. Meanwhile the illuminations were getting nearer and, added to the bonfires, so it seemed to me, was enough noise to wake the entire German force in the Vosges. As one of the Maquis let off a firearm, either out of exuberance or by mistake – a far from infrequent occurrence, as we were to find later – it crossed my mind that the enemy might even be among the reception committee.

Only the bottom leg-strap of my kitbag being secure, I began to haul in the cord attached to the top of the kitbag in order to check its movement, the fulcrum of which was my ankle, before we hit the ground. Progress in this maneuver was barely keeping pace with my descent and I was not feeling too happy about the outcome. But just as the ground started to come up to meet me – that odd impression during

151

the final stage of a parachute jump – I got the kitbag more or less under control. Another couple of seconds and I crashed through the branches of a sapling and landed gently and comfortably on my back in the undergrowth. Before I could rise, a member of the Maquis appeared on the scene and began to help me out of my harness. Out of breath and in my best Wellington French I spluttered out the password, but for the interest he took I might have been quoting the starting prices at the last Plumpton meeting. All he wanted was a cigarette, the parachute material and any items of equipment for which I had no further use.

Greatly relieved to have reached the ground unimpaired and not in hostile society, I extracted my rucksack from the kitbag, of which, together with my helmet, my companion took charge, saving me from burying them. Then I followed him to the clearing where the party were re-assembling.

We were the first parachutists to have dropped into this part of France and from the curiosity we aroused we might have come from another planet. Enthusiastic and curious Maquisards shook us by the hand, fingered our equipment, asked for cigarettes and exchanged greetings. There were no serious casualties: Henry Druce was concussed, Robert de Lesseps seared his hand paying out the cord attached to his kitbag, and one of the SOE team dropped from another plane sprained his ankle.

Gradually some sort of order developed out of the chaos: fires were stamped out and we formed into a semblance of a column, the Maquis taking up part of our baggage. The sky was beginning to pale and with the approach of dawn a sense of urgency to get as far away from the DZ as soon as possible was conveyed finally to the rank and file of the Maquis by their leaders and ourselves.

At last we set off for our rendezvous, some ten hours' walking distance across the mountains. As we left the open, grassed area of the DZ for the concealment of the woods, I felt a certain relief. We had been hanging around too long on the scene of the conflagration and tumult which, I felt, would soon be discovered by the Germans.

In the cool of the early morning, after the long, cramped, stuffy flight, it was pleasant to stretch one's legs and march. Soon we had put one ridge between us and the DZ, so that even if the Germans had learned of our arrival and discovered where we had landed it would not have been easy for them to know where to seek us. As the morning climbed from behind the mountains to mark the new day, it began to get hot, despite the cooling shade of the trees under which most of our path lay. Our guides, used to the mountains, walked swiftly and easily up the steep inclines, but as the hours went by I began to feel the pressure. Apart from the effects of fatigue from loss of nervous energy, which excitement and anticipation had produced, and the weight of my rucksack, the weakness left by the attacks of jaundice and tonsillitis earlier in the year made itself evident. The sweat poured off me in rivulets, I gasped for breath and my limbs felt like lead. After each halt I lay exhausted till it was time to move on, and found it more and more difficult to hoist my rucksack on to my back when I got up. I stripped off my battledress blouse, sweater and shirt from beneath my camouflaged parachutist's jacket, and whenever I got the chance laved my face and neck with the beautifully cool, clear water from the mountain springs which, happily, seemed to be everywhere. At no time has the difference between fitness and lack of it been more deeply impressed upon me. My lamentable condition awakened a foreboding as to how I was going to cope with the exigencies which lay ahead, but the march itself seemed to put me right, because from the next day on I felt a new man. The impurities were sweated out of my system and climbing the mountains cleared my mind and attuned my muscles to a pitch which soon enabled me to return to a physical state which ordinary training had failed to achieve.

By evening we reached our destination. It was an encampment made of logs, on top of a wooded mountain, neatly built and well equipped with tables, benches, sleeping cabins and so on, the whole seeming as if it had been lifted straight out of one of Fenimore Cooper's books. The Tricolor flew from a flag-staff, and at sunset it was hauled down with military ceremony.

The Maquis were quite well supplied with food of a primitive nature: coffee made of acorns, coarse, brown bread, meat and various vegetables. We had brought rations of our own, which we pooled, the Maquis cooking for us.

I slept deeply and well, waking to a beautiful, sunny day, the clear mountain air and the stillness of the forest making it difficult to believe that we were at war.

Our first wireless schedule was due that morning, and guided by one of the Maquis, David and I took the set some seven miles away, preparatory to getting through to base. The Maquis stressed the danger of operating near camp, or in the same place two days running, in case the Germans succeeded in fixing our position through a direction finder.

The place chosen for us was a part of the forest where the trees were tall and deciduous and fairly widely spread, giving a noble, cathedral-like impression. Nearby some woodmen were working with a pair of oxen, and their musical cries, interspersed with the crack of an ox-whip, were the only sounds to break the stillness of the morning.

At the appointed time, we opened up. To the wireless operator this moment, the making of the first call, is a tense and thrilling experience. Hundreds of miles away he can visualize the base operator – probably someone to whom he has often worked in training – tapping out the call sign. And with all senses concentrated he waits for the thin, staccato

154

note, tuned at will between alto and treble, to carry the code to his ears. Straightaway, the first letters of the call-sign spelled themselves out, pure and distinct. Davis held up his thumb to signify the good news, though he had no need, since I caught the welcome sound myself. But the instant we started to answer the set went dead, as a thin, faint needle of smoke emerged from the transmitter, betokening that it had burned out. Mortifying though this set-back was, it was not a disaster, since Jakie had taken the precaution to equip each patrol with two sets. And our Maquis friend nobly volunteered to go back to fetch the second one, so that we could come up on the next schedule.

Davis and I lay beneath the trees awaiting his return, talking, or silently enjoying the peace and beauty of our surroundings. It was an unbelievable contrast to the happenings of the previous twenty-four hours, and feeling that the most should be made of it I clung to the passing minutes with that luxury of enjoyment felt when waking before it is time to get up. Our friend returned in time for the next schedule, when all went well. Indeed, the wireless communication throughout the operation worked perfectly.

Meanwhile, Henry Druce had recovered from his concussion and he, David and Robert began a series of conferences with the Maquis leaders, all of whom were known by pseudonyms, such as Maximum and Felix. The talks were not productive: Maximum, of whom my recollection is of a figure in appearance something between a gamekeeper and an actor, and his colleagues were obscure of purpose, jealous of their position and uncooperative.

It was a difficult and delicate situation. Until we were resupplied we had to rely on the Maquis feeding us, while they knew and controlled the few DZs in the area.

Four or five days passed in this way. Once, a thunderstorm broke in the night, but the next days continued fine, warm

155

and sunny. Each morning at the same time a German reconnaissance plane used to fly over the area. At first there was no sign of its having noticed our camp, but on about the fifth day after our arrival the Maquis reported that the Germans had searched the DZ, thrown a widely dispersed ring of troops round the base of the camp, and were moving more troops into the area. Henry then decided that it was time that we moved out, a point of policy with which, for once, the Maquis leaders were in full agreement. The plan was to split up into two parties and move by separate routes to a rendezvous in a different area. Henry, David and my patrol were to go with one party, Robert, Lodge, Crossfield and Hall with the other, the Maquis being divided equally between the two.

We set off after breakfast, getting out of the immediate area of the camp without seeing any Germans. The route lay along a path through the woods, easy to pick out. David Dill and Dusty Crossfield walked about a hundred yards ahead of the main body, as an advance guard. It was pleasant going: the ground smooth and springy beneath our feet, the branches shielding us from the heat of the sun and the gradations of light, shade and color in the scenery an ease and joy to the eye.

Henry and the rest of the English marched together, the Maquis following in a group behind us, chattering quietly like starlings roosting for the night.

We had been going for about two hours when David and Dusty, who had disappeared round a bend in front of us, came running back. They had caught sight of a German detachment fallen out at the side of the path ahead of them, but had not been seen. At once Henry ordered everyone to get into hiding and stay quiet until the Germans, who evidently were on a route-march, had fallen in again and passed by. His briefing before we left England was to keep our arrival in the area secret from the Germans if possible, and to avoid contact with

156

them until a base had been established and more SAS troops had been dropped into the area.

A hundred yards or so to the side of the track was a small hollow, in which the English party lay down. The Maquis deployed and hid among the trees and bushes on the same side of the track. Behind us the ground fell steeply down to a valley, the hillside thickly covered with trees and scrub. Our hollow could not have been bettered as a hiding place, though badly sited for fighting, since the lie of the land was such that it was impossible to see an approaching enemy until he was right on top of us. But since concealment and not battle was the immediate aim, it appeared to serve the purpose.

After a few minutes, we heard the Germans moving along the track. They were marching at ease, and their voices drifted over to us, interspersed with the clink of equipment.

We listened, still and tense, as the sounds came nearer, drew level, and moved on. Just as it seemed that all was well we heard a shout of '*Achtung!*', so high in note as to give the impression that it was uttered by a eunuch – a peculiarity of the Germans which we found not uncommon. Then came a shot, and the cry ended in a gurgle. At once followed orders shouted in German, firing, and cries from the French. From our position it was impossible to see, though not difficult to surmise, what was going on. It transpired that a curious member of the Maquis had been unable to resist the temptation to look up before the Germans had passed out of sight, was spotted and had shot the soldier giving the warning. Our first visual evidence of the situation was the Maquis dashing by in flight. 'We'll have to leave our kit and run for it,' Henry Druce said. By this time the Germans had set up a machine gun overlooking the hill down which the Maquis were fleeing, this being the only way of escape. Our wireless was packed in the rucksacks, but was useless to the enemy without the crystals and code-book, which I had on

157

me; this was one consolation, as it was impossible to carry the rucksacks or get out and redistribute the wireless. Henry Druce had the presence of mind to leave a stick of explosive timed to go off in half an hour in his rucksack, for the benefit of any German who might carry it off.

Henry directed that we should make a dash in two groups, my patrol in one, he and the rest in the other. Our hollow lay just short of the top of the slope, with a path running across the hillside a little below it. We crept out of our hollow and moved down through the scrub to the edge of the path, which the Germans were covering with intermittent machine-gun fire. I collected my patrol and waited until immediately after a burst of fire had ended, then gave the order to take off. When they saw us crossing the path the Germans opened fire again, but by then we were out of sight in the undergrowth and tearing down the hillside.

I caught a glimpse of Davis just in front of me and to my left as we disappeared into the undergrowth, and the others were close by me. About three parts of the way down the hill, which was some four hundred yards from the path near the top, I stopped to review the situation. The rest of the patrol were beside me, except for Davis, whom I never saw again. So dense was the undergrowth that it was not surprising that he lost touch with us; and there was also the possibility that he had been hit. As it turned out, he was unharmed but lost contact with us. Eventually, he made his way to a village, but was betrayed to the Germans and put to death, which was the fate of all SAS on the operation who fell into their hands.

Besides the other members of our patrol who joined me were three of the French: a young man called Marcel, a boy of about sixteen, and an elderly simpleton, whose presence in the Maquis is difficult to explain; probably he had attached himself to them in the hope of getting better rations than he would have received otherwise.

We lay hidden beneath the bushes, regaining our lost breath; and I pondered the next move. We could hear Germans shouting orders and calling to each other, and every now and then a burst of machine-gun fire.

Gradually, the voices became fainter, the bursts of firing less frequent, and it seemed that the hunt was being called off. Finally there was silence.

It was late afternoon when the Germans appeared to have moved away, but I suspected that they might have left some troops behind to watch the area, so I made up my mind to lie low until just before dawn, when it was light enough to see where we were going, and then slip right out of the area.

For comfort while marching in the heat of the day I had taken off my shirt and battledress blouse, leaving my body stripped to the waist beneath my parachute smock. As night fell and it became colder I began to regret this. Still, it was a minor discomfort, offset by the relief of being safe, at least for the present. At the first glint of light we moved off quietly. Marcel knew the country and volunteered to guide us to another valley, within reach of a village from which we could obtain food and, perhaps, information about the rest of our two parties.

A few hundred yards ahead we came to a path, which was being patrolled by a sentry, who looked cold, sleepy and bored. We slipped across unnoticed when he moved to the far end of his beat, and as we began to climb up the far side of the valley, hidden once more by the welcome undergrowth, I felt the thankfulness of a rider who has crossed the last fence safely in a steeplechase on a bad jumper. We pressed on, resting every now and then for the sake of the elderly man and the boy, till we had put some ten miles behind us. We halted high up on a hill thickly wooded with fir trees and clumps of undergrowth, in which we were able to find a hiding place invisible from a few yards away. There was no sign of any Germans and the stillness of the morning was broken only by the sounds of rural life drifting up faintly from a village in the valley below.

I had a consultation with Marcel, whom I was lucky to have with me. Energetic, resourceful and intelligent, he had refined good looks and an air of sophistication, which suggested the townsman rather than the countryman. We concluded that it would be best if he reconnoitred the village, to see whether he could learn any news of our companions, and find some food. As a Frenchman of the district he would attract little attention, whereas an Englishman in uniform might be received with mixed feelings, and possibly be betrayed to the Germans.

As Marcel began the descent down the hillside, I lay back in the warmth of the morning, letting my thoughts revolve at their will. It seemed that whatever military operation in which I became involved went wrong: first there was Dunkirk, then this. And I pondered the prospects of the immediate future. If Henry and the others had got away safely and we succeeded in finding them, well and good; a plan of operation could be worked out between us. Otherwise, the alternatives seemed to be to join up with the Maquis or try to make our way back through the German lines. For the moment, there was nothing to do except await Marcel's return.

A couple of hours later he came back, accompanied by another Frenchman. The latter was a cheerful, burly, loquacious type, with a full, ruddy, clean-shaven face and an alert, vigorous air. As they approached, I remember wondering about the advisability of his being brought right up to our hiding place, as not all those in occupied France welcomed the appearance of British troops or agents, and it was always possible that he might be in league with the Germans or the Milice. Perhaps the stranger sensed my doubts, for at once, in rusty but comprehensible English, he explained himself. 'Me was merchant seaman. Have been in England; I know Cardiff, Newcastle, Liverpool – I seen the Grand National!' This last observation established him in my estimation: in these circumstances the odds against coming across someone who had seen the Grand National were so remote that the portent could only be favourable. I informed him that I had ridden in the race, which impressed him; and the doubts which had filled my mind changed to a feeling of warmth and trust. He and Marcel had brought some food with them, and the seaman undertook to supply us while we remained in the area, for which I agreed to pay him out of the operational money with which we had been provided, and which, fortunately, I had in a trouser pocket.

I made up my mind to wait a day or two in the area, in the hope of hearing something about my companions: there seemed no point in starting to wander about the Vosges in search of them at once. As it happened, the choice of plan was a happy one. A few days later Marcel, who visited the village daily, returned with the news that Henry and others of the party had been located and that a rendezvous had been fixed for that night.

The respite of those few days was a halcyon calm after the stormy passage of our encounter and escape, which I welcomed. It emphasised, once again, the extraordinary contrasts found in the complex pattern of war. Here was beauty and tranquillity, the hours revolving round us softly and smoothly. From the pearl-grey of first light to the saffron splendour of evening there was nothing to disturb the solitude and peace. The faint sounds of village life rose and fell like the strains of distant music. At the height of the day I would lie full-length in a patch of sunlight, absorbing its warmth and dozing with animal enjoyment. My thoughts strayed down corridors of the past and pondered what lay beyond the door of the future. I repeated in my mind favourite pieces of

161

poetry and memorized others copied into a pocket book which, happily, was in one of my pockets. It contained excerpts from Siegfried Sassoon, Walter de la Mare, W. B. Yeats, one or two of Shakespeare's sonnets, passages out of *The Crock of Gold*, and various other pieces of verse or prose which had caught my fancy. It was to prove a solace both to me and to some of my companions throughout the operation, becoming known as The Anthology.

A further mental standby were the many lines of Milton learned at Wellington for the School Certificate and later in life, through having developed a delight in the beauty of his language. In times of stress it is the resources of the mind rather than those of the body which enable the individual to face the issue.

When we arrived at the rendezvous we found Henry, David, Dusty and the SOE officer, Gough, together with a number of the Maquis. We were also joined by Robert, whose party had fared no better than ours. They had run into some Germans and Hall had been killed, Lodge captured and, as we learned later, murdered. Henry then resolved to attach ourselves to the Maquis, which was the only way of getting any food, and to send a message back to England through the French underground, explaining our position and asking for re-supplies.

By now the Germans were very much alive to our presence, and began to move more troops into the area. We had to keep on the move continually. Every now and then the Germans would find our camp and move on it to attack, but always we got away. The forests of the area were a great boon, since they made it difficult for the Germans to find us and, having done so, to pin us down. They did not seem anxious to stray far from the tracks and never ventured into the woods after dark.

We had enough to eat, our diet consisting chiefly of brown

bread, soup, ersatz coffee, potatoes and an apparently inexhaustible supply of Camembert cheese of a brand called Le Petit Recollet. We built lean-tos beneath which to sleep, laying branches on the ground on which to lie, this being appreciably warmer than lying on the bare ground. When it rained, fires could be lit with safety, as the mist made the smoke invisible. Except for the cold at nights, the chronic diarrhoea produced by the unaccustomed diet, to which the French were immune, and the sudden, periodical appearance of the Germans, life was tolerable, if uncomfortable and somewhat nerve-racking.

When we moved camp, unless surprised by the Germans, we always travelled at night. A Maquis guide would lead the way, sometimes in impenetrable darkness and through thick woods, when we would follow holding on to each other's belts, so as not to lose contact.

Eventually we got in touch with England through the French underground. News came that we would be re-supplied and the map reference of the DZ, code-sign for signals between aeroplane and ground by torch, and the date and time of the drop were given us.

For five or six nights running we sat out on the DZ waiting for the plane. But either there was no sign of it or there was no reply to our signals, and we began to wonder whether the drop would ever materialize. At length, just as we were preparing to leave the DZ after manning it for most of the night, we heard the drone of an approaching aircraft. Our party had been joined by a Canadian pilot who had been shot down over France and looked after by the French Resistance, and he used to accompany us to the DZ, as he was able to tell from the sound of the engine whether an aircraft belonged to the enemy or the Allies. This was a help, as several of the planes to pass over the DZ had been German ones. He identified this as British, and when it was directly overhead we gave the signal. It was answered correctly from the plane, which then wheeled round for the run-in. We waited anxiously and excitedly. Then it was back again, and within seconds dark shapes were floating down towards us. To our surprise, for we had not been warned of this, men as well as containers arrived. Altogether about twenty SAS, including Brian Franks, who had taken over command from Bill Stirling, and Christopher Sykes, the writer and brother of Sir Richard Sykes of Sledmere, also Peter Johnsen and his patrol from Phantom. This changed the whole outlook. Peter had brought two wireless sets and three first-rate men, his patrol corporal, Joe Owens, and two signallers, Bannermann and Bell, so that we could set up direct communication once more. We merged our two patrols, this time so distributing the wireless that no vital part was carried in a rucksack, and if we had to abandon the latter we would still have the wireless.

As quickly as possible we collected the containers and got rid of them and the parachutes. Some confusion resulted from one of the Maquis letting off a Sten gun accidentally, which caused the newcomers to think that the Germans had arrived on the scene – we had become accustomed to this sort of occurrence by now – and to add to the diversion one of the French threw a fit.

It was well after midnight when the plane arrived, and by the time we had cleared the DZ morning was breaking. We moved into the woods and lay in hiding from the rest of the day. The Germans must have heard the plane and suspected that there had been a drop, for a few hours after we left the scene they arrived. After looking round they began to shell an area which, I presume, they thought we might be occupying, but it was nowhere near our position. When evening fell we moved away and set up camp some miles distant, towards the top of a hill above a village called Moussey. So far as anything in our nomadic existence could be so termed, this was to be our permanent base. From time to time we left it, either as a precaution or to operate in different areas. After a few days, and influenced by the unimaginative quality of the German mind, which would lead them to believe that we would not return to the area so soon after the drop, we moved into a farmhouse close to the DZ.

Brian Franks took command and, provided with ample rations, arms and explosives, we were able at last to operate with some effect, instead of being chased about the countryside in the role of what was little more than escaped prisoners of war.

The arrival of supplies made a marked difference to our life. It meant the luxury of a sleeping bag, the warmth of more clothing and the benefit of better rations. While the experiences of the past weeks were not severe, they were beginning to prove wearing. Added to this the uncertainty and lack of purpose surrounding us did not improve matters. The unexpected appearance of Brian and his companions, and the weapons and wireless they brought dispelled this aspect of gloom.

I found Brian, whom I had known slightly before the war, an excellent commander. In build tall, lean and athletic, he was by nature cheerful, understanding, full of initiative and brave, appreciated the exigencies of the circumstances in which we were operating, had a clear and decisive mind and left us to get on with working the wireless without interference. His messages were brief and to the point, as opposed to those from the Brigadier, which tended to be verbose and not always pertinent. As we took down and decoded the tedious contents of his less inspired efforts, we often cursed his lack of imagination regarding the conditions in which we were operating and wished he could be given a course in message writing. Once we had to close down halfway through a call because of the Germans moving in on us. It gave Joe Owens and me the amusement of sending one of the more colorful code-messages on the handkerchief provided by the gentleman in Baker Street. In clear it read: 'Closing down owing to enemy attack'.

Brian had several conferences with the Maquis leaders, but found them no easier than did Henry; so he determined that we would operate on our own, with a small team of Maquis, who would act as cooks, guides and general helpers.

With periodical changes and interruptions, life took on a new set pattern. Twice a day we had a wireless schedule, coding and sending messages, receiving and decoding others. We also listened in to a special channel of the BBC allotted to us and run by the actor John Chandos, who was in Phantom. The messages were always preceded by a few bars of 'Sur le Pont d'Avignon', followed by 'Hello Romo, Hello Romo', and then the message, sometimes in clear, at others half in clear and half in code. If opportunity allowed, lighter features were broadcast, one (chiefly for my benefit) being a repeat of Frankie More O'Ferrall's commentary on the St Leger won by Tehran, a result which gave me a measure of satisfaction, since before leaving I had given a short talk on current racing over the same wavelength and tipped Tehran to win the race.

Parties of the SAS would go out on operations, such as mining roads, reconnoitring concentrations of enemy armour and noting the map reference, which we would send back on the wireless, enabling the RAF to come over to bomb them, and ambushing unsuspecting German troops. Every now and then we would be supplied, when all of us assembled at the DZ to receive the drops. It was hard work, since the place had to be cleared by first light and everything had to be carried to whichever camp we were occupying, these always being high up a mountain.

I learned to adapt myself to circumstances. When it rained,

I found that it was better to wrap my sleeping bag round me instead of getting into it wet, which made it difficult if not impossible to dry. In this way, lying on a bed of branches and covered from head to foot with a waterproof gas cape, I have slept soundly and comfortably through nights of pouring rain.

We had not been in the farmhouse by the last DZ many days when, one evening, a large detachment of German troops appeared down the drive. They had no idea that we were in the area, and approached casually, probably in search of food or billets. They were no more than a hundred yards away when they came into view, but by the time they reached the front door the farmer, his wife and the rest of us were out at the back door and into the woods. Marching through the night, we went back to our base above Moussey unpursued.

Virtually all our movements about the country took place at night, the darkness being one of our best friends. The pitch-black nights, when we had to hold on to each other's belts to avoid losing touch completely, were varied by those of brilliant moonlight. In the forest this gave strange and weird effects of silver and ebony, casting grotesque shapes and shadows, which to the imaginative mind could represent anything from a spectre to a German. For me the scene used to conjure up thoughts of James Stephens' vivid and terrifying story *Etched in Moonlight*.

More SAS were dropped into the area later on, though through losses and departures back through the lines we were never all together at the same time. Several men, including a pre-war racing acquaintance, Denny Reynolds, were captured – all later being murdered – near a lake called Lac de la Mer; 'Lac des Cygnes', Christopher Sykes renamed it. And after being separated from the main body following a skirmish, two of the Phantom men, Bell and Sullivan, went back through the lines, as did some SAS men involved in the same action.

Scope was added to our operations by several Jeeps being

dropped in, landing intact, a parachute at each corner. They were used with great success until finally captured, the star operator in them being Johnny Manners, younger brother of the Duke of Rutland.

The French in the area were extremely loyal to us, though many suffered on our account, an aspect of which Christopher Sykes has written in his excellent book *Four Studies in Loyalty*. One of the sufferers was poor Père Georges, a veteran of the 1914–18 war, in whose farm we sheltered for a while during a spell of wet weather. In the end he paid for his hospitality to us by being shot by the Germans. He lived in a house which might have come out of Grimms' Fairy Tales. It backed on to the forest, the front giving a clear view down the hillside; so that anyone approaching from the only path leading to the house could be seen a long way off. Père Georges was a small, cheery, friendly man, who loved to talk of his experiences in the Kaiser's war and was, I think, glad of our company and conversation.

We used to take it in turns to keep watch from his apple store, the window of which overlooked the path up the hill; and when the memory of those vigils returns the smell of apples and the beating of the rain on the roof provides its accompaniment, giving a feeling of sadness which, perhaps, was the portent of that good man's cruel end.

In the strange and extreme variations of those times were some of the happiest and most tranquil moments of my life. A few hours' rest in safety, a meal, a warm and dry place to sleep; these became every luxury that could be wished for. The worries of ordinary civilian life did not exist, and in my case there was no wife, child or parent dependent upon my existence.

It was pointless to be anxious about the future, because its nature was unpredictable. We lived from day to day, as it were, playing each ball according to the way fate bowled it.

Unreality and incongruity hovered as a Puck-like influence over all our doings. One morning I was alone in the camp above Moussey, when a message arrived from the village that an agent had appeared from St Dié, bringing an important document, which he would hand only to a British officer. The agent was hiding in a cottage a few miles away, and the Maquis agreed to provide me with a guide to it. I was fitted out with a black cloak, which I put on over my uniform and set off with the guide, a demure little country girl of about sixteen. We must have presented an odd couple as we walked along. We skirted the village, which was still occupied by Germans; but by that time we had become contemptuous of their presence, since they had made it clearly evident that they were considerably more frightened of us than we were of them. 'The grey lice', Brian nicknamed them, for so they looked when we watched them from up the mountains, as they moved about in the valleys far beneath. A couple of Frenchmen stared at us suspiciously, and for a moment I wondered whether they were Milice, but they made no further move and we walked on through the mellow autumn morning. Eventually we came to the cottage, which lay by itself just off a track through the valley. All was still and peaceful, but from the precautions which the agent took to hide himself it might have been surrounded by Germans. In the company of a dubious-looking blonde girl – subsequently she proved to have been acting at one time for the Germans – he cowered in the corner of an upper room. He was a thin, pale, nervous man, with hawk-like features and a hunted look. Our hosts, a smallholder and his wife, seemed amused at his apprehension and caution. The document which he had brought was a map of the German defences of St Dié, which Henry Druce, who made trips through the German lines as casually as if he had been crossing Bond Street, eventually delivered to the Americans. The farmer and his wife insisted that my guide and I stay for a meal with them. They gave us an excellent one, asking us to guess what we had been eating. It tasted like venison, which I named it, but in fact it was goat.

'If you and Peter would like a bit of variety you can go out this evening and mine a road,' Brian said to me one day. I was delighted at the offer and so was Peter, both from the aspect of the novelty it represented to us and the excitement of a venture tempered with a minimum of risk.

Our Sapper officer, Dusty Miller, explained exactly how to lay the explosives, fuses and wires, which was a simple and straightforward operation; and Brian showed us the position where they were to be placed, on the map. We loaded the equipment into our rucksacks and waited for night to fall before setting off.

Another and purely selfish reason for our welcoming the expedition was that by this time we were very short of food, and there was the possibility of getting something to eat from the inhabitants of the village through which we had to pass.

It was a fine evening, not cold, and we had plenty of time in which to accomplish the task. So we set off at an easy pace, relaxed in mind, but with the unconscious alertness which the circumstances of our sojourn in the Vosges had developed.

We took the usual, rough track down the hill into Moussey, which at this hour was as dark and silent as a catacomb. In the hope of finding some food we knocked at one or two doors quietly, but either the occupants did not open up or they had nothing to spare. So we went on our way, which led past the house of a friendly buxom woman and her daughter, whom we knew as loyal supporters and good friends. They lived on the outskirts of the village and when we reached the house we made our way round to the back and tapped on the door.

The women opened it cautiously, but recognizing who we were welcomed us in. 'It's good to see you. At first we thought it might be the Germans; they were here a few hours ago, asking a lot of questions and looking round the place, but they won't come back now. Come in and we'll find you something to eat.'

Gratefully we entered and sat down in the kitchen. The room was dimly lit, for security, the windows covered so that no chink of light was visible from without.

The scene had a dramatic quality: the faint, flickering light, which made the objects in its immediate vicinity stand out in unnatural clarity against the blackness of the remoter corners of the room; the unkempt, brigand-like appearance of Peter and me; the neat, clean, simple attire of the two women; the glow of the kitchen stove; and the air of secrecy which our hushed voices emphasized.

At the same time there was about it all a feeling of extraordinary warmth, comfort, friendliness and security. It reawakened an atmosphere of childhood: sitting at home on a winter's evening deep in a story of mystery or danger, which quickened the pulse with excitement and suspense. And if a tremor of fear crept down the spine, a glance at the familiar and comforting surroundings soon allayed it.

So we sat talking, of the war, news of the district, our doings, home and other topics, as the mother prepared us a dish of potatoes. By the standards of peacetime it might have passed for frugal fare, but to us it was a Lucullan repast; nothing could have tasted better.

When we had finished we thanked our hostess, gathered up our equipment and slipped quietly out of the house. *'Bon courage!'* the women whispered before they shut the door after us. Outside there was no sign of anyone. The night was silent and fresh, and we walked comfortably and quickly towards our objective. A couple of miles or so out of the village, two or three hundred yards away to our left, we heard sounds of activity coming from a grove of trees. There was a clanging as if of hammering on metal, sounds of voices and

171

a glare of arc lamps shining through the trees. We moved close enough to recognize the language as German and came to the conclusion that it must be an armored repair unit working.

We made our way back to the road and pressed on, till once more only the sounds of nature broke the night. Eventually we came to the spot where the charges were to be laid. It was a short and simple job, though with the passage of time I am unable to describe the procedure.

When we had finished we set off back to camp, along the route we had taken. When we reached the place where we had heard the sounds of hammering there was no light or anything to be heard. We hurried by and reached our camp before dawn. I never discovered the outcome of our efforts; perhaps the charges did not go off.

Not long after this, we were in our base camp late one afternoon, when several bursts of firing sounded further down the hill. 'John, you might go and see what it's all about, if you can. You'd better take a man with you,' Brian said to me. Accompanied by one of the SAS – so far as I remember his name was Jack Spencer and he came from Spilsby – I started off. I went ahead, placing Spencer to my left and about fifty yards behind me.

It was a damp misty day and the afternoon light was beginning to fade. The firing had ceased and except for the drip of moisture from the trees – the scene brought back passages of *Bleak House* – there was no sound. I walked on quietly and slowly, peering into the Cimmerian gloom. The only sign of life was a figure meandering through the wood, head bent and gaze to the ground, dressed in what looked like a grey dressing gown. 'An old woman looking for sticks for her fire', was the first thought that struck me. Unaware of my presence, the figure moved nearer, until I could see that it was, indeed, a German. I sank into a kneeling position and raised my American carbine, ready to fire. As the German approached, heedless of his peril, I had time to think of what I was about to do. I had no particular wish to take anyone's life, especially in this leisurely and rather cold-blooded fashion, but this, after all, was what I had hired myself to the Army to do, and if I did not kill the German there was every probability that he would kill me. So I aimed at that part of the grey dressing gown behind which I supposed his heart lay, and waited for him to come close enough to ensure his demise. Suddenly he looked up and saw me. An expression of surprise and terror crossed his yellowish face, and the cigarette which he had been smoking fell from his lips as I pressed the trigger – and nothing happened. Desperately I worked the bolt and tried again, while he unslung his rifle shouting '*Hände hoch! Hände hoch!*' But still nothing happened.

All acquainted with the American carbine will know that this estimable weapon has one peculiarity: the safety catch and the button releasing the magazine are placed rather close together. In the heat of the moment I had pressed the latter instead of the former, resulting in the magazine falling out.

Then he started to shoot at me. His marksmanship must have been deplorable, as he cannot have been more than thirty or forty yards away and got off two or three shots without hitting me, before Jack Spencer opened up on him and he ran away. The encounter produced no immediate repercussion, but we left the area before daybreak, to be on the safe side.

As September gave way to October, our position began to deteriorate. The weather broke, making flying impossible, so that we could not be resupplied. Hoping to starve us out, the Germans had stripped the countryside, leaving the French with hardly enough to live on, let alone feed us; we were beginning to run short of arms and explosives; one wireless set was out of action and the remaining one was on its last legs.

173

Also, the Germans were becoming increasingly irritated at our presence and stepped up their efforts to hunt us down, so that we dared not stay more than a day or two in the same place.

About the third week in October we returned to the Moussey base. Late in the afternoon of our arrival we heard an ominous sound – a large number of troops moving round us. We could not see them, but from all sides came faint, though unmistakable noises – steel against stone, the crack of a broken twig and, what was more disquieting, the whine of dogs. We could do nothing but keep absolutely quiet and hope for the best, but the outlook was not pleasant. It seemed impossible that they could not find us; and when they did we would be outnumbered beyond reasonable hope of survival.

I was sitting with Peter Johnsen and an SAS officer, Peter Power, who had joined us after being dropped into another area. At our feet were the embers of a dying fire. Peter Johnsen had been drying a pair of socks at it, and as he turned them over I noticed that his hand trembled slightly with tension. His face, in which the candor and comeliness of youth lay untouched by the erosion of worldly experiences, was pale and taut; and in his eyes was a look not exactly of fear but more of sorrow, as if for the years ahead which he must have realized could soon be snatched from him for ever. He had taken part in a SAS operation before joining Loyton, and had come through the past weeks with a courage, coolness and sense of responsibility beyond his years, standing up to the physical and mental strain, where others of his sensitivity and youth might easily have broken down. To have undergone all this and then be deprived of the fullness of life seemed a bitter injustice. He looked at that moment the personification of Raleigh in *Journey's End*, a symbol of all the anguish, sacrifice and futility embodied in war. And my heart grieved for him.

My case was different. I had to some extent lived my life,

done much of what I wished to do and achieved at least some position in my chosen calling. The past years had smiled on me, and if the end of the road lay just ahead I was entitled to feel no remorse. Peter Power was sitting back, half reclining, against the trunk of a tree, relaxed, motionless and as inscrutable as a sphinx. As ever he was smoking – he could smoke more unobtrusively than anyone I have known, the cigarette barely burning and as still as if it were glued to his lips. His strong, ruddy face with the scar on the cheek left by a bullet received in the North African campaign was expressionless. He might have been engaged in a game of poker, waiting for his opponent to declare his hand.

The Midian-like sounds continued, seeming, if anything to be closing in on us; but because of the thickness of the forest there was nothing to be seen. I thought, 'This looks like the finish', and considered how best I could meet it. I had no illusions as to my probable fate if captured, finding contemplation of that eventuality most distasteful. While not unduly fearful of dying, I had grave doubts as to my ability to withhold information against the Gestapo's methods of extracting it; and I determined that a certain end fighting would be preferable to becoming the subject of their ingenuity in making me talk. To my state after death I gave no thought. While believing vaguely in an afterlife I was sceptical of religion in general. My spiritual problem of the moment was to depart this world in a manner approximating as closely as possible to that expected of a good SAS soldier.

This gloomy reverie was dispelled sharply by a noise, which I felt beyond doubt would bring the whole surrounding force upon us in a matter of seconds: someone dislodged an empty tin, which clattered down the hillside from stone to stone, making as much din as if it had been tied to the tail of a cat loosed in an empty cathedral. Yet, astonishingly, it produced no reaction: the sounds went on as before, then gradually became fainter till finally they ceased. For minutes we dared neither move nor speak, but as the dusk deepened and nothing broke the silence we relaxed, and in hushed voices began to discuss the extraordinary affair. The whole occurrence seemed like a version of Kipling's 'The Lost Legion'.

That night we left the area. It was an opportune move, for shortly afterwards the Germans put in a strong attack on the camp, supported by tanks and guns. This suggested that their previous visit had been a reconnaissance, the result of which defeated their objective, since it gave us sufficient warning to get out before they attacked. The one tragic result of the incident was the capture and subsequent death of David Dill, when he went back to the camp to see if there was any sign of Henry Druce, who was due there on his return from an expedition through the German lines. David was a sad loss and it was ironical that, having survived from the original drop, he should meet this fate on what was to prove the last stage of the operation.

Brian now decided to send a message suggesting that the operation should be brought to an end. Bad weather had made resupply by air impossible, we had almost run out of food, ammunition and explosives, had lost all the jeeps, and in consequence could serve no useful purpose by staying. Besides, the Germans were making renewed efforts against us and it must be only a matter of time before they succeeded.

This news gladdened me. My enthusiasm for the operation was wearing thin, and the prospect of a continued game of hide-and-seek with the Germans, in steadily worsening conditions, made no appeal to me.

John Hislop eventually made it to the American lines. *Loyton* cost the SAS two dead and thirty-one captured, all of whom were executed by the Gestapo as per Hitler's order. Of the 210 villagers from Moussey who were rounded up by the Gestapo for cooperating with the SAS and Maquis, only seventy returned home. At the time, Hislop believed that *Loyton* was an 'expensive failure', but:

It was not until later that the discovery was made of the disruption and alarm to which our presence gave rise among the Germans. The troops in the area were kept in a state of permanent tension, never knowing when they were likely to be ambushed, or blown up by a mine laid on a road, or the strength of our force and how to pin it down. Instead of being able to contain the district with a few sparsely scattered units of mediocre calibre, they had to divert an increasing number of first-class fighting troops from the American front until, finally, an entire SS division was withdrawn for the sole purpose of destroying us. This threw a very different light on the operation, for it showed that the comparatively little material damage we inflicted was more than counterbalanced by the number and quality of the German troops which our presence tied down.

By the time *Loyton* was terminated, the SAS was in danger of becoming the victim of the success it had helped deliver. The removal of the Germans from France left little for the SAS to do. Field Marshal Model, one of Hitler's ablest soldiers, had stabilized the front in north-west Europe, roughly along the Rhine, and behind the lines operations in Germany were not quite unthinkable (indeed, they were entertained) but were eventually ruled out as being suicidal. So far in Europe the SAS had worked in arenas where some support could be expected from the locals; in Hitler's *Deutschland* that would not be the case.

Throughout the winter of 1944–5 the SAS became pre-occupied with finding a role for itself. One squadron, as we have seen, was detached under Major Farran for Operation *Tombola* in

Italy, otherwise the SAS had to wait until fluidity came to the north-west front in March 1945 to rejoin the fighting. At that point the SAS Brigade, now under control of 'Mad Mike' Calvert, was employed by the 21st Army Group for reconnaissance ahead of its drive into the heartland of Germany. Once again, this was not 'traditional' SAS work. 'We were satisfied,' remembered Derrick Harrison, 'if a little perturbed.' As they probed into Germany, SAS units encountered fanatical, if sporadic, resistance from Hitler Youth, the Wehrmacht, the SS, the Volkssturm (Home Guard) – anybody, indeed, the Nazi authorities could place in the Allies' way. When his B Squadron became bogged down at Borgerwald, in the Rhineland, the commanding officer of 1 SAS took charge in his own inimitable fashion. The resulting exploit won Paddy Mayne a third bar to his DSO. Derrick Harrison saw it happen:

From Borgerwald down in the valley came the heavy and sustained fire of machine guns. The radio crackled.

'We've hit trouble. Squadron commander killed. Leading section pinned down. Trying to get them out, but it looks sticky.'

My jeeps were pulled up at the side of the road, looking down on Borgerwald. The firing from the town increased as other B Squadron patrols, trying to outflank the German strongpoint, opened fire. The radio came to life again.

'Another man killed. Two wounded. Still trying to extricate.'

Down the road from the rear of the column came Paddy's jeep in a swirl of dust. Flat out, he flashed past and headed downhill straight for the heart of the trouble. Alone, sweeping past the strongpoint, he raked it with fire, turned, and with guns still blazing swept back again, stopping only to lift the wounded men into his jeep.

A second and a third time he returned, unscathed in the

face of withering fire, to rescue the survivors of the trapped section, and to recover the two bodies.

B Squadron's slog into the heart of Germany, which was typical of the SAS's campaign in the *Endkampf*, carried on. After Borgerwald, Roy Close, who was in Harrison's troop, wrote:

We pushed on through the village, now clear of defenders, white sheets or towels hanging from windows. There was further resistance in the next village which ceased after a short engagement when a number of Germans surrendered. We were making further progress against well-placed nests of resistance. But, as we feared, the land was too marshy to allow us to deploy from the road, so it was easy for small groups of Germans, the fanatical Hitler Youth, to conceal in copses and ditches to cause us trouble. As a result, we split the two squadrons again so that each could push forward on separate routes less vulnerably than in one long column. It was progress, but slow progress. What we did not know then was that, although we could hear heavy firing from the direction of the Canadian armour, their advance was even slower.

Several days into the advance we found the going more and more difficult. The lack of room to maneuver meant we were constantly held up on the roads we were forced to take by well-armed groups determined enough to let us get close to their well-concealed positions before opening fire. I remember one brush we had, when my patrol was once more in 'point' position on a straight stretch of road on either side opened up on us at very short range. Of course we outgunned them and after a few minutes two or three lay dead, others made a run for it and one came limping forward with his hands up. He had a wound in his lower back. He was not able to walk far in the direction of our lines and we could not provide the necessary treatment. There was a farm cottage nearby, so we took him there and handed him over to the two women occupants. The man spoke to them at some length as he showed his wound. The younger woman, speaking in halting English, berated us as cowards for shooting him as he was surrendering. I asked how was it if he was surrendering that we had hit him in the back? The older woman, equally indignant, was shouting at us in German and wielding a saucepan. We decided to leave at that point and get on with our mission. Was this, I wondered, retreating in the face of the enemy?

Two days or so later – we spent nights inside laagers formed by our jeeps – we found ourselves in a more difficult situation. B Squadron were attacking a village along their route but found it strongly held and were bogged down; couldn't go forward; couldn't withdraw to take a better position. They needed support. Tony, our squadron commander, spotted a track leading to the side of the village and asked Derek to take our troop down it to attack from the flank. When we got within sight of the village we could hear heavy firing, but we could not tell which part was occupied by B and which by the Germans. Should we make a blind rush at it and hope we weren't going for our own men? Derek decided to consult Tony.

We had been able to position ourselves in line abreast ready for an assault, but there was absolutely no cover. Sitting there in open jeeps we were completely exposed. That delay for consultation was nearly fatal. Within minutes we heard the tell-tale crump of mortar fire just before the bombs landed among us. The side of the village we were facing was the German side! Fortunately the first barrage landed in front of the jeeps and between them. They had our range not only with their mortars but also with machine guns that raked our exposed position. We were 'sitting ducks', so we did the only thing possible, dive for the nearest ditch!

I managed to crawl into a very muddy but rather shallow ditch. I dragged my .45 from my holster and momentarily lay there wondering which way to crawl to find a position from which I could see where our colleagues were and what was going on. I realized I was alone. I could hear bullets and mortar fragments peppering the jeeps. With no logical or tactical reason, I chose my direction and crawled along. I had to keep very low and the mud almost covered me. The .45 in my hand was also covered with mud, squeezed up into the barrel. Then I was conscious of machine-gun fire from my left just a few yards from where I lay, directed over the ditch at the now-empty jeeps. Someone had got round the back of us. Carefully I raised my head.

On a small mound a yard or two away, just above me, were two Germans with a tripod-mounted machine gun, a Spandau I think. They were talking to each other as they fired. How they didn't see me I shall never know. Moving as carefully as I could I wiped some of the mud off my .45 and examined the barrel stuck with mud. I told myself that the first round would clear it, but suddenly the firing stopped. I looked up again and saw that they had picked up their gun and were making their way quickly towards the side of the village. What seemed to have moved them was the sound of approaching jeeps.

Two B-Squadron jeeps were attacking the village from the flank to rescue the men who had been pinned down. Later we learned that some had been captured with two of our jeeps. With this attack the German firing from the village stopped. I stood up. Other temporary occupants of that long muddy ditch were pulling themselves up, including Tony and Derek, and moving towards our jeeps. Some had been badly damaged by the mortar and machine-gun fire and had to be towed back to where we were to rejoin the other troops of the squadron. The village was no longer a target: our men had been rescued and the Germans had withdrawn. As my section lined up to retrace our tracks I saw movements in the distance beyond the village and to the right. It was long range so I moved forward a few yards and told Chris to loose off a couple of bursts. As he did so a bullet shattered but did not penetrate the semi-circle of bullet-proof glass in front of my face. There was a sniper somewhere. Silently I offered a prayer of thanks to the armourers. There was no more movement in the distance, so we rejoined our colleagues who were delighted to have the proof that the glass on the jeeps was bullet-proof.

By now we were getting worried about supplies. We were thirty or forty miles into enemy territory and food, petrol and ammunition were running low. As we moved we had tried to set up bases, mainly for our workshops. A number of jeeps needed repairs, but we also needed places to which supplies could be sent from a DZ. Unfortunately the 'drops' were delayed.

However, we moved on, wiping out the many pockets of resistance as we went, destroying equipment and taking prisoners. By this time we had too many prisoners, over 300. They did not like being dragged along in our wake as we fought and captured more, and they were increasingly a handicap for us. Moreover, they outnumbered us! However, Paddy decided it might be helpful if we ran into real difficulty to keep some of them with us, so we carried with us what he described as the 'best-looking' ninety and sent the rest walking back to our lines!

We moved on, anxious to keep parallel, as we thought, with the Canadian Armour. But in fact we discovered we were well ahead of them. We were out on a limb and it was not long before the enemy realized it. We were resting in a clearing in a pine forest somewhere on the road from Cloppenburg when we discovered we were surrounded by a well-organized formation of Germans, including Paratroops. Again we formed a laager with our jeeps, manned the perimeter and put our German prisoners in the centre. We were under machine-gun and sniper fire, and the prisoners asked for protection under the Geneva Convention, a request that evoked a short but explicit reply from Paddy. A pine forest with trees close together is not the best place to get a good field of fire, so while the German fire was not very effective, nor our counter-fire, we couldn't move out into more open ground unless we found a route through them or round them. So we organized small patrols to probe through the woods.

One such patrol, comprising two great friends, Tim and Ronnie, and one of their men, went through a part of our perimeter armed with a password for their re-entry. They could not find their way back and, sadly, probably because all pine trees look the same, attempted to re-enter our perimeter at a different point, one where the password meant nothing. They were shot by our own men. Ronnie was not seriously hurt, but Tim was severely wounded. Casualties by 'friendly fire' is not a new experience in war. Paddy could see that Tim needed urgent medical attention, which we could not provide. He immediately arranged for him to be taken out to the German lines in a jeep under a white flag, accompanied by Neville Edwards, an officer from the Royal Engineers who was with us, and a German prisoner who was instructed to tell the Germans that if Tim was not properly looked after eighty-nine prisoners would not get back home, and he was sworn not to give our exact position away.

All this happened while I was away with my patrol looking for a way out on the other side of the perimeter. When I returned I told my patrol to brew up while I went to report our failure to find a way to penetrate the encirclement. As I was talking to Paddy, Neville returned and went straight to him and told him he was fairly sure he saw the prisoner indicate our position on a map. Paddy's reaction was instantaneous, a fine example of his quick tactical brain. Jumping into his jeep, he told us to take as many prisoners as we could and follow him out of the clearing. Because of our position in the laager my patrol was last to follow. I doubt we were more than a hundred yards away when mortar and shell fire landed where we had been. Again, Paddy's quick thinking saved lives.

It was the SAS who were first into Belsen concentration camp. After being inoculated against infectious diseases, the SAS men were requested to enter the camp to see what medical attention was needed. That L Detachment stalwart, Johnny Cooper, who had been commissioned in the field by David Stirling, recalled:

Arriving at the camp, we motored down one side of the perimeter which was screened by tall evergreens, successfully hiding the horrors within. When we reached the main gate we were confronted by what looked like a normal military base with well-tended flower beds and whitewashed kerb-stones. To guard the place, the Germans had left a large contingent of Hungarian and Romanian auxiliaries who patrolled both inside and outside the perimeter. Our mission was to enter the camp to establish the medical requirements and to prepare for the arrival of Army and Red Cross medical teams. We were met by an SS officer by the name of Kramer who introduced himself as the administrative officer. He seemed most willing to oblige and declared that he was not responsible for the condition of the inmates. He was later hanged in Hamelin Prison after a British war crimes court had established his guilt beyond any shadow of a doubt.

Once inside we realized the vast size of the camp, and I will never forget my first sight of the inmates. Ostensibly they were living human beings, but to me, the men, women and even children were just walking skeletons. When they realized that we had come to liberate them, some managed to find enough energy to swarm towards the barbed wire which contained them. In fact, in their joy, some impaled themselves on the barbs without any apparent registration of pain. Moving on, we then discovered a whole series of communal graves, consisting of trenches about a hundred yards long and twenty feet deep, which were being steadily filled with naked skeletal bodies. Lime was casually thrown over them, presumably to try to contain the danger of infection.

We stood aghast! We simply could not comprehend how it was possible for human beings to treat their fellow men in such a brutal and heinous way. I walked into one of the barrack huts, a long, low, wooden affair which was crammed with bunks one on top of the other in four tiers. Many of the bunks were occupied with dead bodies, as the other inmates had been too feeble to pull them out for burial. One man I was able to speak to was a Belgian journalist who said that he had been there for some time. He told me that we might be able to restore some of the inmates to bodily health but that their minds would be distorted for years to come – perhaps for ever.

Gradually the medical teams assembled and it became possible to set up soup kitchens. The poor wretches could only take in a limited amount of liquid nourishment as solid food would have killed them. The more we witnessed the living proof of human beings' capacity for ill-treatment of their fellows, the more we found it difficult to keep control of ourselves. The effect on Reg Seekings was one of utter rage. I could see that he was on the verge of pulling out his pistol and shooting the first German guard he came across. The Hungarian auxiliaries were just as bad. A woman prisoner thrust her hand under the wire to try to grab a rotten turnip and one of them shot her dead.

Three weeks later the war in Europe was over. Reg Seekings who, like his friend Johnny Cooper, had been one of the very first volunteers for L Detachment, was filling up with petrol outside Brussels when a young girl came running out, and told him, 'The war is finished.'

Seekings replied, 'I've heard that before.'

'No, it's true,' she insisted. 'Your prime minister, Mr Churchill, is speaking now.'

Seekings ran into the garage, where the wireless was tuned to the BBC. Sure enough, the war with Germany was over. Some SAS troops celebrated in Brussels, but Seekings decided to join those in Poperinge, which had been a recreational centre for British troops in the First World War. He declared later:

I was glad I did, because it was just as my old man had described it, hadn't changed at all. They were all sitting outside on the pavement, having a drink. All those old girls were there and we kept running out to the gents. Then we heard this old girl say, 'They're just like their fathers, drink-drink-drink, piss-piss-piss.'

The partying continued when the SAS returned to Britain. Paddy Mayne drunkenly drove a jeep up the marble stairs of 1 SAS officers' mess at Hylands Park, where it got stuck and had to be freed by fitters the next morning. On another occasion he made an emergency call to the local fire brigade. When they turned up, they found they had been invited for a drink.

The partying came to an abrupt end at the beginning of October, when the SAS was ordered to disband.

PART II

THE LITTLE WARS OF PEACE

The SAS, 1947–81

On the morning of 8 October 1945, 1 SAS paraded at Hylands Park for the last time. 'The whole regiment was drawn up,' wrote Johnny Cooper, 'squadron by squadron, in front of the main house, with Paddy Mayne out in front.' Mayne was the only one present wearing the sandy-colored beret of the desert; everyone else was wearing the red beret of the Airborne divisions.

The salute was taken by Mike Calvert. He and Mayne had 'history' – only months before they had brawled in the mess – however, today both men had other things on their mind beyond their personal enmity. Despite their best efforts to find a role for the SAS in the peacetime army, they had failed. On the same day that 1 SAS was disbanded, 2 SAS took its farewell parade at its Colchester HQ. The French and the Belgian regiments had already been returned to their respective countries.

Johnny Cooper, like many other SAS stalwarts, found the end of the war 'an anti-climax'. His old partner-in-arms, Reg Seekings, said, 'It [was] like the bottom dropping out of the world.' For his part, Paddy Mayne found the idea of a return to the law unappealing. 'The more I think of being a solicitor again,' he wrote to his mother, 'the less I like it.' Paddy Mayne never did settle to 'civvy street'; he was killed in a car accident in 1955 following another of his mammoth drinking sprees.

Officially, the SAS founded by Stirling, Lewes and Mayne

ceased to exist on 8 October 1945; in actuality, it remained alive. Just. A team of SAS men, including L Detachment Original Bob Bennett, were attached to the Military Reparations Committee in Greece, where they proudly sported their winged-dagger badge. Brian Franks, still pained and outraged by the murder of SAS soldiers during *Loyton* and other operations, organized a team to investigate the crimes and bring those responsible to justice. This became the SAS War Crimes Team, which operated for four years and successfully identified several Nazi perpetrators. Beyond these two small SAS remnants, the Regiment's veterans kept in personal contact. Johnny Cooper was invited by David Stirling, long since released from Colditz, to lunch at White's in London. Stirling, thought Cooper, 'looked none the worse' for his stay at Hitler's pleasure. Also in attendance were George Jellicoe, Fitzroy Maclean and Randolph Churchill. Such social occasions were pleasant chances to air memories. They were also opportunities for ex-SAS men to plan the Regiment's rise anew. Eventually, lobbying of the War Office by SAS veterans, chiefly Mike Calvert and Brian Franks, brought its reward, and in 1947 an SAS unit was formed within the Territorial Army. It was attached to a former officers' training unit, the Artists' Rifles, to become 21 (Artists) TA, based at Duke's Road, Euston. The commanding officer was Lieutenant Colonel Brian Franks, 2 SAS's sometime commander during the Second World War.

Wartime SAS soldiers flocked to the new TA SAS, so many indeed that Johnny Cooper found the first training camp 'a splendid reunion'. This TA SAS unit, which still exists and is complemented by another TA SAS unit, 23 SAS, provided many of the volunteers for a long-range patrol Franks raised for Korea, where the first major war since 1945 was being fought between the Communist North and the UN-backed South. Before Franks' jeep patrol could be sent to Korea, though, the UN commander, General McArthur, decided he had no use for it.

What was McArthur's loss was Britain's gain. A communist

insurrection – known as 'The Emergency' for insurance-claim purposes – had broken out in the British dominion of Malaya. From hide-outs in the jungle, Communist Terrorists ('CTs'), led by Chin Peng of the Malayan Races Liberation Army (MRLA), were murdering British rubber-plantation owners and their families. The Commander-in-Chief Far East, Sir John Harding, summoned Mike Calvert to Malaya and asked him to find ways of dealing with the CT campaign. Before becoming commanding officer of the SAS Brigade during the Second World War, Calvert had commanded 77 Chindit Brigade. Mad Mike, along with Freddie Spencer Chapman, soldier and author of the memoir *The Jungle is Neutral*, was as close to an expert jungle-fighter as the British possessed. Looking at the situation in Malaya, Calvert realized that The Emergency required the British to have a special force that would 'live, move, and have its heart in the jungle' just as the enemy did. His proposal for a new unit, the Malayan Scouts (SAS), was accepted. For personnel for the unit, Calvert milked three sources: A Squadron was formed from 100 volunteers in the British Army already in the Far East; B Squadron was comprised of soldiers from 1 SAS, primarily those who had put up their hands for the Korean job; and C Squadron was made up of Rhodesian volunteers.

Unfortunately, while B Squadron – thoroughly marinated in SAS philosophy, discipline and training either by war service or Brian Franks' Duke's Road regime – was the right SAS stuff, the Rhodesians were keen but undertrained. But the real headache was A Squadron, who, save for a few good apples, were poseurs and party-animals. It did not help that Calvert himself was keen on wild drinking parties. So notorious was A Squadron's indiscipline that the Malayan Scouts were almost disbanded. Instead, Calvert was sent home with a convenient (and fictitious) kidney illness, and Lieutenant Colonel John Sloane was brought in as commanding officer. A straight-backed, by-the-book officer from the Argyll and Sutherland Highlanders, 'Tod' Sloane unsentimentally returned to unit misfits and implemented proper admin. He was ably assisted in his makeover of the Malayan Scouts by John Woodhouse and Dare Newell, men who were both to become legendary figures in SAS history. To make the regiment more attractive to volunteers, its name was changed from Malayan Scouts – which, after all, suggested members would only serve in Malaya – to '22 SAS'.

And yet, for all Calvert's waywardness he was, more than Sloane, Woodhouse and Newell, the architect of the modern SAS. Quite aside from creating a unit to bear the appellation 'Special Air Service', Calvert proposed that the SAS should work in three- or four-man patrols, the SAS should win over local tribes by kindness (what later became known as 'hearts and minds'), notably by setting up medical clinics, and that the SAS should establish long-term counter-guerrilla bases deep in the jungle. All three of these principles still shape the modern SAS.

The men of the 22 SAS Regiment underwent an experience in Malaya that their successors down the decades would empathize with: fighting in appalling conditions. Johnny Cooper, who had transferred to 22 SAS as 8 Troop's commander (thus becoming, by his reckoning, the oldest lieutenant in the Army, at 29 years of age), was dismayed by the rain. 'If there was no great downpour after three or four days, it was reckoned a drought.'

There were other unpleasantnesses in the jungle. After communist terrorists, Cooper wrote, leeches were the main adversary:

They would fall off the leaves and latch on to one's softest area, around the neck, behind the ears, under the armpits, and on a long patrol they would even find their way to one's private parts. You couldn't feel them, but as they slowly sucked blood they enlarged into horrible black swollen lumps.

Sores festered, clothes and boots rotted in the damp, and fevers such as Weil's Disease abounded.

Lying in an observation post or in an ambush could be particularly trying, as Trooper Geordie Doran, a recent recruit, found:

The duty was set in pairs for four-hour stags, or watches, during which time all SAS soldiers involved had to lie perfectly still, watching and listening, rifles loaded and at the ready. Conversations were in whispers. If a man wanted to relieve himself, he would first indicate to the others what he intended, then slither slowly and silently to the rear. Washing and shaving in the jungle, especially on ambush duty, was sometimes banned. The CT, with their sharpened sense, could pick up the odour of soap from quite a distance. Also, soap suds in rivers could be seen a long way downstream before they dispersed. Lying in ambush I was again conscious that the jungle is never quiet, nor still. Among other sounds, a troop of gibbons entertained us with their hooting most days. There was also the constant falling of leaves and debris from trees, and nearby a regiment of ants went about their business. Leeches gathered expectantly, and pig flies fed on the backs of my legs. Luckily we hadn't disturbed any red tree ants when getting into position. They are vicious little buggers and have a pair of pliers for a mouth. We had to take all the bites and stings in silence, as a slap or curse could have alerted an approaching enemy and been fatal.

By the end of a patrol, a soldier would have lost on average ten pounds. Despite the hardships, however, patrols stayed out in the jungle for longer and longer periods, as the Regiment's jungle education grew. Johnny Cooper once led a 122-day patrol in the jungle to establish a military fort in the region of Sungei Brok. Cooper recalled:

The first job was to clear a small area and then we radioed for confirmation that we were on the correct site. An Auster aircraft came over and we were informed that we were at least in the right place. To secure the place from the attentions of CTs, I placed three screens out on the most dangerous approaches to our clearing. Then the heavy work began, blowing down the huge jungle trees, clearing the area of bamboo and building a wooden bridge over the river which was at that point about thirty feet wide. In the latter job, our local Iban trackers were of great help with their skill in splicing creepers to tie the bridge together. The structure lasted for many months, although only two men could cross at any one time, and one had to get used to the swaying motion in midstream over the raging torrent.

By the middle of November we had cleared the site for the building of the fort and also constructed a helicopter landing ground as there was not enough room for a proper airstrip. This gave us the opportunity for more active patrolling into the aboriginal areas. Bruce Murray had a great success when he sorted out a complete CT gang, killing some and dispersing the others from our immediate area. To the west, however, we suffered a tragedy when another patrol under the command of Corporal Digger Bancroft ran into an ambush. Digger, who was in the lead, was killed and Trooper Willis behind him was also shot. Fortunately the rest of the patrol reacted promptly, engaged the enemy and drove them off. I received the news by runner, immediately informed our headquarters of the casualties and requested a helicopter to bring out the bodies. Volunteers stepped forward to carry out the dead men; one of them was Bill Speakerman, the Korean War VC who was doing his jungle training with C Squadron. This party disappeared off to Bancroft's old base and I ordered others to search for further traces of the enemy.

In the dark and the tangle of the Malayan jungle, contacts with the enemy were fleeting. On his epic patrol Cooper lost just two of eighty men to enemy action; nearly forty, meanwhile, had to be helicoptered out because of illness. Cooper's Sungei Brok patrol also advanced the 'hearts and minds' programme by establishing 'diplomatic relations' with a tribe previously under the spell of the communist terrorists, by befriending the aboriginals and giving them medical and food aid.

Perhaps fortunately, Cooper's Sungei Brok patrol went into the jungle on foot; during the Malayan campaign the SAS experimented with parachuting into the jungle. A successful jump by fifty-four troopers of B Squadron ('Big Time Bravo', as it was known by envious troopers in the other squadrons) in the Belum Valley in 1952, persuaded senior officers that 'tree-jumping' was viable, even desirable. Numerous personnel were thereafter injured, among them Johnny Cooper, whose arm was broken when it became entangled with a fellow parachutist's static line. Disabled, Cooper crashed into the treetops; due to his broken arm he was unable to tie his scaling rope to a branch and climb down its 150-foot length to the ground. Thanks to clever thinking and climbing by the medical officer, Freddie Brunton, Cooper's scaling rope was attached to a piton in a tree; Cooper then cut himself free from his parachute and fell sixty feet before the rope pulled him up. He was lowered the remainder of the way. The wrenching action of the fall, however, added nerve damage to his list of injuries. Cooper was far from being the only casualty of tree-jumping. Another high-profile victim was Lieutenant Colonel Oliver Brooke, who took over from Sloane as 22 SAS's commanding officer; Brooke broke his ankle.

By 1956, the Regiment was up to a strength of 560 men and was making a real contribution towards containing The Emergency; its tally of communist terrorists killed was eighty-nine. Captured communist terrorists confessed that the SAS patrols, even when failing to make contact with the enemy, were so disruptive as to render guerrilla warfare all but impossible. Four years later, The Emergency was over. The leaders of the MRLA had fled to Thailand, and the murders of civilians had almost ceased. After its eight years in Malaya, the Regiment had, despite an inauspicious start, become a highly professional unit. In 1957, in recognition, 22 SAS was placed in the order of battle of the British Army, and as a result was able to readopt both the beige beret and the winged-dagger badge. For all this, the future of the Regiment was far from assured: the whispers from Whitehall were that 22 SAS would be disbanded when it was finally pulled out of Malaya.

History, however, was on the side of the SAS. In the death agony of Empire there came other small wars. Malaya was not a one-off; it was part of an historic trend. Even as the SAS was mopping up in Malaya, another little war in a British-dominated corner of the world was beginning. The SAS, which had begun life as a poacher, was turning gamekeeper. The next peace-keeping job was far from the green jungles of Malaya, it was on the Green Mountain, the Jebel Akhdar, in Oman.

The ancient Sultanate of Muscat and Oman is a small arid country of such extremes of weather that, according to a Persian proverb, a visit there is a foretaste of Hell. Oman, however, has a strategic importance in inverse relation to its size; it lies aside the Hormuz Straits, through which pass 30 per cent of the world's oil tankers.

In 1954 a rebellion against the autocratic (but pro-British) Sultan, led by Ghalib, the Iman of Oman, and his brother, Talib, threatened to destabilize the country and interrupt the oil supply to Great Britain. With understandable *realpolitik*, if with questionable morality, the British government determined to back the Sultan. An RAF bombing campaign of the rebel stronghold on the Jebel Akhdar failed. An infantry assault on the Jebel failed. A plan to drop the Parachute Regiment was cancelled, because the Prime Minister thought the committing of a world-famous regiment over-emphasized the importance of the situation.

And so the shadowy SAS was given the job nobody else could

194

or should do. Lieutenant Colonel Anthony Deane-Drummond, the commander of 22 SAS, was given fifteen days to round up D Squadron from Malaya and deploy it in Oman. David Smiley, the Sultan's British chief of staff and a former SOE operative, planned and oversaw the SAS's campaign in Oman:

A week later they came – some eighty officers and men comprising D Squadron, under Major John Watts; they were organized in four troops, or patrols, of sixteen men each, together with Squadron Headquarters. Despite their small number they wielded formidable fire-power, with their Browning machine guns, FN rifles and Energa grenades. We had built them a camp at Beit al Falaj, but Watts, a stocky, tough and dedicated professional, sensibly decided to lose no time in making them familiar with their new conditions; for he realized that the steep bare rocks and sharp outlines of the Jebel would require tactics quite different from those they had learned in the swamps and jungles of Malaya. We therefore split the squadron, sending two troops on fighting patrols among the giant slabs above Tamuf and Kamah, and the other two to join Tony Hart [a British contract officer with the Muscat Regiment] at Awabi. Men from the Sultan's Armed Forces accompanied the SAS on all their patrols, an arrangement which greatly improved the morale and fighting skill of my own soldiers, who in their turn provided the SAS with valuable local knowledge.

The need for different tactics struck the SAS forcefully and tragically on one of their first patrols in the Tanuf area. In a skirmish with the rebels one of their best NCOs ['Duke' Swindells MM] incautiously showed himself on a skyline and was shot through the heart by a sniper. This sad incident at least gave them a healthy respect for the enemy, whom they had been inclined to underestimate.

The other two troops, with Hart and some of his men,

195

climbed from Awabi by the Hijar track to the top of the Jebel, which they reached undiscovered. They then pressed on across the plateau until they came under attack from some rebels entrenched among caves in a cliff known as the Aquabat al Dhafar; although held up, they inflicted severe punishment on the enemy without loss to themselves. While a platoon of the Muscat Regiment dug themselves in at the top of the Hijar track to establish a base for further operations, the SAS tried to work their way round the Aquabat al Dhafar. But the rebels had strengthened their positions, and as we were unwilling to commit the SAS to a full-scale frontal assault, a role for which they were not intended, we contented ourselves with strengthening our new base on the plateau, in the hope of demoralizing the enemy and encouraging him to divert troops there from other sections of the Jebel. At least we were firmly on the top.

Action flared again at the end of November around Tanuf, where some forty rebels suddenly launched a determined attack, supported by heavy mortars, on a company of the Northern Frontier Regiment and our troop of 5.5s. At first the defenders wavered, and almost broke, but they rallied under the spirited leadership of the Royal Marine NCOs, until the timely arrival of a troop of Life Guards racing up from Nizwa turned the scales. After a fierce battle, in which the machine guns of the Life Guards' Ferrets took a heavy toll, the enemy withdrew; but the NFR had four men wounded, and we lost two of our gunners when one of their shells failed to clear their sangar and burst on the lip.

On 1 December the SAS troops in that area took the offensive. Eager to avenge their dead NCO and acting on the information they had gleaned on that unlucky patrol, they attacked one of the caves held by the rebels and, supported by a strike of Venoms, killed a number of the occupants; they claimed to have killed eight of them, but subsequent interrogation of prisoners revealed that only two had been killed and three wounded. All the same, it was a useful action, which raised their spirits as much as it must have depressed the enemy.

This morale-boosting action was led by a young troop commander, Captain Peter de la Billière, later, of course, to become the Regiment's commanding officer:

On the night of 30 November we set off at 1930 with two full troops: my own, 18 Troop, was to carry out the assault, and 19 Troop was to give us cover from a higher outcrop. Tanky Smith was carrying the main part of his .30 Browning (his partner Curly Hewitt carried the tripod for it, and hence was known as 'Legs'). We were all heavily laden with water bottles, extra ammunition for our SLR rifles and rockets for the 3.5-inch launcher.

It was a dark night, with little moon, but enough ambient light for us to pick out salient features. The ascent was uneventful but tough: to be sure of reaching our assault position in the dark, we had to press on hard, but at the same time make no sound. Even with commando boots this was difficult, for as the rubber soles wore down – which they did at an astonishing rate – the screws securing them grated on rock. After a while the troops separated, each heading for its own objective.

Steep escarpments delayed our advance. Several times I feared we had lost our way. The moon went down, leaving us in deeper darkness. But by 0530 we had reached what seemed to me the right place, so I sent a couple of men forward to make sure that the position was the best available. A few minutes later they came back, affirming that all was well. I crept forward and placed every man, spaced out in a line, with a party to guard our rear.

The ground was ideal for our purpose, with plenty of big

197

rocks to give cover. All we had to do was wait. Having sweated pints on the way up, we now began to shudder in the icy pre-dawn air. I pulled on the thin jersey which was all I had in the way of extra clothes, and still kept shivering. The sky started to lighten. We were facing north, so that dawn stole up on our right. I thought about Tanky, somewhere above us, and hoped that the strike by Venom fighter-bombers, which I had laid on with the RAF, would come in on time.

As the light strengthened, I was disconcerted to find that we were farther from the caves than I had hoped. The distance which during our reconnaissance I had reckoned as two hundred yards turned out to be three hundred, the limit of accurate fire for our weapons. Still, we could not move.

The sky paled. Light stole on to the mountain. Now at last I could see the black mouth of the main cave, with smaller openings beside it. The air was absolutely still. The cold bit more fiercely than ever. My watch said 0610 . . . 0615 . . . 0620. At last a white-robed figure appeared in the cave-mouth. The Arab looked round, yawned and stretched. When he spat, we heard him as clearly as if we had been in the same room. He moved off to one side to urinate. Another man appeared, then another.

I looked to right and left. Everyone was poised for action. The rocket launcher crew, Troopers Goodman and Bennett, were on their feet behind a rock with their weapon levelled. I waited until four or five Arabs were in view together, then at last gave the signal.

Pandemonium erupted. With a *whoosh* the first rocket flew straight into the cave. A flash lit up the entrance, and the boom of a heavy explosion came back at us. The rattle of our small-arms fire echoed harshly round the rock walls. Several Arabs fell, and for a few seconds we had things to ourselves. Then suddenly the whole mountain came to life as shots began to crack out from above us on both sides. What we had not realized was that other caves high in the rock faces were also inhabited. Far from bolting when taken by surprise, the *adoo* counter-attacked with commendable resilience.

The ricochets were prodigious: bullets whanged and whined in every direction, and chips of rock flew. All at once we were in trouble. Where were our Venoms? From high on our left came the comforting, heavy rattle of Tanky's Browning, firing in short bursts. Then I heard the roar of jets, and saw a pair of Venoms high overhead. I put up a Very light to indicate the enemy, and within seconds the aircraft made their first run. Cannon-fire and rockets tore in, helping to keep the enemy's heads down.

With the advantage of surprise gone, the battle degenerated into a long-range sniping match, as both sides took snap shots at fleeting targets. With fire and movement, one group covering another, we pulled back. Still from above came the hammer of the Browning. So great was the noise, and so intense the fire, that when we reached a relatively safe position, over a ridge, I was amazed to find that we did not have a single casualty. Except for cuts caused by flying rock splinters, nobody was any the worse. By then we were short of ammunition, and in no state to run into an ambush. Once on to the big slab, we spread out well and hurried down, reaching base at 0800. After more than twelve hours on the go, everyone was exhausted; even so, we held an immediate wash-up, or debriefing, sitting in the sand, to make sure we recorded everything of importance while events were fresh in people's minds. Then we had some food and went to sleep.

The raid went down as a major success. Early reports indicated that we had killed twenty of the enemy, including the rebels' chief expert on the .5 machine gun. Later it seemed that the number of dead may have been exaggerated; even if it was, the attack gave the enemy's morale a jolt. We had taken them by surprise in one of their strongholds, an area which until then they had thought impregnable, and we had given them an unpleasant glimpse of what we could do.

David Smiley takes up the story of what happened next in the battle of Jebel Akhdar:

In the ensuing weeks we strengthened our positions on the other side of the Jebel. At the end of December the Trucial Oman Scouts put a squadron into the village of Hijar, out of which they maintained two troops at our new base on the top, to reinforce the existing garrison of the Muscat Regiment and SAS. A platoon from the Northern Frontier Regiment joined them, and to provide additional fire-power a dismounted party of twenty Life Guards under a Corporal of Horse carried up eight of their Browning machine guns. We never ceased to bless the authorities for giving us these Life Guards; they really entered into the spirit of our war and, when not engaged in a protective role with their Ferrets, were happy to turn themselves into infantry and carry out arduous and dangerous duties up the mountain.

The SAS now felt they had sufficient support to mount a strong night attack on the Aquabat al Dhafar. They excelled in night operations, and under a protective barrage from the Life Guards' Brownings and the heavy mortars of the Muscat Regiment, they scaled the steep cliffs with ropes and came to close quarters with the rebels in their caves. A wild *mêlée* ensued in the darkness, with bullets, grenades and insults flying between the combatants, but the rebels fought back stubbornly and held their ground until we called off the attack. Although once again they had inflicted casualties without loss to themselves, the SAS emerged from the battle with an even greater respect for the enemy.

Although our situation was immeasurably better than in

the summer, we were still a long way from victory. John Watts and I agreed that our chances of storming the Jebel with a single squadron of SAS were pretty slim, but that with a second squadron we could be reasonably certain of pulling it off. We therefore sent a signal to Deane-Drummond asking if he was prepared to let us have another squadron; he not only agreed but added that he would come himself with a small headquarters to take over command of both squadrons.

Our next problem was to secure the approval of the War Office and the FO. We put our case to the Political Resident on one of his visits to Muscat, and obtained his promise to forward it to the Foreign Office; and in Aden the military authorities agreed to back us with the War Office. With all this support we won our clearance but, needless to say, the FO modified it with a proviso of their own: all British troops must be out of Muscat by the first week in April. The significance of this deadline, apparently, was that the United Nations were to discuss the Middle East situation soon afterwards, with Oman featuring large on the agenda; British diplomacy must not be embarrassed by the presence there of British troops.

Deane-Drummond arrived on New Year's Day, 1959. Our first decision was to set up a joint headquarters to coordinate the operations of the Sultan's Armed Forces, the SAS and the Royal Air Force, and we co-opted a senior RAF officer from Bahrain to serve as our Air Liaison Officer. We installed this 'Tac HQ', as we called it, in the Northern Frontier Regiment's Camp near Nizwa, and I moved there from Beit al Falaj on 9 January with John Goddard and a small staff.

My next problem was the chain of command. Officially all British troops serving inside the country came under my orders, and hitherto my second-in-command had been Colin Maxwell. But Deane-Drummond had to be in a position where he could give orders to his own troops, and so, to avoid complications, I appointed him my Deputy Commander. From anyone less generous-hearted and unselfish than Maxwell this arrangement might have aroused strong resentment, but he accepted my decision with his usual amiability, well understanding the reasons behind it.

On 12 January A Squadron, 22 SAS Regiment, flew in from Malaya under Major John Cooper, one of the longest-serving officers in the SAS. As a corporal, Cooper had been David Stirling's driver in the Western Desert in the earliest days of the regiment, and had taken part in some of its bloodiest actions in Sicily, Italy and France. Dark and thin, with strong, expressive features and a quick though short-lived temper, he was a brilliant soldier whose thirst for adventure and danger was to bring him under my command again in the Yemen.

We sent the new arrivals to relieve D Squadron, who came back to Beit al Falaj for a few days of rest and refit; the special SAS boots had lasted only a few days on the sharp rocks of the Jebel – to the incredulous dismay of the experts in the Quartermaster General's department who had designed them – and so we replaced them with hockey boots, which were much more satisfactory. Fresh from the heat of Malaya, A Squadron needed time to adjust to conditions on the Aquabat al Dhafar, where it had turned very cold, with hail storms and even snow; water bottles froze at night and fires were a necessity, even at the risk of snipers' bullets; although, in fact, both sides took this risk and nobody ever shot at the fires.

Because of the imposition by the Foreign Office of an April deadline we had about three months in which to assault the Jebel. We had agreed that the attack must be launched at night and during a period of full moon – it would be impracticable in total darkness; the full-moon period came at the end of each of the next three months, which meant that the last weeks in January, February and March were the vital ones. We would make our first attempt at the end of January, which would give us two more chances if we failed. We must therefore plan on a very tight schedule, for we had a bare three weeks before our first attempt in which to move all troops to their take-off positions, organize their reinforcement and supply, redeploy our garrisons, find reliable guides and coordinate the support of loyal tribal irregulars – in close consultation, of course, with Sayid Tarik.

At the same time I was faced with a difficult problem in diplomacy. The OC Northern Frontier Regiment, a British Seconded Officer, had an unfortunate habit of quarrelling with everyone with whom he came in contact. Already his Contract Officers had formed up to me, one after the other, to tell me they would 'soldier no more' under him; I had to transfer them and replace them with seconded officers, which meant there were no Arabic-speaking officers in the regiment. Next he alienated the Life Guards at Nizwa, giving them orders which he was not empowered to give them but which, presented with even a minimum of tact, they would almost certainly have accepted; it is only fair to add that, in return, the Life Guards officers baited him unmercifully. The consequence for me was that I had to spend precious time smoothing ruffled feelings as well as preparing for war.

The primary object in all our planning was to gain a foothold as quickly as possible on the top of the Jebel, near the rebel headquarters, and hold it for the reception of air supply drops and as a firm base for further operations. Surprise was obviously essential in order to avoid the heavy casualties that we must expect if the assault were opposed. The Aquabat al Dhafar was too far away from the main rebel strongholds of Habib, Saiq and Sharaijah, and in any case the enemy was already well entrenched on the Aquabat, where he

203

was expecting us to attack; we must encourage him in that expectation and hope he would concentrate the main body of his forces on the northern side of the plateau. On the other hand the shortest approaches to the rebel villages, the tracks leading from Tanuf and Kamah, were known to be guarded.

Deane-Drummond and I made several flights over the Jebel, cruising slowly just above the ground and scanning the smooth faces of rock to find a route that men and donkeys could climb. At length Deane-Drummond made his choice, a sloping buttress thrusting out above the Wadi Kamah on its eastern side. We sketched it, mapped it, studied photographs of it, and imprinted every detail of it on our minds; there appeared to be no track, but the slope looked feasible for the pack animals except in one place – a sharp ridge connecting the two main features – where we hoped the Sappers would be able to improve the going.

This approach had two main advantages: first, it was unguarded, so far as we could see, and it was most unlikely the enemy would expect an attack by such a route; secondly, our men could climb it in one night – in about 9½ hours by our reckoning – and so by dawn the leading troops could be in position on the top, where they could receive supplies by air.

Following standard Army practice, we gave a codename to each of the tactical features on the way up. Our principal objective, the top of the Jebel, we christened 'Beercan'; the first prominent peak on the approach to it became 'Pyramid', while the sharp ridge connecting the two, which we had already noticed from the air, received the name of 'Causeway'. There was a lesser crest about a third of the way up to Pyramid, which we called 'Vincent', and our final objective, a peak beyond Beercan overlooking the village of Habib, went down in our operations plan as 'Colin'.

The two SAS squadrons would lead the assault, for I had

received strict instructions from Aden that all other troops – Life Guards, Trucial Oman Scouts, and Sultan's Armed Forces – were to be used only in support of the SAS. These orders caused some natural disappointment to the Sultan's forces, who had tried for so long to reach the top, and who had in fact been the first to get there – when Tony Hart had taken his platoon of the Muscat Regiment up the Hijar track. However, they accepted the situation philosophically, especially as they themselves had important roles to play: first, they would make diversionary attacks before the main assault; secondly, they would follow closely upon the heels of the SAS and take over successive features as they were captured; and thirdly, they would consolidate the top of the Jebel and hold it against attack while the SAS pressed forward.

'Once we're on the top,' I told Deane-Drummond, 'and the aircraft have made their supply drops, we'll have to play things off the cuff. It'll depend on a lot of factors we can't foresee at this stage, such as the rebels' reaction and the whereabouts of their leaders. Remember, from our point of view – that is, from the Sultan's – the capture of Talib, Ghalib and Suleiman is very nearly as important as the capture of Beercan.'

We agreed that if there was no serious opposition Deane-Drummond would push his patrols on to Habib, Saiq and Sharaijah, while our supporting troops cleared the enemy from the Kamah track and opened it up for the donkey columns.

We planned to launch our attack on the night of 25 January, at the beginning of the full-moon period, which would allow us to postpone the operation if the weather forecasts were unfavourable. It was vital for us to have at least twenty-four hours of good weather following the assault, to allow the RAF to drop their containers accurately; otherwise the leading troops would arrive on the plateau short of food, water and ammunition, for we couldn't expect the donkeys to get there in time.

Talib must by now have realized that an attack was imminent, but he had no idea from which direction it would come. In order to confuse him we mounted a series of diversions during the weeks before 25 January in different parts of the Jebel. Between 8 and 22 January D Squadron of the SAS and A Company of the Northern Frontier Regiment carried out offensive patrols from Tanuf, and drove the rebels from some high ground they were using as an observation post. From 18–22 January A Squadron of the SAS, supported by the squadron of Trucial Oman Scouts, made probing attacks against the Aquabat al Dhafar; but on the night of 23 January A Squadron disengaged all but one of its troops and, after a forced march across the mountain, came down to join D Squadron near Tanuf. The following night A Company of the Northern Frontier Regiment engaged the enemy again near Tanuf, while C Company put in an attack from Izki. On every occasion we met strong opposition – C Company had a particularly hard time, losing one soldier killed and several wounded – which showed us the enemy was reacting as we hoped.

But the most brilliant, and one of the most successful of our deceptions involved no fighting at all. 'I'm prepared to bet,' said Malcolm Dennison, my Intelligence Officer, 'that if we call leaders of the donkey men together on the night before the assault, and tell them in strictest confidence and under the most ferocious penalties that the following night they'll be leading their donkeys up the Tanuf track, Talib will have the news within twenty-four hours.' In fact, we learned afterwards, Talib received the news in twelve hours.

Our plan of attack was necessarily simple, even primitive. The operation was essentially a straight slog up the mountain face, and everything would depend on whether we achieved surprise; even when we postponed it for twenty-four hours because of a poor weather forecast – a wise decision, as it turned out – there was no need to alter the details. There were to be three phases: in the first, A Squadron of the SAS would capture Vincent, and D Squadron would occupy Pyramid, Beercan and Colin before first light. In the second, C Company of the Northern Frontier Regiment would relieve A Squadron on Vincent, while the dismounted troop of Life Guards took over Pyramid; and lastly, A Squadron would consolidate their position on Beercan and D Squadron on Colin.

Two groups of irregulars would be taking part: on the southern side fifty Beni Ruawha tribesmen under Major John Clarke, a Sultan's Contract Officer, would accompany the SAS squadrons, while a force of 200 Abryeen and a platoon of the Muscat Regiment, under the command of Jasper Coates, would create a diversion in the north and, if unopposed, would climb the Jebel by two tracks leading from Awabi. These two tribes were hereditary enemies of Suleiman and his Beni Riyam, and welcomed a chance to pay off old scores; the Abryeen, in particular, needed to restore their honour after their failure the previous summer to protect the lines of communication with the Muscat and Oman Field Force.

There would be air support the following morning: Venoms from Sharjah would strafe any pockets of resistance, while three Valettas from Bahrein would make a total of nine container drops on Beercan. We also had two helicopters ready at Nizwa to evacuate casualties to our field hospital there. If the weather was still bad we should be absolutely dependent for supplies on the donkey columns; the prospect worried me and my only consolation was that we had a few Omani jebel donkeys to supplement the poor little Somalis.

Such was the preparation for the assault on the Jebel Akhdar. The course of actual events, in all their intricacies, can be seen in the report of Major J. S. Spreule:

D-Day 26 January, 1959. Both squadrons were in camp at Tanuf. Donkeys and handlers brought from the Aqabat under an animal transport officer provided by the Trucial Oman Scouts were at Tanuf. All ranks were briefed by Colonel Deane-Drummond in the morning. The donkeys left at 1000 hours to walk to the donkey assembly area at Kamah Camp. Both squadrons left Tanuf in transport and arrived at Kamah after last light at 1930 hours. Troops debussed in the assembly area where there was half an hour's wait for the moon to rise. The squadrons then re-embussed and were driven to the start line. The start line was crossed as planned at 2030 hours. Owing to a strike by donkey handlers, the F echelon donkeys, which were to follow A Squadron and precede the Commander's HQ party, failed to arrive at the appointed time. These 25 donkeys, 10 for each squadron and 5 for HQ, were to carry the squadrons' Browning machine guns and ammunition and HQ's wirelesses. The donkeys eventually followed 15 minutes behind the Commander's party. At 2030 hours the diversionary attack by 4 Troop was put in. This could be heard by the assaulting troops. The climb was without incident, but the going was harder than expected. A few unfit or overladen soldiers were left behind to make their own way, while the squadrons pushed on.

27 January. By 0500 hours 27 January, progress had been slower than expected. A Squadron was in position on Vincent, but D Squadron had one troop on Pyramid and three troops bunched round the point where it was thought a track began to lead to Beercan. It was vital to reach the top – Beercan – by first light and so D Squadron commander made two troops leave all their extra loads behind and push on. They reached Beercan at approx 0630 hours. By 0645 hours the first of the Valletas began the resupply drop . . . The troops were too exhausted after 10 hours' almost continuous climbing to do more than collect sufficient ammunition to hold off an expected counter-attack. At 0700 hours they were joined by the Commander's party carrying equipment, with an Air Liaison Officer and ground to air radio. The third troop was left to deal with a rebel .5 machine-gun team, which they did by 0630 hours. They then moved up the ridge, arriving at 0800 hours. The .5 machine gun was in a perfect position commanding all approaches. Had it been manned, the outcome might have been very different. During the morning snipers in caves to the east put up desultory fire at troops on the machine-gun position and on troops moving to Beercan. These snipers were attacked by Venoms and were not eventually silenced until about 1430 hours after holding up the leading troop of A Squadron, which reached Beercan by midday. A grenade, exploded by a chance shot, wounded Troopers Carter, Hamer and Bembridge. Carter and Bembridge later died of their wounds. By 1500 hours the last troop of D Squadron on Pyramid was relieved by the Life Guards and rejoined its squadron at 1630 hours. At 2130 D Squadron moved to occupy a feature overlooking the Kamah Wadi, leaving A Squadron to hold Beercan. The Commander went with D Squadron and later returned to Beercan. A Squadron sent a troop reconnaissance patrol out at last light to the village of Habib. In the event it went to an unmarked village on the far side of Nantos because of an inaccuracy of the map. Going was difficult and the village was reported deserted.

28 January. D Squadron took an airdrop and later pushed forward to a feature overlooking Kamah Wadi. A Squadron collected previous airdrops and accepted further drops. Offensive air support against rebels throughout the day . . . a 62-set was manpacked from Pyramid and with this the Forward Observation Officer was able to range the guns. A request was made to begin psychological warfare. 15 Tribals arrived and spent the night on Beercan. On the night 28/29 January D Squadron with Squadron HQ and two troops occupied a feature which overlooked the village of Habib. The same night, half A Squadron occupied a feature called Nantos, 1,500 yards in front of Beercan.

29 January. D Squadron now had positions overlooking the Kamah Wadi and Habib. They took an airdrop at 1100 hours. Half A Squadron was on Nantos, the other half on Beercan. Colonel Deane-Drummond with his HQ accompanied a patrol of D Squadron which together with 15 Tribals entered Habib at 1200 hours. The village was deserted and had been damaged by bombing. A Squadron troops on Nantos detained 38 Arabs including women and children. They were sent under escort to Beercan for interrogation where a PW compound was set up.

30 January. Colonel Smiley and Said Tariq, Wali of Nazwa, landed at Beercan by helicopter and spoke to prisoners, who were later released. Half of A Squadron joined half of D Squadron, and together they occupied the village of Saiq. Later HQ was helicoptered to Saiq, which was deserted. A number of prisoners were taken and Suleiman's cave was located and searched. Vast quantities of documents and a substantial number of weapons were collected. A further supply drop took place at Saiq. Some prisoners were taken at Sharaijah, and a number of Talib's manacled prisoners released.

31 January. One troop of D Squadron was left at Saiq, while two troops of A Squadron, one troop of D Squadron, Squadron HQ and the Commander's Tactical HQ moved to Sharaijah. All resistance on the Djebel had ceased, except for a few minor pockets on the south slopes. These were dealt with by SAS and Sultan's Armed Forces. SAS troops started work on landing strip between Saiq and Sharaijah. A report was received that Talib and Suleiman were in the Wadi Salut area with their families. A party of A and D SAS troops from Sharaijah searched south and a composite patrol from HQ searched north from Mi'aidin. The search was fruitless and was abandoned on 1 February.

The SAS had done what no other military force had done in 1,000 years; it had captured the Jebel Akhdar. More than that, the Jebel Akhdar assault had secured the future of the SAS. As Peter de la Billière wrote, Oman, more so Malaya, was a turning point in the history of the SAS:

We had shown that we were a flexible force capable of adapting quickly to new conditions. We had demonstrated that a small number of men could be flown into a trouble spot rapidly and discreetly, and operate in a remote area without publicity – a capability much valued by the Conservative Government of the day. Above all, we had proved that the quality of the people in the SAS was high indeed, and that a few men of such calibre could achieve results out of all proportion to their numbers.

The SAS would return to Oman a decade later, to counter an insurgency by communists in Dhofar. But first, the drums of war summonsed the Regiment back to the jungles of the Far East.

From 1963 to 1966, Borneo was the scene of a bloody conflict between Malaya and Indonesia, both of which claimed ownership

211

of the mountainous island. To counter the infiltration of guerrillas from the Indonesian side of the island (Kalimantan) into the northern Malaysian side, the British – Malaya's former imperial masters – organized a border guard of Malaysian, British and Commonwealth troops. A main constituent in this guard was 22 SAS. For the most part, SAS effort in Borneo consisted of the insertion of four-man patrols into the jungle, often for weeks at a time, gathering intelligence and implementing 'hearts and minds' programmes. Frequently, as one trooper wrote in the Regimental journal *Mars and Minerva*, patrols lived in the longhouses of the tribes:

Where, day by day, the sick come for treatment, the women to bring news, the children to watch silent-eyed and the leaders of the community to discuss their problems and to ask for and offer advice. The patrol slips as easily into the primitive rhythm of the day and season as the people themselves; soon the cycle of burning, planting, weeding and harvesting becomes a part of life itself and customs, rites and celebrations as familiar as the Cup Final or Bank Holidays at home.

Some of the medical problems presented to the patrols were unusual to say the least:

I was attached to a 'hearts and minds' team as a specialist in combat intelligence. It was my job to talk – usually via an interpreter – to the head man of any village we came to and find out if there was any activity in the area. Gradually I'd hope to build up some sort of picture of any terrorist organization, figuring out who they were, where they were based, what weapons they had and so on. As well as myself, we had a signaller, a medic, four minders who could act independently if they had to, an interpreter/tracker who spoke

212

some of the local dialects a young captain, who came from the same regiment as the minders.

All in all, it was one of the best jobs I ever had – we were on our own and I got to see the kinds of people who you only ever read about: the Aborigines. Lovely, gentle people they were, but a little confused by some of the medical practices they were being taught.

I remember one village we came to, the head man came out to meet us and the old boy had a very well-developed chest – a sort of geriatric Page Three. It worried our medic quite a bit until finally we found out what had happened. Apparently a government team had been there about a year before, preaching the virtues of birth control. Then, when they left, they gave the village a year's supply of birth-control pills. Well, there was no way the head man was going to let valuable medicine be used by mere women, so he scoffed the lot himself. As a result he developed breasts as well as beginning to talk in a high-pitched voice. Our medic explained that an enemy had cursed the medicine and with great ceremony the remaining pills were burned.

As the 'Confrontation' wore on, however, the Indonesians began committing units of their army to the frontier war, and in response the SAS stepped up its activity with offensive patrols into Indonesia itself. Codenamed 'Claret', these operations were top secret. The codename was apposite; much blood was spilled. Like Malaya, the jungle-fighting in Borneo was split-second and close-up. A report in *Mars and Minerva* gave a flavour of the combat:

On a recent February morning [1965] a small SAS patrol was moving down from a ridge on a jungle track towards an old Indonesian Border Terrorist camp. This camp had been found the day before and appeared as though it had not been used for some six months. As the leading scout, Trooper

Thompson ducked under some bamboo across the track – there was a lot of it in the area – a movement attracted his attention. He looked up and saw an Indonesian soldier six yards away to his right, just as the latter fired a burst at him. Several other enemy opened fire simultaneously. Thompson was hit in the left thigh, the bone being shattered, and was knocked off the track to the left. He landed in a clump of bamboo two yards away from another Indonesian soldier lying concealed there. As the latter fumbled for his rifle, Thompson picked up his own, which he had dropped as he fell, and shot him.

The second man in the patrol, the commander, Sergeant Lillico, was also hit by the initial bursts and had collapsed on the track, unable to use his legs. He was still able to use his rifle, however, and this he did, returning the fire. The remainder of the patrol had meanwhile taken cover. Thompson, unable to walk, hopped back to where Sergeant Lillico was sitting and joined in the fire fight. As he had seen Thompson on his feet, Sergeant Lillico was under the misapprehension that he could walk and therefore sent him back up the track to bring the rest of the patrol forward and continued to fire at sounds of enemy movement.

As Thompson was unable to get to his feet he dragged himself along by his hands and, on arriving at the top of the ridge, fired several bursts in the direction of the IBT camp. Whether the enemy thought that this fire came from reinforcements moving into the area is not known, but about this time, some ten minutes after the initial contact, they apparently withdrew. During the remainder of the day Thompson continued to drag himself towards where he expected to find the rest of the patrol. He had applied a tourniquet to his thigh, which he released from time to time, taken morphia, and bandaged his wound as best he could with a shell dressing.

After sounds of enemy movement had died down, Sergeant

Lillico pulled himself into the cover of a clump of bamboo, took morphia, bandaged his wound, and passed out until mid-afternoon. He awoke to hear the sound of a helicopter overhead. Realizing that it would never find him amongst the bamboo he decided, in the morning, to drag himself to the top of the ridge which was covered in low scrub. The balance of the patrol had decided that the best course of action was to move to the nearest infantry post, close by, and lead back a stronger party to search the area. This they did, starting back towards the scene of the contact late that same day.

The following morning Thompson continued on his way and by evening had covered 1,000 yards, about half the total distance he had to cover. However, soon after he had stopped for the night, a short while before last light, he heard the search party and was found about 1800 hours. An attempt was made to winch him out by helicopter but this failed due to the height of the trees. The next day, therefore, he was carried to a larger clearing nearby and was successfully evacuated at 0930, 48 hours after the contact.

Meanwhile, Sergeant Lillico had dragged himself to the ridge as he had planned – a distance of 400 yards – and on arriving there at 1500 hours, had fired some signal shots to attract the attention of the search party which he expected to be looking for him. These were immediately answered by three bursts of automatic fire some few hundred yards distant. Not by the search party, however, which at that time was too far away to have heard him firing. He therefore hid in the scrub as best he could and was able both to hear and see the enemy looking for him. One man climbed a tree about forty yards away and remained there for about half an hour in full view as he looked around and about.

While this was going on, he heard a helicopter close by but because of the enemy's nearness and obvious risk to the aircraft, he decided to make no use of the means at his disposal to attract it towards him. Not until the observer climbed down from his tree was he able to drag himself further away from the enemy and out into the scrub. The helicopter, continuing its search operation, returned in the early evening. This time he signalled to it and without delay it flew over, lowered the winch and lifted him out. In all, a rescue operation reflecting great credit on both RAF and Infantry, but most of all on Sergeant Lillico and Trooper Thompson for their courage and determination not to give in.

For this action Lillico was awarded the Military Medal and Thompson a Mention in Dispatches.

One desired 'Claret' objective was the Koemba river inside Kalimantan, suspected of being a major enemy supply route, but teams from B and D Squadrons had failed more than once to reach it. In May 1965 Sergeant Don 'Lofty' Large and three other SAS men left Squadron HQ to have their go. The journey got off to a miserable start when, en route to the airfield, Trooper Pete Scholey realized that he had been issued with the wrong self-loading rifle by the armoury:

> I knew, liked and trusted my particular gun. It never got a stoppage. I had it set for just the right pressure. I knew if I had it set on gas regulator 4, it would work. I cleaned it and looked after it . . . I started honking. I was Lofty's cover man. If I saw anything I was the first one to fire . . .

On board the aircraft, Scholey stripped down the strange weapon and set it as best he could. There was no time for a test firing when they landed, because a chopper was ready, rotors whirring, to drop them off at a 'hot' landing position just on the border. From there the patrol set off on a bearing west of their intended course, so as to confuse any Indonesians who might discover their tracks. On the second day out, Large heard a faint sound ahead; cautiously edging forward through the jungle, he discovered an Indonesian Army platoon directly in their path. Edging away and around the Indonesians, the SAS patrol headed for a spur of high ground they hoped would lead them to the Koemba. To their dismay, their way ahead lay through thick swamp, tangled with roots and curtained by hanging moss and vines. A particular hazard was a carpet of huge leaves which lay on the surface of the water and crackled loudly when stepped on. Progress was exhausting. Failure seemed certain. Lofty Large called a 'Chinese parliament' – a meeting in which any team member, no matter how lowly his rank, can have a say. 'No one considered going back,' remembered Pete Scholey. 'Our objective was clear.'

They pushed on and finally stumbled upon the spur, rising fully thirty feet above the swamp, which led them directly to the Koemba. Without wasting a moment, Large set up an observation post, closing a place on the river bank bounded by a ditch and covered by trees. To celebrate their arrival, the team disregarded all Standard Operating Procedures, cooked curries, brewed tea and smoked cigarettes. Don Large wanted 'morale at its peak' for the action that was sure to come.

The days passed with a steady amount of boat traffic passing along the team's view, all of it reported back to base via radio. As the Regiment's intelligence officers had suspected, the river was a major communications line for the Indonesian military. After several days Large considered that the patrol had done enough observation, so he sent off a signal requesting permission to carry out their secondary task: an ambush of a boat carrying troops or war cargo. The signal read: 'Request 00 licence.'

Unfortunately the officer in charge of the Operations Centre was the only person in the world not to have read a James Bond book or seen a James Bond movie, and sent back a signal saying, 'Message not understood.' Cursing the Ops Centre officer, Large sent another – and longer – message, hoping against hope that it would not be intercepted by enemy signals and give a fix on the patrol's position. Eventually they received permission to ambush a riparian target. The best tactic, decided Large, was to hit a military boat when it had gone past them. 'That way,' said Large, 'we don't get a broadside back from them.' Raking the aft of the boat with fire should also ignite the fuel tanks. Pete Scholey said:

Next morning we lay in wait. The boats normally started coming past about one thirty, two o'clock. It started to rain which is good for cover but not so good for the swamp levels. Just after two we heard the chug, chug, chug of a diesel. It wasn't a very big one and it was pulling two canoes behind it.

Lofty shook his head. It wasn't big enough for him.

Three o'clock came and went.

Half past three, chug, chug, chug.

I tapped my watch, indicating that it was time to start thinking of going, but Lofty held up his hand, telling us that we had to wait. Kevin grimaced. He was thinking, he told us later, What's he waiting for? The fucking *Ark Royal*?

A couple of minutes later we heard another boat coming. It was a good 'un. About forty foot and gleaming white. Lofty gave the ready signal, then he noticed a woman on the bridge between an army officer and a naval officer. She was wearing a long white chiffon dress. He signalled for us to hold our fire. In that situation, where there is one woman, there is likely to be others, and maybe children, and the British Army does not make war on women and children.

Time was moving on and there was a storm brewing, when all of a sudden an even larger boat appeared. We could see two soldiers in the stern.

This was it.

Lofty took out the two soldiers at the stern, the only ones visible because the drapes were down along the sides of the boat. The boat got arse-end and I opened up. Bang, bang,

bang, click. Stoppage. I cocked it double quick and then it fired again. It was the weapon I'd been honking about on the way in. It was lucky all four of us were lined up, firing at once, and that we hadn't been caught short in a head-on contact.

The boat took sixty-nine rounds in only a few seconds. The odd nine came from me. Next moment there was a great flash, then a jet of flame and smoke and the boat began to list.

Time to bug out.

Collecting their packs, the team made a hasty getaway towards the spur. As they went up a short slope, they found their exit blocked by a snake. Large recalled:

I immediately brought up my rifle sight, and it reared up four or five feet so that with the slope, we were eye to eye. It was a king cobra, ready to strike. I aimed at the centre of its hood but I didn't dare shoot. The Indos might have been just ahead.

The 'Mexican stand-off' continued for several long seconds, before the snake dropped down and slithered off. Hurrying on, they reached a track, crossing as one, not in single file, since the latter maneuver simply allows an ambusher to sight all those following in the leader's footsteps. Towards nightfall there came the sound of mortars, but the mortars landed far down river.

The next day they reached the border, where a helicopter arrived and winched the team up to safety.

Sergeant Large's ambush was a resounding success. To guard their now demonstrably vulnerable supply route, the Indonesians had to redeploy 700 frontline troops. Indeed, so many troops had to be diverted that the Indonesians never mounted a major attack across the front thereafter. The Indonesian generals began to lose faith in President Sukharno, and in March 1966 he was overthrown in a coup. Five months later Indonesia made peace with Malaya.

The grey dawn on 19 July 1972. In the fishing port of Mirbat, Oman, a nine-man SAS detachment known as 'BATT' (British Army Training Team) slept in a small mud-and-brick building, save for three troopers who were awake talking and keeping guard. In command of the detachment was twenty-seven-year-old Captain Mike Kealy of B Squadron, known as 'baby Rupert' because of his inexperience. As the smear of light on the eastern horizon grew brighter, 250 communist guerrillas, known as *adoo*, stole to within 400 yards of the SAS 'BATT house' and opened fire with mortars, machine guns and small arms.

The battle of Mirbat, one of the most storied actions in the history of 22 SAS, had begun.

Despite the success of the SAS attack on the Jebel Akhdar in 1955, Oman had lurched from instability to instability, particularly in the southern province of Dhofar, where a full-scale communist insurrection had blown up, helped by some flame-fanning from the neighbouring state of Yemen. Qaboos, a new, more moderate Sultan of Oma had wooed over some of the insurgents and begun the training of a loyal militia, the *firqa*. Acting as bodyguards, intelligence-gatherers, 'hearts and minds' campaigners and military trainers, the SAS had been committed to Oman since 1970. Such had been their success that the communist adoo had been pushed on to the back foot. To regain the initiative the adoo needed a stunning victory. Hence the attack on Mirbat.

Inside the 'BATT house' Captain Kealy tumbled out of his sleeping bag, pulled on some flip-flops, seized his rifle and ran up the stairs to the roof. Kealy had never been in action before, and as he climbed up he was desperately worried about how he would behave under fire, how he would command men technically below him in rank but high above him in experience.

Reaching the roof, Kealy was astounded by the sheer intensity of the assault. Previously the adoo had satisfied themselves with desultory mortar and shell attacks, then hastily withdrawn, now they had descended the nearby escarpment of the Jebel Ali and were on the open ground just outside the perimeter wire, which flanked the north and west of Mirbat. Through the half-light, Kealy could see that a picket manned by the Sultan's Dhofar Gendarmerie (DG) had been overrun, and the adoo were pounding the small stone fort held by twenty-five gendarmes which dominated the town and was about 400 yards away from the BATT house. Like the BATT house, the DG's fort was inside the perimeter wire. Also inside the wire, almost at the water's edge, was Wali's Fort, occupied by a small force of Askari tribesmen loyal to Qaboos. The Askaris were returning accurate but slow fire from bolt-action .303 rifles.

Shells began landing everywhere inside the town, throwing up plumes of dust. The noise was deafening. An 84mm anti-tank round scorched low overhead to explode behind the BATT house.

For a moment Kealy thought a blue-on-blue, or 'friendly fire', situation had occurred, and that the Gendarmes' picket and a returning firqat patrol were blasting away at each other. However, his radio operator, Trooper 'Tak' Takavesi, a Fijian, soon disabused him of this notion; the firqat were still out somewhere in the back country. Assessing the situation in a manner he found almost a reflex, Kealy ordered Trooper Harris to start returning fire with the team's own mortar from the sangar below. Meanwhile, Trooper Pete Wignall opened up with his .5 Browning, mounted on sandbags on the roof, and Corporal Roger Chapman poured out fire from his general-purpose machine gun. Other SAS men calmly picked off the advancing adoo with Armalite automatic rifles.

To Kealy's consternation, the adoo continued to move forward, doing so in textbook manner: fire and movement, fire and movement. The discipline and vigour of the enemy advance suggested that they knew the strength of those within Mirbat – a bare fifty men. Next to Kealy, Trooper Takavesi talked urgently over the radio to a gun pit in front of the DG fort manned by another Fijian SAS trooper, Corporal Labalaba. The gun in the pit was a 25-pounder of Second World War vintage. Labalaba, with the 25-pounder's barrel almost horizontal, was *whumphing* out round upon round.

Then Labalaba called on the radio to say he had been 'chinned'. Takavesi asked permission to go and join his friend. Kealy agreed. Picking up his rifle, Takavesi ran to join his fellow Fijian in the gun pit:

I ran up the hill, dodging as much as I could, taking cover when I had to. They were advancing, and the firing was getting heavier all the time, but I had to get there because Laba was on his own with the Omani artillery, and I didn't know how many of them were with him at the time. I got to the top and crawled in to where Laba was and he was alone. Normally it takes three men to fire the gun and he was doing it all by himself. When he said he'd been chinned he meant he'd been grazed by a bullet, either a ricochet or a direct hit.

I started banging on the door of the fort, trying to get the DG to come out. Only one emerged, the gunner Khalid. I got back to the sangar wall but Khalid was hit. From then on it was just the two of us.

By then it was getting light. We could see figures or bodies everywhere, some still a long distance away towards the coast, along Jebel Ali, and some on the plain due north of us. There were people advancing with machine guns, some running, some firing heavy machine guns, mortars and rocket launchers. All Laba and I did was fire close to Jebel Ali. We couldn't fire at the Jebel because the Omani soldiers were protecting one of our high grounds.

At the same time some of the firqas were coming back into Mirbat, and we were worried about firing on them. So we fired towards the plain. That's where most of the guerrillas were coming from, doing a frontal attack.

It was just like watching a movie. It was about 6 a.m. and it was very, very cloudy and misty too, so they were lucky they had lots of cover and lots of time to make their way in. When Laba and I were firing, we were really under heavy attack. As soon as you put your head up, you could hear the bullets whistling by. It was so close. We literally had to crawl to be able to do anything. We'd crawl and load the gun, fire it and then crawl down and do it again.

It was ridiculous. They were almost on top of us, shooting from all directions. At least we could hear on the radio that our comrades back in the house were still okay. It was getting very, very fierce, and Laba and I were joking in Fijian. All the fear seemed to go away.

We knew the gun was their main target and we were still firing at point-blank range. We had no time to aim. All we could do was pick up a round, load it in and fire as quickly as we could. But the guerrillas were coming closer and closer towards us, and at the end we had to abandon it. You can't fire a 25-pounder at 50 metres. You'd just get metal fragments in your face. And we had to cover ourselves.

I heard the crack of a gun. Something hit my shoulder and the shock knocked me out for a few seconds. I really didn't know where I was. I totally curled up. The clearest way of describing it is like an elephant charging at you at 120 miles an hour with a sharp, pointed trunk.

Laba, still bleeding from the graze on his chin, crawled across to give me a shell dressing to cover the wound which was on my left side. After that I had to fire my rifle single-handed with my right hand. I still wasn't frightened. It was us or them. I always had a feeling we would survive in the end. So we just fought on.

Then the rebels reached the wire. Kealy and Corporal Bob Bradshaw started potting adoo as they monkey-climbed up the wire. One fell, then another, but others reached the top and jumped down. The adoo were inside the compound. To protect the fort, where the main weight of the adoo attack was falling, Kealy switched the 'Gimpie' and Browning to cover it.

Shinning down the ladder, Kealy went to the communications room. He had already sent a contact report, but it was clear that they needed air support. They also needed a casevac chopper for Labalaba.

Back on the roof, Bradshaw told Kealy that he could not establish contact with the gun pit. Something like an argument broke out when Kealy insisted that he should be the one to make the dangerous dash to the gun pit to find out what was going on. Finally, Kealy agreed to take Tommy Tobin, the medical orderly, with him. Bradshaw pointed to Kealy's feet and said, 'You won't get far in those.' Kealy was still wearing his flip-flops. He quickly pulled on desert boots.

An eerie lull suddenly descended on the battlefield. Having loosed off so many rounds, the adoo were having to wait for new supplies of ammunition. Kealy decided that this was the moment to make the run to the gun pit. As they left the BATT house, so did Roger Chapman, who sprinted towards the helipad 200 yards away.

For the adoo, the appearance of the helicopter was a signal to renew battle. A ferocious barrage of bullets and shells went up from the adoo positions, and Chapman had to warn off the helicopter by detonating a red smoke flare. The unwelcome restart of the fighting found Kealy and Tobin halfway to the gun pit. Takavesi in the gun pit watched their approach:

I could hear the radio going but I was too far away to call for help. Then I saw Mike Kealy and Tommy Tobin coming towards me, dodging bullets. As they approached, the adoo were getting nearer the fort, advancing. They were so close you could almost reach out and touch them.

Tommy was the first to reach the sangar and as he climbed over, he got shot in the jaw. I heard machine-gun fire and all I could see was his face being totally torn apart. He fell, and Mike Kealy dragged him to a safe area. Then Mike spoke to me. He decided we'd be better off if he got himself into the ammunition pit a few metres away. It was four feet deep. He ran to it and jumped in and landed on the body of a DG soldier, a 'powder monkey', one of those who had been detailed to carry the ammo to the gun pit. There was another soldier cowering in the corner. Kealy told him to move the body and checked our situation.

Mike and I were now about three or four metres away from each other. We couldn't see each other but we could talk. I was shouting at him to tell him that I was running out of ammunition. Luckily, he was with one of the local Omani artillery who still had loaded magazines, so he started throwing them to me. At last I could reload my magazine and keep on firing. The battle was really getting heavy. Mike and I could see two or three people on the corner of the fort throwing grenades only about four or five metres away from us. Mike said, 'Look, we'll take one each on each corner.' When he was firing I was covering; likewise when I was firing he was covering me. We managed to kill a few.

A snap shot by Kealy felled an adoo who had Tak in his sights; adoo light machine-gun fire was now passing so close to Kealy's head that he could feel the vibrations from the spinning bullets.

A grenade landed on the lip of the ammo pit, the explosion almost bursting Kealy's eardrums. The adoo were almost on top of the pits. There was only one hope; Kealy spoke into the short-range radio and told the BATT house to spray either side of the gun pit with machine-gun and mortar fire. To shorten the mortar range, Bradshaw had to hug the huge tube vertical to his chest as Trooper Harris dropped the shells down the barrel.

At the moment when it seemed that Kealy and Takavesi could hold on no longer, when they would surely be overrun, a Strikemaster of the Sultan's airforce appeared on the scene, its pilot steering under a cloudbase a mere 150 feet above the ground. Then another Strikemaster, cannons blazing, screamed over the battlefield. Seizing the ground-to-air radio in the BATT house, Chapman began passing targets to the jets: the shallow wadi near the fort where the adoo were massed for shelter; the adoo's 34mm Carl Gustav; the 7.62mm machine gun near the perimeter wire. Shells and rockets rained from the sky. To identify his friendly status, Kealy broke out a fluorescent marker panel.

The adoo were not finished yet. On the south-east of the town, they began organizing a counter-thrust.

By pure coincidence, another SAS detachment was in Dhofar that day. These were twenty-three men of G Squadron waiting to take over from Kealy's team, who were due to end their tour the very morning of 19 July. At 09.15 a.m. a G Squadron patrol arrived on the beach at Mirbat and surged towards the town; a second wave of G Squadron reinforcement landed and engaged the adoo on the seaward side. Another relay of Strikemaster jets attacked adoo positions on the Jabal Ali.

Perceptibly, the tide of battle turned and the adoo began to slip away through the shallow wadis around the town. Even so, it was 10.30 a.m. before the helicopter evacuation of the wounded could commence. For a while it was hoped that Tobin would survive by emergency first aid, but he died of his wounds shortly after arriving at the Salalah Field Hospital.

Tobin and Corporal Labalaba were the sole SAS fatalities incurred during the 22 SAS Regiment's hardest test. For this loss the SAS took the lives of more than thirty-nine adoo. They also delivered a telling blow to adoo morale. Proud warriors all, the adoo had been beaten by fighters better than they. The adoo ceased hostilities four years later.

For his bravery and leadership at Mirbat, Kealy was awarded the DSO. Trooper Tobin and Corporal Labalaba were posthumously awarded the DCM and a Mention in Dispatches.

Tragically, Mike Kealy died of hypothermia during an exercise on the Brecon Beacons in 1972.

The origins of SAS counter-terrorism work in urban areas lie in the mid-1960s when A Squadron SAS was sent to Aden, the unlovely scene of an Arab nationalist insurgency which was sweeping both the hinterland and the back alleys of Aden town. During this so-called '*Keeni Meeni*' (Swahili for snake) period, when Yemen-trained insurgents were trying to assassinate British officials, A Squadron set up a Close-quarter Battle Course for a selected team of troopers. Thereafter, SAS Counter-Revolutionary Warfare (CRW) work evolved through sheer Darwinian necessity. Oman aside, the Regiment was desperately short of work in the early 1970s; so short of work, indeed, that training the bodyguards of foreign VIPs became a major strand of regimental activity. In the same period, the camp of 22 SAS, now based after a period of itinerancy at Bradbury Lines (later christened Stirling Lines), saw the construction of a special house to train marksmen in the skills of shooting gunmen in the confines of a room without hitting VIPs or hostages. Formally called the Close-quarter Battle House (CQB), the building is more usually known as the 'Killing House'. One significant spur to the development of CRW work came in September 1972, when Palestinian terrorists from the 'Black September' group seized the dormitory occupied by Israeli athletes at the Olympic games. The West German government allowed the gunmen and hostages safe passage out of the country, but as the group moved through Munich airport the German security forces opened fire. In the wild gun battle that followed they mistakenly killed all the hostages. Alarmed by their incapacity to deal with terrorism, European governments began developing elite anti-terrorist units. The British government was no exception.

Following a direct request from the Director of Military Operations in September 1972, the new commanding officer of 22 SAS, Lieutenant Colonel Peter de la Billière, reorganized the CRW cell into 'Op Pagoda'. In charge of Pagoda was Captain Andrew Massey, who selected twenty troopers from all sabre squadrons for special CRW (sometimes CT, for Counter Terrorist) training. The Pagoda team was put on constant standby. Later, the Pagoda role became rotated through the squadrons – so every trooper in the Regiment had a turn – and the team was issued with black overalls and Ingram sub machine guns. However, following their observation of the successful German GSG9 storming of a hijacked aircraft at Mogadishu airport in 1977, SAS Major Alistair Morrison and Sergeant Barry Davies recommended adopting the GSG9's main firearm, Heckler & Koch MP5A2. Tests confirmed its superiority over the American Ingram sub machine gun, and the 650-rpm, 2kg Hockler was adopted by the Pagoda troop.

The Pagoda team's first major call to action came in 1975, when an IRA active-service unit machine-gunned a Mayfair restaurant and then took hostages in a flat in Balcombe Street, London. On hearing on the radio that an SAS team was preparing to storm the flat, the IRA gunmen surrendered without a fight.

The Balcombe Street siege ended without bloodshed, but it ignited a bloodbath of violence in Northern Ireland, starting with the 'Kingsmill Massacre' in which IRA terrorists pulled Protestant line-workers from a bus and mowed down ten of them in the road with machine-gun fire. On 7 January 1976, Prime Minister Harold Wilson publicly committed the SAS to patrol the 'bandit country' of South Armagh.

Northern Ireland would never be a happy hunting ground for the SAS. The orthodox regiments of the Army already deployed to the province were suspicious and resentful – after all, SAS deployment suggested that they themselves had failed – and there was little possibility of implementing the SAS's by now stock 'hearts and minds' campaign. Aside from patrolling, the SAS men in Northern Ireland set up covert observation posts and established a new undercover spying squad known as the Army Surveillance Unit (later 14 Intelligence Company).

The Regiment did not limit itself to these prescribed and lawful activities. In March 1976 a Provisional IRA (PIRA) gunman and bomber, Sean McKenna, was abducted from his home in southern Ireland by masked men, almost certainly SAS, holding Browning 9mm pistols and was taken over the border to Bessbrook RUC station. IRA members who lived by the gun could expect to die by it. Unfortunately, SAS soldiers in Northern Ireland – eventually organized in Ulster Troop – took a steady toll of the innocent. By the end of 1978 the SAS had publicly killed ten people in Northern Ireland, of which three were guiltless and one, a PIRA quartermaster called Patrick Duffy, was shot twelve times in the back. The slaughtered innocents included a sixteen-year-old boy, John Boyle, exploring a churchyard where the IRA had cached arms, and a Belfast Protestant pedestrian, William Hanna, in an incident in which the Army rules of engagement in Ulster – by which soldiers could only open fire if they believed a person was about to fire, endanger life and if there was no other means of stopping them – were ignored. Even the SAS's greatest ever blow against PIRA – the killing of eight PIRA terrorists as they attacked the police station at Loughgall in 1987 – was marred by the shooting of two blameless villagers driving by, one of whom died. Accusations that the SAS were 'shooting to kill' amplified in the following year, when three PIRA members, Danny McCann, Sean Savage and Maired Farrell, were shot dead by an SAS team in Gibraltar. SAS claims that the trio were warned to surrender were challenged by witnesses. When the families of Savage, McCann and Farrell took the case to the European Court of Human Rights, the court found that the British Government – in the shape of the SAS – had violated Article 2 of the Convention, and deprived the trio of their right to life. The court also ruled that, since the three PIRA members had been engaged in an act of terrorism, the applicants' claims for damages and costs be dismissed.

If SAS black ops in Northern Ireland were controversial, they were also deadly dangerous for the Regiment's troopers. Trooper Tom Read recalled a bog-standard undercover SAS operation in Northern Ireland, in which he and his team were tailing a van suspected of carrying PIRA members:

The Escort van has double doors at the back with rear windows covered in what looks like silver paper. I pull away and slip in behind it, putting it between myself and John's car. The dicker sees me leave and gets on his radio – the game is up!

Suddenly the van spears off to the left, giving up on the target. As they take the turn, they drop the galvanized tin covering the rear windows and open fire.

'Contact! Contact!'

I can see black masks and the muzzle flashes of an automatic rifle.

Within seconds we are hurtling along a narrow country road at 70 mph. I fight with every corner in the low gears. The van is much faster around the bends and keeps disappearing from view and then reappearing. Beside me, Cyril opens up with the MP-5 and punches a dozen neat holes in the laminated glass. He's trying to aim at the target at the same time as holding on as we swerve around corners.

Ernie is leaning over my shoulder, with his elbows braced against the two front seats and the HK-53 pointing directly out through the windscreen. When he opens up with his cannon I think my head has exploded. I half expect to see the van disappear in a ball of flames.

He keeps firing and the red-hot cases spit out of the breach, bouncing off my left ear. Two of them fall down the front of my shirt where I've loosened my tie. Shit, they hurt!

230

The Renault leans heavily on the bends and surges over dips as I try to create a stable platform for the lads to shoot from. Trees and hedges flash past in a blur, but all I care about is not losing sight of the van.

At the same time, I'm constantly trying to transmit our location and direction, but part of the windscreen has been shot out and the noise of the rushing air and gun-fire means I can't hear any incoming calls. Each time we swing into view, the terrorists keep firing with what seems to be an Armalite and a shotgun. One round hits the dashboard and severs the electrics for the Renault's windows and sun-roof. Another goes straight through the windscreen and hits the back window, passing between Ernie's head and mine.

They're edging ahead . . . thirty metres, then forty. The IRA have selected a good vehicle. I could thrash them on a motorway, but the Renault doesn't like the tight corners and I'm hammering the low gears.

The van keeps weaving from side to side; it only needs something to be coming the other way.

'Where's a tractor when you need one?' yells Cyril.

Ernie: 'Don't lose them, Tom. Don't lose them.'

The windscreen is a mass of holes and cracked glass. I lean back and kick it with my left foot. My side flies out, but the other half blows back into Cyril's lap. A wall of rushing air explodes into the car, lifting debris from the floor.

Suddenly, we emerge back on to Dungannon Road, taking a sharp right. I see uniforms and a bus stop. A half-dozen schoolchildren are crawling out of a ditch where they've thrown themselves to get away from the van.

'Oh, shit!' Wrenching at the wheel, I feel the weight of the Renault shift beneath me. For a split-second, I think I've lost it. I drop a gear and accelerate. Everything happens in slow motion – a young girl with muddy knees looks at me; she's

231

got a red ribbon in her hair and her school books are scattered at her feet.

With every fibre, I will the Renault to turn. The tail-end is sliding. At the last instant, the wheels grip and the Renault responds. We go hurtling past the bus stop and along the old Dungannon Road.

It's a long straight stretch running parallel to the motorway. Now the Renault has the advantage. Flooring the accelerator we begin closing the gap. The van is weaving from side to side as Cyril and Ernie open up.

Fifty metres . . . forty metres . . . thirty metres . . . twenty . . .

Recognizing where we are, I call in our position. John's car is on the same road, up ahead of us, with the van heading directly towards them.

Fastening his seat belt, John yells at Chris behind the wheel: 'Ram it!'

'You must be fucking joking,' he says. It doesn't make sense – at a closing speed of 170 mph they'd all die.

Chris slams on the brakes and throws the Lancia around, side on, trying to block the road. The van is almost on top of them and swerves up a right bank around them, like a wall-of-death stunt. John tries to get out of the front passenger seat with his seat belt still buckled. It forces him backwards at the precise moment that two PIRA rounds hit the window of his door. If not for the seat belt, he'd certainly have been hit.

Chris is out of the driver's side and takes up a firing position, kneeling down near the front right headlight. Jocky scrambles out a back door and also opens fire. I aim the Renault directly at Chris with my foot to the floor and just before I hit him I tweak the wheel and send the car into the ditch and up the bank, riding on the same near vertical wall as the PIRA van.

Again I close the gap, but the van is zigzagging from side to side. I keep a steady line, giving Ernie and Cyril a platform,

232

even though it makes the Renault an easier target. The van is now on the wrong side of the road, risking a head-on collision with anything coming the other way. I can't understand why. Suddenly, it brakes and spears across in front of me, taking a sharp left turn into Washingbay Road. In a fraction of a second, I realize my mistake – the PIRA driver had been setting himself for the corner. He almost rolls the van but makes the turn. I start pulling the wheel, but at my speed from the left side of the road I have no chance. At the precise moment that I decide not to go for it, Cyril screams, 'No way!'

I hit the brakes in a controlled skid, overshooting the junction.

'John, it's gone left! John, it's gone left!'

The Lancia makes the turn but we've lost a crucial twenty seconds. Over the road, turn right, then left, where's it gone? The van has simply vanished. There's a Cortina with a single occupant parked opposite a muddy farm track.

'Which way did the yellow van go?' asks Jocky. The driver motions down the road and the Lancia takes off in pursuit.

They've been sent the wrong way by a dicker. The van has turned off along a gravel farm track. We scour the area for twenty minutes but all of us know it's too late – the terrorists have gone.

The RUC find the van later, full of empty shell cases, abandoned at the back of a farm. The IRA had taken a hostage, cut the phone lines and made their way on foot across several fields to Derryavena before taking another car. That's how they avoid the police road-blocks.

I'm exhausted and bitterly disappointed, but the news is about to get far worse. An innocent civilian has been killed in the operation. Frederick Jackson had been pulling out of a lumber yard in his car, with his foot propped on the clutch as he looked left and right. One of our rounds had ricocheted off the road and gone through the car door. It hit Mr Jackson in his body and exited through his neck. The car rolled back and re-parked itself.

Three months later, in December 1984, one of Read's team, Al Slater, was shot dead by the IRA after getting out of his car in a lane where an IRA team happened to be hidden behind a hedge. Corporal Slater joined a roll of honour of SAS dead in Northern Ireland, the most senior name on which was Captain Richard Westmacott, killed by IRA gunfire in May 1980.

The cat-and-mouse game between the SAS and IRA continued until 1997 when the IRA announced a ceasefire which has held to this day.

The reputation of the SAS was tarnished by Northern Ireland. Another anti-terrorist operation, however, would burnish it bright. This same operation would also draw the SAS out of the world of the shadows into the public view.

Number 16 Princes Gate, home of the Iranian Embassy, overlooks the peaceful green expanse of London's Kensington Gardens. At 11.25 a.m. on the morning of Wednesday 30 April 1980, this leafy tranquillity was rudely shattered as six men wearing shamags sprayed Number 16 with bullets and stormed through the front doors. The gunmen – Faisal, Hassan, Shai, Makki, Ali and Salim – were members of Mohieddin al Nasser Martyr Group, an Arab group seeking the liberation of Khuzestan from Ayatollah Khomeini's Iran. The siege of Princes Gate had begun.

The police were on the scene almost immediately, alerted by an emergency signal by Trevor Lock, and were soon followed by Scotland Yard specialist units including C13, the anti-terrorist squad, and D11, the elite blue-beret marksmen. The building was surrounded, and Scotland Yard hastily began putting in motion its siege-negotiation machinery.

While no siege is ever the same as the one before or after it, most follow a definite pattern: in stage one, the authorities try to pacify the gunmen (usually with such provisions as cigarettes and food), and allow the release of ideological statements; in stage two, the hostage-takers drop their original demands and begin negotiating their own escape; stage three is the resolution.

The Princes Gate siege moved very quickly to stage one with Salim, the head Arab gunman, announcing his demands over the telephone just after 2.35 p.m.: autonomy and human rights for the people of Khuzestan, and the release of ninety-one Arab prisoners held in Iranian jails. If his demands were not met he would blow up the Embassy, hostages and all, at noon the following day.

Meanwhile, the SAS had been alerted about the siege within minutes of its start. Dusty Gray, an ex-SAS sergeant and now a Metropolitan Police dog handler, telephoned the Officers' Mess at Bradbury Lines, the SAS's HQ near to the River Wye in Hereford, and said that the SAS would probably be required at the Iranian Embassy, where gunmen had taken over. That night, SAS troopers from B Squadron left for London in Range Rovers, arriving at a holding area in Regent's Park Barracks in the early hours of Thursday morning. The official authority from the Minister of Defence approving the move of the SAS teams to London, arrived at Bradbury Lines some hours after they had already left.

Over the next few days the Metropolitan Police continued their 'softly, softly' negotiating approach, while trying to determine exactly how many hostages were in the Embassy and where they were located. Scotland Yard's technical squad, C7, installed microphones in the chimney and walls of Number 16, covering the noise by faking Gas Board repairs at neighbouring Ennismore Gardens. Gradually it became clear that there were about twenty-four hostages (as they discovered at the end of the siege, the exact count was twenty-six), most of them Iranian Embassy workers. Also hostage were PC Trevor Lock and two BBC sound engineers, Sim Harris and Chris Cramer. The latter, who became seriously ill with a stomach disorder, was released by the gunmen as an act of good faith. It was a bad mistake by the Arab revolutionaries: a debriefing of Cramer gave the SAS vital information about the situation inside the Embassy as they planned and trained in a new holding area only streets away from Princes Gate itself.

Inside the holding area a scale model of the Embassy had been constructed to familiarize the SAS troopers with the layout of the building they would assault if the police negotiations were to break down.

As the police negotiating team located in a forward base at Number 25 Princes Gate (of all places, the Royal School of Needlework) anticipated, the gunmen very quickly dropped their original demands. By late evening on the second day of the siege, the gunmen were requesting mediation of the siege by Arab ambassadors – and a safe passage out of the country. The British Government, under Margaret Thatcher, refused to countenance the request. To the anger of the gunmen, BBC radio news made no mention of their changed demands, the broadcast of which had been a concession agreed earlier in the day. Finally, the demands were transmitted – but the BBC got the details wrong.

For some tense moments on Saturday, the third day of the siege, it looked as though the furious Salim would start shooting. The crisis was only averted when the police promised that the BBC would put out the demands accurately that evening. The nine o'clock news duly transmitted them as its first item. The gunmen were jubilant. As they congratulated themselves, however, an SAS reconnaissance team on the roof was discovering a way into Number 16 via an improperly locked skylight. Next door, at Number 18, the Ethiopian Embassy, bricks were being removed from the dividing wall, leaving only plaster for an assault team to break through.

On Sunday 4 May, it began to look as though all the SAS preparation would be for nothing. The tension inside the Embassy had palpably slackened, and the negotiations seemed to be getting somewhere. The gunmen's demands were lessening all the time. Arab ambassadors had agreed to attend a meeting of their COBRA committee in order to decide who would mediate in the siege.

And then, on the morning of Bank Holiday Monday, 5 May, the situation suddenly worsened. Just before dawn the gunmen woke the hostages in a frustrated and nervous state. Bizarrely, Salim, who thought he had heard noises in the night, sent PC Lock to scout the building to see whether it had been infiltrated. The hostages in Room 9 heard him report to Salim that there was nobody in the Embassy but themselves. Conversations between the gunmen indicated that they increasingly believed they had little chance of escape. At 11.00 a.m. Salim discovered an enormous bulge in the wall separating the Iranian Embassy from the Ethiopian Embassy. Extremely agitated, he moved the male hostages into the telex room at the front of the building on the second floor. Forty minutes later, PC Lock and Sim Harris appeared on the first-floor balcony and informed the police negotiator that their captors would start killing hostages if news of the Arab mediators was not forthcoming immediately. The police played for time, saying that there would be an update on the midday BBC news. The bulletin, however, only served to anger Salim, announcing as it did that the meeting between COBRA and the Arab ambassadors had failed to agree on the question of who would mediate. Incensed, Salim grabbed the telephone link to the police and announced: 'You have run out of time. There will be no more talking. Bring the ambassadors to the phone or I will kill a hostage in forty-five minutes.'

Outside, in the police forward post, the minutes ticked away with no news from the COBRA meeting, the last negotiating chip of the police. Forty-two minutes, forty-three minutes . . . The telephone rang. It was Trevor Lock to say that the gunmen had taken a hostage, the Iranian Press Attache, and were tying him to the stairs. They were going to kill him. Salim came to the phone shouting that the police had deceived him. At precisely 1:45 p.m. the distinct sound of three shots was heard from inside the Embassy.

The news of the shooting was immediately forwarded to the

SAS teams waiting at their holding area. They would be used after all. Operation *Nimrod* – the relief of the Embassy – was on. The men checked and cleaned their weapons – 9mm Browning HP automatic pistols and Heckler & Koch ('Hockler') MP5A3 sub machine guns. Frank Collins was one of the SAS assault team waiting in the holding area in the Royal School of Needlework. He recalled what happened next:

Instantly the room's full of movement. Not fast, panicky movement. It's quick but it's deliberate. People are grabbing their weapons, putting on their belts, fitting their respirators. Nobody runs out of the room but within seconds we're gone. Outside, the policemen who brought us the food press against the wall as we pass. Now they stare.

Everyone goes in their own direction, some upstairs, some down, some along this floor. I go up. There are twelve of us. As we climb the stairs they get narrower and more secret. After one flight they aren't grand any more and after two there's no carpet. We reach the top. It's our first position. We're grouped right under the roof now and a sliding wooden ladder will take us up there when the word comes. But the word doesn't come. We wait.

At first I'm tense and my heart is beating fast but as the minutes go by I relax. My weapon feels a little heavier. It's an MP5, a little Rolls-Royce of a machine, smooth with no rough edges. It's my own gun and I know it well. Slowly, quietly, hoping no one's looking, I check the safety catch. I don't want to be the one to screw up. It's the most public operation yet, there are lines of camera crews at the end of the street and, although I have no interest in the politics of this operation and don't even care who the terrorists are or why they're there, I know that mistakes could have repercussions, serious repercussions, for the Regiment. If anyone makes mistakes, I don't want it to be me.

We wait in silence but it's a noisy silence. The gas masks magnify our breathing and there's a slight echo here on the landing so the whole place sounds like one big dirty phone call. The rubber diaphragms on the respirators click each time we breathe and with every breath I take there is a smell of rubber and traces of old gas. It's a peppery, pungent odour. The lenses steam up a little. I start to get that detached, underwater feeling. I think of yesterday's training exercise, when I last wore this mask. Was it only yesterday? I remember that Claire is coming down to Hereford this weekend. She would have arrived by now and found me gone and known better than to ask where. If she switches on the TV she might guess.

Via my earpiece a voice brings me back here to London. We're being told to stand down.

We return to the long room and wolf La Pierre's pork in cream sauce. Something cold and gooey for pudding. I take off my holster but not my boots and lie down feeling full. Another couple of bobbies have arrived.

'Pizza. From Carlo's around the corner,' they say. 'The boys thought you'd like it.'

I sit up. I can smell the pizza and it smells good. Someone tells him that we've already eaten but the copper shrugs, nearly upsetting the trays, and then puts them down on the floor.

'I was told to bring it in here,' he says.

So we eat the pizza too. Garlic, tomato, wedges of gooey cheese. Bottles of cold water. More tea. Overhead the chandeliers are going tinkle, tinkle. Life's pleasant. I almost forget what we're here for. We've just finished when we're told to stand-to again. This time, I grab a pillow as well as my weapon. We're supposed to be alert up there but I like to think I can be alert and asleep at the same time. It's another false alarm. When we return a copper comes in.

239

'The outer police cordon hasn't been fed,' he says. 'We bought them pizza from a restaurant down the road.'

'Oh yeah?' we say pleasantly.

'It's not in here by any chance?'

'Oh no,' we say. He looks at us hard and doesn't argue.

Over the next few days we stand-to and stand down again and again. My pillow earns me a reputation and the nickname Forty Winks Frank.

Sometimes my team goes back to the barracks in Regent's Park where we get in a few hours' training and build a model of the next-door building using wood and sack. The abseilers find similar buildings elsewhere in London and go out training in public without anyone realizing why. We get bored. Most of us don't believe we'll be called in next door to do the business and even the TV people are sounding less excited now. Our plan is constantly upgraded. Briefing follows briefing.

Then, suddenly, there's an alert. Television reporters under makeshift lighting start jabbering at the entrance to the street. The terrorists have killed a hostage. There's rustling and readiness. I know the word's going to come soon and when we're told to stand-to again I suspect it's for real. Over the earpiece there are more voices than usual and their pitch is different, more urgent.

I have no idea of the day or the time of day when we take up our first positions under the roof for the umpteenth time but there's something electric in the air which tells me that now, at last, we'll move to deliberate action. It's coded black amber and when I hear black amber, although I'm not surprised, there's a lurching feeling inside my ribs and my heart starts to thud.

Up the sliding ladder, I await my turn and then I'm up so fast that I'm outside before I know it. Out here it's light but not bright. Even through lenses I can tell it's the soft light of

240

an early May evening.

The first thing I see is a London bobby. He's young, fresh-faced and his cheeks look smooth under his helmet. He's been patrolling the roof all day, probably, thinking about what's for dinner, and suddenly here are twelve men in black advancing towards him, dehumanized by gas masks, weapons wrapped around their bodies. Which side are we on? Are we going to kill him? His face goes through an interesting range of emotions from horror to terror. We give him the thumbs-up to reassure him but he's already fingering his radio, so nervous he can hardly work it. Er, are there supposed to be a bunch of men up here with sub machine guns, er, sir? He's trying to control his voice but it's slipping up and down a few octaves. We tell him as kindly as we can in the circumstances that there is going to be a big bang and he should get his head down. He looks at us in disbelief. He's sweating now.

We are to storm the building from a number of different points simultaneously and my team is going down through the roof. My heart is still thumping. I'm not scared, just scared I'll make a mistake. We've trained for this and we're good, the best. The dry spot in my throat is self-doubt.

We're on the roof of the adjacent building now and the abseilers are already starting to drop their ropes down the front. My team are lowering the detonator on to the roof. While I wait I look across the back of the building, down on to a kitchen, a restaurant kitchen. Perhaps it's Carolo's or La Pierre. A couple of elderly women are standing over the sink. One has her sleeves rolled up. Her arms are frozen in the water by the sight of us. The other is pointing and shouting. A few more people come running into the kitchen, flapping their elbows and shaking their heads like chickens. I cannot resist it. I raise my arm, at the end of which there happens to be an MP5, and give them a jaunty oh-I-do-like-to-be-beside-the-seaside wave.

241

There's no time to see their reaction. Our ball of plastic explosive is in place, so is the detonator. We're waiting for the go, knowing there should be a delay of a few minutes while everyone else gets into position. When the word comes I'm to be first in. A ladder will be lowered for me and I'll go down into the building. I'd like to use these few moments to prepare myself but, before we expect it, things are happening. We're waiting for, 'Stand by, stand by . . . go!' but instead we get a voice over our headphones yelling, 'Go, go, go!' This is it. Bang. We hit our explosives device. There's a *woomph* of smoke and dust.

I feel misgivings. Everyone can't be in position by now, something must have gone wrong. My heart's hammering. I hear the words, 'Go, go, go' again inside my head.

Alpha-three is hooking the caving ladder on to the roof rails for me to climb down but there's a problem: it won't hook. I tell him to hurry but he fumbles some more. It's essential to take everyone in the building by surprise by attacking simultaneously so I decide to go down with the ladder only half-stabilized. Alpha-three stands aside for a moment. I lower myself into the dark hole at the heart of the building. I have never felt so alone.

I'm twenty-four and have smelled my own fear on occasions, but this isn't one of them. Once the action starts and I'm climbing down the rope ladder, hand under hand because it's so unstable, I'm no longer aware of my heartbeat, my breathing. I'm working now.

I'm waiting for my feet to touch the ground. When they do, I'm in half-darkness. There is smoke and dust and the smell of explosives. Silence, for a split second. Then the bang and shudder of the building rearranging itself around our bomb. I can't hear the rest of my team behind me or the other lads storming in through the windows at the front. Am I the only one in? Have the terrorists guessed what's happening? I feel vulnerable. I know the others will be inside in a few seconds but I slide a couple of stun grenades out of their holders and chuck them down the stairwell. They're a spectacular light and sound show. Fairly harmless, but guaranteed to terrify the uninformed.

I enter the telex room. The windows have been blown out. I cover the hall, down on one knee. By now the team has sorted out the rope ladder and my partner, alpha-three, is there behind me. The building is smoking. Perhaps my stun grenades have caused a fire.

When alpha-three taps me on the back, I go. We know the layout of the fourth floor. Our job is to comb this area for people, terrorists or hostages. I burst out, sweeping my gun ahead of me. I stop at each door until my partner taps me on the back. I open it, my gun goes in first, then me, then my mate, and it all happens in a split second. I decide on the instant whether to go right or left and he covers me while I search behind curtains, and I cover him while he searches the cupboards and under desks on his side of the room. We've done this back in Hereford a thousand times. It's like clockwork. He yells, 'Clear, clear, out, out, out!' We shut the door behind us.

Below us is the sound of gunfire, screams, a cloud of CS gas. In my earpiece voices are shouting. Sixty men, one radio channel. What's happening? a voice is saying. The politicians and top brass are anxious for news but they're blocking the channel with their questions. Shut up, someone tells him, we're trying to carry out an operation here.

My mate and I find no one. One door is locked and alpha-three tells me to shoot the lock. I use my MP5. You'd expect a sub machine gun to deal with a lock. Guys in detective movies are always shooting them off with 38s, but I feel splinters of brass bouncing off it into my legs and the lock hasn't budged. I use my axe and in a few swings it's off. We open the door. It's empty. It's a loo. I've shot the lock off the Ambassador's toilet.

'Congratulations, alpha-three-bravo,' says alpha-three.

We've cleared the floor now, our team. The boys upstairs have cleared the fifth. We all go down to the third.

This floor is chaotic. There's a lot of screaming, more gunfire, a strong smell of burning, voices yelling at each other inside my ear.

Someone, I can't tell who, one of the team, runs up to me. My gun is equipped with a streamlight, a powerful torch which is zeroed to my weapon and illuminates the target in the dark. He says, 'You've got a torch, come with me.' I leave my partner as we run downstairs.

He leads me to a door. 'There's a terrorist in here,' he says. 'Not sure if I killed him or not.'

We hit the door. Darkness. Nothing. No noise, no movement. Torches on, I go left, he goes right. I run the beam over the floor and chairs and we advance on the curtains. They're big, heavy velvet curtains and they swish as we rip them down. A yell from the other lad. He's found the terrorist. We both shine our torches on his body. He's dead, fallen back across a sofa, blood on his face, a small sub machine gun cradled in his arms, grenades strapped to his body. His eyes and mouth are open. Outside, we tell the team leader about the body. We know the next man who goes into that room will be a scenes-of-crime officer.

We join the human chain on the stairwell. The boys have already started grabbing the hostages and passing them from man to man down the stairs. I seize each warm, sobbing body and throw it to my left. Some of them are trying to hug me, but I am not gentle. We're trained to handle hostages and I know that any one of these grateful, sobbing people could be a terrorist acting as a hostage. And then I pause. I'm holding a man by the lapels. He is wearing a green denim jacket. He

244

has bushy hair. Instead of passing him along, something about him stops me. His eyes aren't saying, thank God, I'm rescued. He's afraid. We look at each other but I can't hesitate for longer, the next hostage is being passed to me. I hand him on. A few seconds later a yell comes.

'That's him! That's Salim!' Salim is the leader of the terrorists. I feel sure that this is a man with the fight gone from him, a man whose bravado has been replaced by terror. But intelligence tells us that he is carrying grenades and he is thrown up against the wall to be searched.

He is shouting, '*Taslim, taslim.*' No one understands him. The firing begins. His body is rapidly riddled with bullets. A question comes into my head: why so many? But, there's no time to ponder further. The embassy is on fire and we are ushering the hostages out through the back door.

The building blazes. There are big flames in the rooms behind us. Outside in the garden we lay all the hostages down, handcuff them and search them. We are still wearing our gas masks. Anyone who takes off their respirator rapidly puts it back on when they see the TV crews. We climb into police vans and are driven away from Princes Gate.

When we return to the Regent's Park Barracks we're jubilant. We push aside our life-size model of the embassy. We're too busy finding out who was who behind those masks and who did what. We learn that the order to go came early because one of the abseilers put a foot through a window upstairs and alerted the terrorists to the fact that something might be going on. About three people claim to have shot Salim there on the stairs. Eventually the meaning of his last words is revealed to us: he was surrendering. But for all we knew it could have been an Islamic battle cry, particularly since he was believed to be carrying grenades. Most of us speak at least some Arabic but he was speaking Farsi.

Margaret Thatcher arrives with Willie Whitelaw, the home

secretary. It's an emotional occasion: Whitelaw is crying openly. When the bangs, flashes and gunfire started they thought it must be carnage in there. To find out that the hostages were alive, we were alive and most of the terrorists were dead was a huge relief for them. The prime minister congratulates us, not in a formal line-up sort of a way but just mingling in amongst us. Then someone shouts, 'It's on the telly,' and we all of us sit down and watch it, including Mrs Thatcher. There are cheers as we see the boys going in.

Later that night, when we're driving back up to Hereford in the Range Rover, we're stopped on the M4 by a police car. We're still wound up and we just want to get back and we've been driving at 110 m.p.h. We have blue lights which we can use in an emergency but going home doesn't really qualify.

The policeman says, 'Bit of a hurry, sir?' and we say, 'Well, yeah.' We tell him we're an army team and give him the special codeword and then watch his face. He says, 'You're the boys!' and he and his copper mate shake us by the hand, congratulate us, and radio ahead, 'The boys are going through, don't pull them no matter how fast they're going!'

In the weeks following the Iranian Embassy operation, the SAS received 2,000 applications from regular soldiers wishing to join the Regiment. Of these, five passed selection.

SAS Selection Training is based on a course devised in 1953 by D Squadron commander Major John Woodhouse, and is designed to enlist only those who have the physical toughness to become an SAS trooper. The egalitarian, unorthodox culture of 22 SAS, together with the closeness of the basic four-man patrol and the frequently isolated nature of special forces' work, also requires a special mentality and character. In the words of Major Dare Newell:

Selection is designed rather to find the individualist with a sense of self-discipline than the man who is primarily a good member of a team. For the disciplined individualist will always fit well into a team when teamwork is required, but a man selected for teamwork is by no means always suitable for work outside the team.

The selection course for 22 SAS lasts for one month. Although the regiment is now based at Credenhill in Herefordshire, with a satellite training facility at Pontrilas, much of selection training takes place on the bleak terrain of the nearby Black Mountains and Brecon Beacons, particularly the 3,000-foot peak called Pen-y-fan. As it is impossible to enter the SAS directly, every volunteer must be serving with a regular British military unit. The only civilians allowed to try for selection are members of the SAS's two part-time Territorial regiments: 21 and 23 SAS. Officers must be between twenty-two and thirty-four, other ranks between nineteen and thirty-four. The selection course is run twice a year, once in summer and once in winter.

Selection consists of a three-week build-up (two weeks for officers) to allow each volunteer a chance to get up to the physical standard required, followed by a Test Week. The emphasis is on cross-country marches over the hills and mountains in which the distance covered, carrying SLR rifle and rucksack (Bergen) increases every day. So does the weight of the pack – from 11 kg to 25 kg. In the 1950s and 1960s the Bergens were filled with bricks, today they are filled with more useful items, such as sleeping bags. Candidates are also issued with a webbed belt, two water bottles, a brew kit, ration packs, map and compass. As SAS troopers must be proficient at navigation, basic tuition in map and compass work is given to those who need it. At the beginning of Selection the marches are done in groups, but from week three candidates go solo. Each man is given a rendezvous to head for. There is a time limit for the march but the candidate is not told what it is. For much of the march he will have to jog. When he reaches the rendezvous he is given another rendezvous. To increase his anxiety and to test his ability to deal with the unexpected when tired and stressed, the candidate will be asked to perform a task at the rendezvous, such as stripping down an unfamiliar weapon.

By the fourth week, Test Week, the numbers on the course will have dropped significantly. Many will have left of their own accord, while others will have been rejected ('binned', in SAS parlance). At the training wing the photos of the rejects will be scored with a red line: what the SAS jokingly calls the 'SAS plastic surgery'. Those who remain are exhausted by twenty-one days of exercise and training beginning at 4 a.m. and ending at 10.30 p.m. Officers are expected to participate in 'staff exercises' every evening, in which they plan – and defend under interrogation – operations such as deep-reconnaissance patrols. At the end of Test Week comes an endurance march, known as 'The Long March' or 'Fan Dance'. This is a forty-mile navigation exercise in the Brecon Beacons which must be completed in twenty hours or less; due to map and navigational errors in the mountain terrain, most candidates will end marching/jogging considerably more than forty miles. The Long March goes ahead whatever the weather. Paul Bruce recalls his Long March:

We all knew that at the end of the endurance training we would face the biggest test of all, what the SAS term 'the long drag'; a forty-mile endurance march across the mountains with 60 lb on our backs and carrying an SLR. To put added pressure on us, the march would have to be completed in eighteen hours.

We were woken by the duty guard at 5 a.m. and given a full breakfast. By 6 a.m. we were in the trucks, headed for Talybont reservoir, our starting point. On this march we were all alone, with no one for company. We began at ten-minute intervals and were given twelve map references to check into

248

before completing the forty-mile test.

As we started out, the wind was blowing a gale and sleet and bitterly cold rain beat into our faces. It would have been difficult to have found a worse day to undertake such an exercise. We cursed the weather but knew we had to put it behind us and concentrate on the job in hand.

Each reference point was situated at the top of a hill or mountain so we were marching through horrendous terrain, the gradient making life very difficult and very testing. At each reference point an instructor waited to check us in, to see if we were fit to continue.

Despite the terrain, we had to average three miles an hour, which is only walking pace. However, when a 60-lb pack and mountainous terrain are added to the equation, three miles an hour is so tight that, at every possible opportunity, it becomes necessary to run just to keep up the average. On one occasion, as I clambered up a slope, I lost my footing and found myself rolling over and over down the hill. I managed to stop and looked up to see that I had fallen perhaps sixty feet. I was covered in dirt and mud, my clothes sodden to the skin and I still had twenty miles or more ahead of me. As I struggled to my feet, I really didn't think I would complete the march.

On a couple of occasions panic gripped me. I could hardly see in front of me because of the sleet slicing into my eyes, mingling with the sweat dripping down my forehead from beneath my woollen commando hat. I found it all but impossible to read the map and I was exhausted.

On the mountain peaks the sleet gave way to swirling mist, which made it extremely difficult to check one's route with the compass. On those occasions I had to put all my faith in the compass because there were no visible signs to which I could refer. I managed a wry smile, believing that the instructors must have prayed for such appalling weather conditions to make sure we were given the toughest possible test. Being totally alone made one feel more exposed, more vulnerable, and that increased the psychological pressure.

To cap it all, I slipped on a stone as I was descending a hill at the double, and fell over, twisting my ankle. I swore like a trooper, angry that I had missed my footing and fearful that they would fail me. I got to my feet and tried to put my foot down but the ankle hurt. Gingerly I continued down the hill, hoping the pain would go away. Thankful that the ankle could take my weight, I determined to carry on. I had only a mile to go and knew that I had to make it.

Many didn't. Twenty per cent of those who began failed this test and every one was sent back to his unit the following day. It didn't matter that, until that moment, they had passed the course with flying colors. Failing that very stiff trial was sufficient for the instructors to fail the recruit. It seemed a tough decision but that is the SAS. Failure will never be tolerated. There are no excuses.

Even during that gruelling march our instructors hadn't played straight for, after we had completed the march within the eighteen hours demanded, they casually let us know that we had, in fact, been given twenty hours to do it in. They hadn't told us because they didn't want it to seem too easy!

That particular year the 'long drag' had been one of the toughest ever, but that march has never, ever been postponed or cancelled because of bad weather. Indeed, it seems that the worse the weather, the happier the instructors become because it then becomes a true test of a recruit's physical and psychological stamina.

That night there were many long faces. The six who had failed were upset and annoyed as they faced being sent back to their regiments. Besides myself, there were others carrying minor injuries, and everyone had walked himself into the ground. As we changed and showered an instructor came in to congratulate everyone who had succeeded in conditions which he described as 'horrendous'. We had passed the toughest test the SAS ever throws at recruits.

Undergoing his Long March, Robin Horsfall witnessed the death of Mike Kealy who, after an office job with the SAS, had decided to test himself physically:

It was raining when we left the truck and started up the hill. The wind, although strong, felt warmer than it had all week. In the valley a thaw had set in, and the snow was melting fast. As we climbed higher and higher above the tree line, the temperature dropped and the wind increased in velocity. Soon it was impossible to hear the man standing next to you, even when he shouted. The rain was hitting us from the left. To our right the cliffs dropped 200 feet, and we had to lean heavily into the wind to travel in a straight line. The snow was still thick on the ground but underneath it water was running in great streams, soaking our legs and letting in the cold. The wind-chill factor in such high winds is enormous. Although the temperature was probably about one degree Centigrade, it felt like minus thirty.

As I broke the ridge-line the wind hit me like a hammer. I locked my eyes on the man in front and plodded forward. After about an hour I saw three men walking back down towards me. One had collapsed with exposure and the others were taking him to safety. A short time later I saw Major Kealy shouting at two of the students. They were trying to get him into some spare waterproof clothing which one of them had been carrying. He was refusing, and I saw the waterproofs blow away over the cliffs and into the dark.

I struggled on, but the cold was beginning to prove unbearable. I tried eating and I tried walking faster, but I couldn't focus on my compass and I started to feel nauseous. I had nothing else to wear and the wind was cutting through me like a knife. Sitting down, I realized that if I didn't keep moving I would go down with exposure. I got up and stumbled on for another half-hour before I found myself alone and going in completely the wrong direction, straight towards the cliffs. I've got exposure, I thought. I asked myself whether I was bottling out again, and struggled with the choice of pushing on or accepting that I was ill and going back down. I think now that I made a good decision, the decision to live. For the second time on a selection I turned back.

When I got to the bottom, I was on my last legs. I reported to the truck, where I was met by Lofty, the training-wing sergeant-major. He simply wrote down my name and told me to get in the back. I told him I thought the weather was so terrible up there that somebody could end up dead. In the thawing valley it looked, if anything, as if the weather was better than before, but up on top it was the worst I had ever experienced in any mountains, anywhere.

I wrapped myself up in my sleeping bag and went to sleep. I was upset that this selection had come to an end, but I didn't feel that I had let myself down. I knew that my decision had been the correct one. If the weather had not been so extreme I would have been successful. A few hours later, I woke up to find the truck moving off towards Hereford. We stopped briefly and I asked Lofty what was going on. He was very concerned. It was now six hours since the group had set off, and so far not one person had reached the first checkpoint at the Story Arms. They were going to alert the Mountain Rescue Service and get A Squadron up to the Story Arms to mount a search-and-rescue operation.

We got back just in time to see the squadron departing. I wanted to go back with them but was told that I couldn't be of any help and was ordered to remain behind. The searchers were out for most of the night, but when they eventually came down, exhausted, they had found no one. It was their guess that the troops had taken shelter somewhere. They would try again at first light.

The next morning all but two were found. Only a short time after I had turned back, the remainder had decided to get off the mountain as well. They had gone down to a water pumping station and broken in. Once out of the cold, they had bedded down for the rest of the day. The roads were impassable. It was a question of survival, pure and simple.

The two missing men were Major Kealy and Simon. Apparently, when I had seen the major shouting at the men, he had been showing the first signs of hypothermia. They had tried to help him get his spare clothing on, but when they opened his Bergen they discovered that instead of emergency equipment and waterproofs, he was carrying only bricks and some rations. He had pulled rank when they had tried to persuade him to go back and, as he was an SAS major, they had finally given in. A short time later he collapsed and lost consciousness. The troops that were with him dug a shelter and put up some overhead cover, then got him into his sleeping bag; they donated their own survival gear to try to keep him alive. Simon stayed with him and snuggled up to him to transfer his body heat. Now that he was unconscious, there was no way that fuel could be put into his body. He could not eat or drink; his only hope was that help would arrive soon.

A Squadron found the shelter at about lunchtime. Simon was in a bad way, but Major Kealy had died in the night, of exposure. He had been a hero at the defence of Mirbat in Oman in the early 1970s, and was highly thought of by all members of the unit. He just didn't have the kit for the terrible weather conditions we'd encountered. It was a terribly sad end to the week.

Looking back, we had been lucky not to lose more men. Scouse could have been lost on the night march. Andy could have walked over the cliff, and the loose cornice could have turned into an avalanche. It was only with hindsight that I realized what a truly dangerous week we had all experienced.

Those who survive and pass the endurance march are then gathered in Stirling Lines, where they are told that they are not yet in the SAS. They must now undertake, after just a week's leave, fourteen weeks of Continuation Training.

Continuation Training lasts for around four months and tutors the potential recruit in all the SAS patrol skills: Standard Operating Procedures (SOPs), weapons training, demolitions and reconnaissance. Each student receives instruction in signalling, a vitally important skill for long-range patrolling. All SAS troopers pretty much achieve the British Army regimental signaller standard, which includes being able to transmit and receive Morse code at a minimum of eight words a minute. In addition, tuition is given in SAS field-medicine techniques.

After these fundamentals, the candidates then undergo Combat and Survival Training, which lasts three weeks. Here the prospective troopers learn all the aspects of living in hostile environments: laying traps, building shelters, finding food and water. The Combat and Survival phase ends in an Escape and Evasion exercise, in which candidates must not only live off the land but do so for three days while being hunted by the 'enemy', usually soldiers from local infantry battalions. On the conclusion of the exercise, candidates are subjected to twenty-four-hour realistic interrogation of the sort they might face if captured by the forces of an enemy nation. The interrogation includes elements of physical hardship, sensory deprivation and psychological torture. Any candidate who 'breaks' is rejected.

Paul Bruce recounts his interrogation:

I woke with a start, with the hut in pitch darkness and someone shaking my arm, telling me to get up. Luckily, I had gone to bed in my underpants because I was given no time to put on anything, not even a T-shirt or trousers.

I was still half-asleep as two men pushed me towards the end of the hut and out of the door. I couldn't see their faces but something told me they were probably the two strangers who had interrogated me earlier that day. I was half-dragged, half-pushed across the open ground and into another hut. I was roughly pushed into a chair. I began to come to and reckoned that I was probably in the same hut where I had been questioned the previous day.

They shoved a black bag made of cotton material over my head. My hands were tied with cord behind the chair and then there was silence. I tried to hear what was going on; I strained to listen in case they spoke, to give me some idea of what was happening. For all of five minutes I was left alone with not a word or a sound coming from inside that room. My heart began to thump.

'What was this parachute course like that you've just been on?' one man asked.

Remembering what my SAS instructor had advised me, I denied I had been on a parachute course.

He said, 'You've been in the SAS for eight fucking months and you haven't been on a parachute course. That's bollocks.'

'I ain't been here for eight months, I've only just arrived,' I lied.

'Bullshit,' one replied. 'Don't you lie to us.'

'I'm not lying,' I protested.

For the next two hours the two men kept up a relentless barrage of questions, sometimes asking me things about my life in the army which I knew to be true but which I denied vehemently to them. They even questioned me about my time in the REME, about things I had done, all of which were true.

I kept wondering what the hell all this questioning was for; convinced that they still believed that I had been in a Hereford pub boasting about being a member of the SAS.

Then the insults really began. They were fucking and blinding, calling me all the names under the sun, insulting my parents and all the time calling me a lying bastard. Then, suddenly, I heard a woman's voice in the room. She was saying, 'Who's this old slag Maria from Tidworth?'

'I don't know who you're talking about,' I lied. 'I don't know anybody called Maria.'

The foul-mouthed bitch continued: 'Don't you fucking lie to me. Not only do you know this Maria but we know that while you have been here she has been fucking every Tom, Dick and Harry around Tidworth. She's nothing but an old slag, nothing better than a fucking whore.'

Like a bolt from the blue I understood. I knew Maria wasn't like that. I knew this bitch was telling lies. The penny dropped; this was the feared interrogation training we had heard rumours about but never been told about officially. Our instructors had never mentioned interrogation training but we knew, from what we had heard, that one day we would be put through this training. I did not know what to expect but I convinced myself in that instant that this was it.

They kept asking me questions. I would answer whatever came into my mind but I did not tell the truth. I found my mouth had become dry and was feeling terribly thirsty. I asked if I could have some water.

'You're getting fuck all, you lying shit, until you start telling us the truth,' they replied.

They continued asking questions, about the training, the SAS, my past, everything and anything. I started to get angry. Suddenly, I felt a shot of pain across my legs as though I had been struck with a cane. Then another swish and the cane hit my other leg. 'What the fuck's that for?' I asked.

256

'Every time you lie to us you'll get another one. And they'll get harder and harder until you tell us what we want to know.'

'I've told you everything,' I lied again. The cane swished again, cutting across my naked thigh.

I had a sudden fear that they would hit my bollocks. I thought of crossing my legs to protect myself but realized that if I did that then they were certain to go for my balls and I knew that would really hurt.

They began to slap me across the face whenever I answered them. It didn't matter what I said but, every so often, with no warning, one of them would smack me across the face or use the cane on my legs. Neither was really painful but what shook me was the fact that there was no warning; every hit or slap came as a shock and that disoriented me.

I don't know how long the interrogation and physical abuse went on because, after an hour or so, I lost track of time. I judged it must have continued for about two more hours but I may have been wrong. It could have been longer. I began to lose touch with reality. I kept telling myself that this was only interrogation training, that it would soon be over, that they would take off the hood and tell me everything was fine and I could go back to my billet and get some sleep. And yet part of my brain began to doubt that because the blows and the questions were very real indeed.

I wanted to go for a piss. Suddenly, all I could think about was wanting to go for a slash but I kept my mouth shut because I knew that they wouldn't let me go; indeed, they would probably have loved to see me pissing in my pants while they laughed at me and took the mickey. I was determined not to give them that pleasure.

It seemed odd because I was both desperately thirsty and desperate for a piss. I kept asking for a drink but they never once gave me even a sip of water.

I began to have doubts about what was going on. I couldn't believe that this was only training. I knew the SAS was tough and the training rigorous but this seemed beyond credibility. But if it wasn't training, what the hell were these people after; what did they want with me; why were they determined to slag off poor Maria and insult me and my parents.

At times I became angry. I swore at them, told them I was telling the truth and told them, including the woman, that they were all a bunch of cunts. I told the bitch: 'How dare you slag off Maria. You have no right to do that. You're calling her names because you're probably the biggest whore around Hereford.'

For that I earned three hard swishes with the cane across my thighs. They hurt. Not once did they laugh; not once did they change their approach to me; not once did they give me an inkling that this was all a game and that it would soon be over. Occasionally, throughout the interrogation, I told myself that, once I was free, I would kick the shit out of these three bastards, particularly the bitch who had been slagging off Maria.

Then one said casually, his voice filled with menace, 'We're going to leave you here to think about things. When we return we want you to tell us the truth, or else. Do you hear? We haven't touched you yet. Tell us more lies and you'll really pay for it. We're fed up with all your fucking lies.'

They must have been gone for the best part of an hour. During that time I tried to rationalize what was happening. Deep down, I suspected that if they were determined to hurt me they would attack my bollocks. That worried me.

They returned and immediately resumed the same relentless questions that they had asked a thousand times before. The blows came raining down on my face and my legs and thighs were hit repeatedly with the cane. I came to fear the swish, knowing that a split second later I would feel the cane cutting across my legs and thighs. It was not knowing where or when I would be hit next that upset me, not the actual pain. I could take that. But I didn't know whether I would be able to stand it when they began grabbing, kicking or hitting my balls. I just hoped to hell they would leave them alone.

I lost track of time; I lost track of what to say to try to put an end to this bloody agony. I thought of telling them the truth; sometimes I was within an ace of jacking in the whole bloody interrogation and telling them truthfully the answers to all the questions they had asked about the SAS, the training, the parachuting, everything. And yet something made me keep up my tissue of lies. I kept thinking of the advice my SAS instructor had given me, 'Tell them nothing'.

And it worked.

Suddenly, I felt the hood being taken off my head and I blinked at the light. I looked around and saw the two men and the woman who had been tormenting me. I was trying to pull myself together, to gather my strength, when one of the men said, 'It's all over. You did well.'

The sense of relief was unbelievable. All thoughts that I had nurtured of kicking the shit out of them vanished in a second. All I wanted to do was have a slash. I was near to bursting point. I also desperately needed a drink.

One told me it was ten o'clock at night; that I had been under interrogation for twenty hours; that now I was free to go and do whatever I wanted, have a meal, have a drink, have a shower or just go to sleep. All I wanted was a slash, a shower and bed.

As I drifted off to sleep, my thoughts returned to the interrogation. On the one hand, I was happy that I had survived without breaking down but on the other I thought that if ever I found myself in a situation where I needed to break someone to find out information, I wouldn't be as gentle as my interrogators. I would go straight to the balls and inflict as much pain as possible as quickly as possible to get the result I needed. Then I fell asleep wondering what the hell I was doing in the fucking SAS.

Those who do not break have finished Continuation Training. However, they are not yet members of the Regiment. There is still six weeks of jungle training, usually in the Far East or Belize. Finally, there comes a four-week parachute course at Brize Norton. Those who are left return to Credenhill, where they are 'badged' SAS.

Their advanced training then begins.

Each SAS trooper is assigned to one of the four sixteen-man troops in the squadrons: boat troop, mobility troop, air troop and mountain troop. Even men who are 'badged' will be swiftly returned to unit and sent off to Hereford railway station if they fail to keep the Regiment's standards.

PART III

BACK TO THE FUTURE

The SAS, 1982–2010

The Falkland Islands, specks of land almost lost in the vastness of the South Atlantic, had been British owned since 1833. Argentina, however, had long laid claim to the 'Malvinas', and on 2 April 1982 the leader of the nation's military junta, General Galtieri, decided to back that claim with a full-scale invasion of the islands.

Immediately on hearing the news of the invasion, the Director of the SAS Group, Brigadier Peter de la Billière, and the commander of 22 SAS, Lieutenant Colonel Mike Rose, put the Regiment on standby and lobbied hard for a role in the military campaign for the islands' recovery, should one be launched. It was. The Argentinian junta was not minded to give up their new possession; the British prime minister of the day, Margaret Thatcher, was equally determined that the islands should become British once more. War was on. The Special Air Service, de la Billière intended, should share the burden of war and – dare it be said – the limelight, in what might be Britain's last colonial war.

The SAS appeal fell on favourably inclined ears. Three days later, after SAS soldiers had been frantically summonsed back from leave, training courses and patrolling in Armagh's bandit country, an advance party from D Squadron flew south to Ascension Island. A small D Squadron contingent also embarked the carrier HMS *Hermes*, sailing from Portsmouth Harbour. The remainder of D Squadron, together with all their kit, was airborne for Ascension twenty-four hours later, and so was G Squadron and the regimental headquarters. The swift send-off was a telling tribute to the efficiency of the quartermasters at Stirling Lines.

Although Ascension Island, pinned in the middle of the Atlantic just below the Equator, was 3,885 miles from the Falklands, it was the nearest British territory of serviceable use. Hot and cramped, the island had little to recommend it and D Squadron's ninety troopers were not sorry to find that their sojourn was soon curtailed. Margaret Thatcher was keen that a dramatic and immediate military action was undertaken against the illegal occupiers of Britannia's southern outposts. The chosen target was Grytviken, the former whaling station on the island of South Georgia, 870 miles south-east of the main Falklands group.

The execution of Operation *Paraquet* (soon corrupted to Operation *Paraquat*, after the branded weedkiller) fell to D Squadron, alongside a patrol from M Company, 42 Royal Marine Commando ('The Mighty Munch'), and a section of the SBS – some 235 men in all. On 21 April the small assault force, carried in HMS *Endeavour*, HMS *Antrim* and HMS *Plymouth*, came in sight of South Georgia, an ice-bound mountainous wilderness which formed, before the Argentinian occupation, the base for the British Antarctic Survey. Little was known about deployment of Argentinian forces on the island, so Major Guy Sheridan RM, the commander of the assault force, ordered covert recces. Captain John Hamilton's 19 Troop of D Squadron was inserted by helicopter in near white-out conditions of driving snow. Carrying 77 lb of kit and hauling heavily laden pulks (sledges), the troops inched down the Fortuna glacier, but after a night of hurricane-force winds Hamilton had no choice but to request extraction. Three Wessex helicopters successfully landed on the glacier. The weather conditions were so extreme, though, that the take-offs were blighted. Corporal Davey, Squadron SAS, recorded:

The helicopters lifted off, the Mark 3 Wessex with

262

navigational equipment leading and the two Mark 5s following. I was in the first Mark 5. The flight plan was to follow the glaciers down to a land fall and then out to the ships. The Mark 3 put in a shallow right-hand turn, height probably about 200–300 feet, the first Mark 5 started the turn but was hit by a sudden white-out in which the pilot lost all his horizons and we crashed into the ice. The pilot managed to pull the nose up before impact so that the tail rotor hit first and the helicopter rolled over on its left-hand side. The main door being uppermost everyone got out quickly, the only injury being Corporal Bunker who had hurt his back.

The remaining Mark 5 and Mark 3 then landed and we transferred to them . . . the two helicopters lifted off again and exactly the same thing happened, white-out followed by crash. This time the Mark 5 rested on its right-hand side. The Mark 3, unable to return because of extra payload, then flew back to *Antrim*. I and the other passengers were taken to the wardroom where an emergency medical room had been set up. After refuelling, the Mark 3, with the same crew still aboard, returned to the area of the second crash, but was unable to land because of weather. It returned to the ship, having contacted the troops on the glacier who had no serious injuries. They had in fact managed to erect a survival tent carried by the helicopter and had also retrieved equipment from the first crash.

The Mark 3 then returned again to the second crash, and this time picked everyone up and returned to *Antrim*. It had seventeen passengers, very much overloaded, and the pilot had to fly the helicopter straight on to the flight deck as he was unable to hover and approach normally. It was now 22 April.

The pilot of the returning Mark 3 Wessex was Lieutenant Commander Ian Stanley RN. For his valour and professionalism, Stanley was awarded the DSO.

With the South Georgia Task Force's helicopter capability reduced by two-thirds, the planners decided to launch D Squadron's boat troop. Although two of their five Gemini inflatables suffered engine failure, three crews got ashore to set up watch on Leith and Stromness on the night of 22 April. Three days later, Ian Stanley successfully inserted an SBS patrol a few clicks below Grytviken. Choppering back to *Antrim*, Stanley spotted the Argentinian submarine *Santa Fe* on the surface; he immediately attacked, straddling her with a pair of depth charges. These inflicted sufficient damage to prevent her diving, and she was shortly attacked by helicopters from *Endurance* and the frigate *Brilliant*. The *Santa Fe* limped into Grytviken, where her condition, plus the sight of pursuing British helicopters, caused panic among the 130-strong enemy garrison. Despite only having seventy-five men immediately available, Major Sheridan and D Squadron's commanding officer, Major Cedric Delves, decided to exploit the Argentinians' set-back. To the roar of supporting gunfire from *Antrim* and *Plymouth*, an SAS composite troop and two composite RM/SBS troops landed in the vicinity of Grytviken. Screened from the settlement by a small mountain, the SAS struck out for the port. Some elephant seals, mistaken for Argentinian troops, were shot up and a suspected enemy position was promptly demolished by a Milan missile; the stronghold, alas, turned out to be a piece of scrap iron. These hazards negotiated, the SAS team ascended to the top of Brown Mountain to see the wooden buildings of the port below festooned with white flags. The garrison surrendered without a shot being fired. With barely a pause to get his breath, SSM Lawrence Gallagher of D Squadron hauled down the Argentinian flag and raised the Union Jack. To their incredulity, the SAS assault party discovered that they had blithely trolled through the minefield ringing the Argentinian weapons pits. The next morning, 26 April, two troops from D Squadron, together with an SBS team, took the peaceful surrender of the Leith garrison. South Georgia was once again in British hands.

While D Squadron had South Georgia on its mind, G Squadron 22 SAS was sailing towards the war zone on the RFA *Resource*. Since there was little in the way of aerial or satellite pictures of the Argentinian positions on the Falklands, G Squadron was earmarked for some old-style 'eye-ball' reconnaissance. Beginning on 1 May, four-man patrols were inserted by Sea King, an earlier plan to parachute them in being cancelled at the last moment. The forward observation posts in the featureless terrain often consisted of a mere shallow depression covered with ponchos. Life in the hides was unrelentingly grim, with little or no chance to brew up hot food or drink, and with cold, wet weather that seeped into the bones. The record for staying in a hide was twenty-eight days, set by Sergeant Mather and his team above Bluff Cove.

There was always the danger of discovery. On 10 June an SAS covert 'hide' containing Captain John Hamilton – who had rejoined the main task force after the successful taking of South Georgia – and his signaller was uncovered; in the ensuing firefight with the Argentinians, Hamilton was killed as he tried to cover the signaller's escape. For his bravery, Hamilton was awarded a posthumous MC. On more than one occasion SAS and SBS patrols ran into each other and opened fire. One such 'blue-on-blue' incident ended tragically, with the death of SBS Sergeant 'Kiwi' Hunt.

Despite these set-backs, the recce teams achieved conspicuously successful results. One four-man patrol, led by G Squadron's Captain Aldwin, set up a hide on Beagle Ridge, directly above Port Stanley, in an area heavily patrolled by the enemy. From the hide, the team spotted a night dispersal area for helicopters between Mounts Kent and Estancia; when the intelligence was relayed back to the fleet, two Harrier aircraft attacked the site and destroyed three enemy helicopters.

Besides reconnaissance, the regiment was tasked with the carrying out of its quintessential activity: offensive raiding behind the lines. An early target was the Argentinian airstrip on Pebble

Island, off the northern coast of West Falkland, the base for 1A–58 Pucara aircraft. Sergeant Peter Ratcliffe was among those slated for the Pebble Island job:

At about eleven o'clock on the morning of 15 May, the Boat Troop commander sent a signal which will go down in the annals of the Regiment. Coded and transmitted in Morse, once deciphered it read, 'Eleven aircraft, repeat eleven aircraft. Believed real. Squadron attack tonight.'

The timescale was very tight – clearly Ted saw the matter as urgent. In the light of this, the squadron commander and the senior planners got together and worked out that any attack launched against the aircraft on the Pebble Island airstrip would have to be completed by 0700 hours the next day to allow sufficient time for the raiding parties to be recovered by helicopter. The reason for this was because the Task Force ships closed up to the islands at night, but steamed away into the South Atlantic so that they should not be vulnerable to air attack when daylight came some time after 1100 hours. As they sailed out of danger, so the distance the helicopters would have to fly back to the ships increased.

The plan began to go wrong from the first. Because of bad weather conditions and *Hermes* miscalculating her run in to a position eighty miles offshore, which would bring Pebble Island within helicopter range of the ships, the operation started running late almost from the start. The South Atlantic lived up to its foul-weather reputation, and the aircraft carrier had to sail in fierce headwinds and mounting seas. Movement on board was risky, which meant that the Sea Kings on the hangar decks could not be safely readied by the technical crews in the time allowed. Once they were ready, there were more delays while the choppers were brought up to the flight deck for lift-off.

The helicopters were carried up from the hold of *Hermes*

by huge lifts let into the flight deck, for all the aircraft, Sea Harriers as well as Sea Kings, were kept below deck at all times when they weren't flying. The mood and atmosphere among D Squadron was electric, with everyone raring to go. By then our faces were covered in cam cream and we were all tooled up. Each SAS man tasked for the raid carried an M16 rifle with three spare magazines taped to the butt, and another 200 to 400 rounds of 7.62mm GPMG ammunition in belts. Everybody carried two mortar bombs, one of high explosive and one of white phosphorus, which we were to drop off when we reached the mortar pits that would be established near the airstrip. Several of the guys also carried LAWs – M72 light anti-tank weapons – which are extremely effective against aircraft on the ground.

Adrenalin raged through our systems like rivers of fire, giving us an enormous rush. Armed to the teeth, forty-five of us boarded the Sea Kings; with us also went a naval-gunfire support team from 148 Battery, 29 Commando Regiment, Royal Artillery, whose task was to direct the bombardment from the 4.5-inch guns of the ships lying offshore. We all embarked on the hangar deck, and eventually the Sea King that my troop was to fly in was brought up to the flight deck. The helicopter's engines roared into life. We waited on deck for at least fifteen minutes, only to be told that one of the Sea Kings carrying another troop had developed mechanical problems and would have to be replaced. All in all, this took over an hour, leaving our time on the ground less than adequate, as everything had been planned on the basis of the distance between *Hermes* and Pebble Island and the range of the Sea Kings, making timing absolutely critical.

At last we lifted off, flying low-level over the sea in blackout conditions, occasionally gaining fleeting glimpses of the waves below. I had never experienced surges of adrenalin to the same extent. To be part of the largest SAS raid since the Second World War was something that I would not have missed for anything, especially when I remembered that I should have been back in Birmingham drill hall completing my two-year stint as an instructor.

The navy pilots were terrific, lifting off in the dark and, despite very high winds, flying only forty or fifty feet above the waves to dodge any enemy radar cover. For all their efforts, however, because of the atrocious weather we were already running an hour late when they dropped us off three miles from the airstrip. We estimated that it would take us about two hours to reach the target.

On landing we were met by Captain Ted, the Boat Troop commander, and his men. They had spent the last four days lying up on Pebble Island, watching the enemy without being seen; now it was their job to lead us to the target. The squadron commander and the 'head sheds' of each troop were briefed by Ted. Once the briefing had finished, we were told that this was not a night for tactical movement; instead, we had to get our arses in gear and get to the target as quickly as possible, since otherwise we wouldn't have enough time to carry out the mission and rendezvous with the helicopters before the latter had to return to *Hermes*. The plan was for Mobility Troop to attack the eleven aircraft on the ground and destroy them with plastic-explosive (PE) charges. Air Troop was tasked to mask off the settlement, and Mountain Troop was to be held in reserve at the mortar pit, from where they would be able to go instantly to the aid of any troops that might be in trouble.

My troop, Mobility, was commanded by Captain Paul and his number two was Bob, a staff sergeant; I was number three in the pecking order. Considering the ground and the darkness, we got off pretty quickly. It was not quickly enough, however, for the going was against us. The ground was mainly of peat, spongy stuff that made walking difficult, especially in the dark, and there were lots of fences and walls to cross. Just the kind of thing you'd expect around a sheep settlement.

Realizing that precious time had been lost, the squadron commander decided to speed-march in single file, one man behind the other. As a result, rather than observing patrol procedures, which would normally involve a stealthy approach, we often broke into a run. But when we came to a wall or a fence, we adopted 'obstacle procedure', which dictated that each man should be covered by others while he crossed, and this slowed us considerably.

When moving in an extended single file, the soldier in front is responsible for the soldier behind. So long as he can see the man ahead of him and the man behind, then everything is fine. That's the theory, anyway, but what we didn't know was that while we were painstakingly crossing obstacles, the squadron OC and the other troops were leaping walls and fences and racing towards the target as though their boots were on fire.

Inevitably, we lost contact with the troop in front. They were travelling much faster than we were, and before long the man at the head of our troop could no longer see the last man of the troop ahead. Going over undulating ground at night, you can simply disappear into the darkness, and once the chain is broken you are as good as lost. In the pitch blackness we couldn't see a thing, even through our night scopes, so our only means of contacting the leading troops was by the radio carried by the troop signaller. When Captain Paul realized our predicament he radioed the OC, who was somewhere up in front of us in the dark, and asked him for a steer. The squadron commander came back on the radio and said he didn't have time to wait for us – if we didn't catch up with him by the time we reached the rendezvous position, we were to stay in reserve by the mortar pit, the task originally given to Mountain Troop.

We didn't catch up. However, a contingency plan had been agreed before we left *Hermes*. Under this, if anything happened to Mobility Troop prior to our reaching the target, then Mountain Troop was to pick up the baton and lead the attack. Its members were carrying enough explosives to complete the mission.

By the time we reached the mortar pit, we knew we had lost our starring role in the attack. Almost beside ourselves with anger and disappointment, we realized that we had been relegated to being just a bunch of extras.

Looking back on that night, the troop sergeant should have detailed someone to be in front as the lead scout. Captain Paul was a good officer and was trying to do things properly, and it was not his fault that a gap had developed, for on this particular night there was drifting mist that continually came and went. To make matters worse, we were the only troop that didn't have a member of Boat Troop attached to us as a guide – a mistake, since by then they knew the way to and from the airstrip better than the backs of their hands.

Nevertheless, there can be no excuses. Mobility Troop's delay in arriving at the target was the result of incompetence, and it should not have happened. The important thing to remember, however, is that the Regiment is not infallible. We do sometimes make mistakes. In this respect the SAS is like any other regiment, and its soldiers are not immune from sometimes getting things wrong, especially in the confusion of war.

'David', a soldier with another troop, takes up the story:

At this point it became apparent that we had lost the troop that was supposed to carry out the attack on the actual planes. In all fairness to them, it is sometimes quite hard to locate a six-figure grid reference in the pitch-dark in the middle of nowhere in a place where everything looks the same. And they were one of the troops who did not have a guide. Nobody knew they were missing until we arrived at the forward RV. We had assumed they were out in front of us. We had to change plan immediately. We waited for a bit to see if they would reappear but they didn't. We now had exactly thirty minutes to complete the assault.

Mountain Troop, led by John Hamilton, was designated to do the assault. My troop became the fire-support team for the assault. Thank God for that. We were so lucky. It meant we didn't have to do the house-clearing assault on the settlement. We later found out that there were 200 Argentinian soldiers in the wool shed, which was the starting point for our operations. There were sixteen of us. That would have been interesting.

The attack opened with a naval bombardment on to the feature directly overlooking the settlement. Then our own mortar opened up, lighting the whole place up like it was bright daylight. The mortar man was having a lot of trouble. Every time he fired the bloody thing, the whack of the pipe was kicking the base plate further into the ground. If the angle of the plate changed, he lost his trajectory and elevation. Despite this he kept up continuous fire, eventually giving the order 'check fire' before we withdrew.

After a few more minutes the assault troop went in. As they reached one end of the airstrip they got into a firefight. An Argentine officer and an NCO were in a bunker to the side of the strip and opened up. They were rapidly dealt with. After that there was virtually no enemy fire on us, so the boys got stuck into the planes.

They split into seven two-man teams. It was a bloody big strip and they had a lot of ground to cover. It's not as if the planes were all parked in a nice neat row. They were all over the strip. And all the time the boys were running against the

271

clock. Five planes were destroyed using the explosive charges that they had with them. The Pucara was the tallest of the aircraft. As they approached each plane, one bloke would give the other a leg up on to the wing. Once up, he then leaned down and hauled the other one up to join him. The Skyvan was not a problem. The Mentors were very small, and with one great leap the guys got themselves up on to the wings.

The other six planes were attacked at close quarters by hand. It's not like in the movies, when you shoot the fuel tank of a plane and it explodes. Planes are built to withstand bullet holes, at least up to a point. Still, the lads used their initiative. They riddled the planes, especially the cockpits, with machine-gun fire and chucked in grenades for good measure. Some of the lads, including Paddy A., got so worked up with adrenalin and enthusiasm that they actually ripped instrument panels out of the cockpits with their bare hands.

During the withdrawal there was suddenly this almighty explosion. The Argies had planted command-detonated mines, and as we were leaving someone on their side decided to get brave and initiated one of them. We had no knowledge that they had even been planted. The guys who had done the assault were withdrawing in groups of four. Fire and maneuver. One team of two is on the ground providing cover for the other two as they move. One foot on the ground, one moving. Leap-frogging. Two of our guys were caught in the blast of the mine. One had shrapnel wounds and the other was just winded. They were recovered and helped to the original central rendezvous point near the mortar. The base plate had to be dug out, it had sunk so deep. As soon as we could, we set off back to the coastline. There was so little time.

I was in the last chopper to leave. As we were taking off I remember looking back over my shoulder. I'll never forget

272

it. The whole place looked as if it was burning. It was terrific. We all went nuts.

Corporal Davey was one of two SAS men injured in the raid. He wrote of his part in the operation:

Captain Burls led 19 Troop on to the airstrip via the forward RV manned by Captain West and Sergeant Major Gallagher. Once on the edge of the airstrip we began to engage visible aircraft with small arms and 66mm rockets. By this time naval gunfire and illumination were being produced by HMS *Glamorgan* and our mortars also fired some illuminating rounds. We were aware of some incoming enemy small arms fire, but it was totally ineffective.

I was a member of Staff Sergeant Currass's patrol and was the extreme right-hand man. I was hit in the lower left leg by shrapnel at about 0700 hours. Staff Sergeant Currass helped me put a shell dressing on the wound. The troop moved on to the airstrip and started systematically to destroy the aircraft with standard charges and 66mm. Captain Hamilton covered Trooper Armstrong who went forward to destroy the last aircraft. The troop then shook out and started to fall back off the airstrip. We were at this stage silhouetted against the burning aircraft. A land mine was command detonated in the middle of the troop, Corporal Bunker being blown some ten feet backwards.

I was beginning to feel faint from loss of blood and consequently was told to head back towards the forward RV with two others. Just off the airstrip we heard Spanish voices, at least four or five, shouting some fifty metres towards the settlement. I opened fire with M203 and put down some sixty rounds in the direction of the voices. Two very pained screams were the only reply. The troop came down behind us and we moved back through the forward RV at about 0745 hours.

273

During the move back I was helped over various obstacles and so was Corporal Bunker. The helicopter pick-up was on time at 0930, and the flight back to *Hermes* lasted about one hour twenty minutes. Corporal Bunker and I went directly to the sick bay where we were looked after admirably.

It had been a textbook job. It passed through the thoughts of more than one SAS trooper that night that, swap the South Atlantic for the desert, the Argentinians for the Germans, and the RAF helos for the LRDG taxis, 22 SAS was doing exactly what Stirling, Mayne and Lewes had done forty years before.

Presumably, the 'Head Shed' at Stirling Lines felt the daring hand of L Detachment's history on their shoulders when they conjured up Operation *Mikado*, in which B Squadron would attack Exocet-carrying Super Etandard fighters on Rio Grande airstrip on the Argentine mainland. In one fell SAS-swoop the war would be shortened. Some members of the squadron thought the operation suicidal – the airstrip was defended by 1,300 Argentinian marines and state-of-the-art AA guns – and the squadron sergeant major even resigned over the issue. When the squadron's commanding officer, John Moss, showed less than requisite enthusiasm, DLB summarily returned him to unit. If not a death wish, others in the squadron considered that the Paras would be better equipped to undertake such a *coup de main*. The pessimists grew gloomier when the helicopter inserting the recce team was compromised; the Sea King, at the very maximum of its range, tundra-hopped to plop down just over the Chilean border. At best any attack would henceforth be blind. Tom Read of B Squadron recounts the plan, preparation and frequent postponements of *Mikado*:

Apart from the various troop briefings, we have larger squadron meetings to discuss the full operation. The initial patrol will set up the LZ on the dual carriageway, allowing the RAF pilots to bring in the C-130s.

The squadron will then brass-neck it, driving straight along the main road on motorbikes and in right-hand-drive Land Rovers. I like the audacity of that. Our intelligence lads have interviewed a Canadian who used to work at Rio Grande airfield. He's given us details of the layout and the location of the local military base. There are two guards on the security gate and Des has been assigned to take out one of them, while Harry McCallion takes care of the other.

The open-top Land Rovers have mounted machine guns as well as Browning 30s and a handful of M-202s – American-made white phosphorus grenade-launchers that look like something out of a James Bond movie. They're only as long as a shotgun, but they have multi-barrels and when you squeeze the trigger there's a gentle explosion and a wall of flame. It can destroy an aircraft in seconds.

At H-hour we'll pour through the front gate and spread out, splitting into smaller groups and hitting different targets. One patrol will take out the control tower, another will blow the fuel tanks and a third will attack the accommodation bunkers and try to kill the pilots. My Land Rover is to head for the aircraft hangars and use the M-202 to destroy the Super Etendards.

'Okay, you're probably wondering what the enemy will be up to while we're doing all this,' says Ian C., the new OC of the squadron. 'Our intelligence says the airfield has a limited troop presence. About two miles away there's a military base with about 1,800 Marines. That's why one of the primary targets is the comms centre. Assuming these troops are alerted, hopefully by the time they get their shit together and weapons out of the armoury we'll have finished and gone.'

Discussion turns to our escape, but the options are limited. The nearest Task Force ship will be 500 miles away, and the choppers on board have the fuel capacity to reach us but not get home again. This leaves us with a dash towards the

Chilean border, forty miles away. Basically we'll have to drive as quickly as possible towards the border on one of two roads until we hit road-blocks or are compromised. After that, it may be a case of tabbing over the tundra.

'Take any vehicles you can get, but try not to kill any civilians,' says Ian C. 'Once you're across the border, surrender to the Chilean authorities.'

It's not much of an escape plan and Rhett, one of the older lads, pipes up, 'Boss, I think I should point out that I shouldn't be here, because I cheated on Combat Survival.' Everyone laughs.

Call it youthful enthusiasm, but I don't even contemplate failure. More experienced heads than mine are going to decide what's right. There are no escape maps or cover stories in case of capture. The Argies will doubtless seal off the roads and put up helicopter gunships. Once the element of surprise has gone, we'll be deep in hostile territory and vastly outnumbered.

Until the green light is given, we spend our time going on runs over Green Mountain and doing weapons training. I take the M-202 down to the beach, loading up the barrels and firing it at various rocks. A lot of the lads want to have a go because it's a new weapon. On another day, I go fishing with Charlie and we catch enough red snapper for a squadron barbecue.

A week later, the operation is confirmed. We leave in twelve hours. The compo boxes are opened and we sort out rations and ammunition. I'm jumping with the minimum of kit, just a chainsaw. The rest of my gear is in one of the Land Rovers.

After packing everything away and writing letters home, we get word of a hold-up. Twenty-four hours later it's on again and then off again. This happens all week, and each morning B Squadron goes for a run, trying to work off the frustration. Apparently, there's disquiet in Downing Street about the predicted 60 per cent casualty rate of a mainland operation. Prime Minister Thatcher isn't happy with the odds. Equally, the RAF isn't thrilled about abandoning a burning aircraft and leaving the crews to tag along with us.

The mainland option seems to be falling apart when, on 8 June, the *Sir Galahad* and *Sir Tristram*, both British transport ships, are hit by Argentinian Skyhawks and Mirages in Bluff Cove. The ships are torched and dozens of soldiers die, most of them Welsh Guards. Some of the injuries are truly horrific. Suddenly, the mainland operation is back on again. We are due to leave on a flight at 0700. I'm in the baggage party, humping all the gear into the cargo hold in the pre-dawn cold. The sky is growing light but I'm sweating. A lot of the younger lads like me are raring to go, but the older blokes are more circumspect. Maybe their instincts for self-preservation are more acute.

A Land Rover arrives beside the aircraft and the news is broken – the operation has been cancelled. Apparently, a British newspaper had published a story saying that a SAS squadron based on Ascension Island was practising for a mainland operation. Within hours the Argentinians had started moving their planes away from the airfields and scattering them about the countryside, parked under camouflage nets. The chance of striking a blow against the Super Etendards had been lost.

Mikado might have been aborted, but there was plenty of 'old-style' SAS stuff to come. On the night before the main Task Force landings at San Carlos, the SAS mounted a series of diversionary raids. These included the landing of sixty D Squadron men, who then marched for twenty hours to reach the hills north of Darwin and attack the garrison at Goose Green. To put the wind up the Argentinians they simulated a battalion-sized (600 men) attack, raining down a torrent of LAW rockets, Milan missiles, GMPG rounds and tracer into the Argentinian positions. So ferocious was the barrage that the enemy failed to probe the SAS positions and could only manage desultory return fire. By mid-morning, the main landings accomplished, the SAS disengaged from Goose Green, 'tabbing' (only Marines 'yomp') north to meet up with 2 Para as they made their way inland. En route, the SAS were intercepted by a Pucara ground-attack aircraft. Fatalities seemed certain, but as the planes winged in an SAS trooper launched a heat-seeking Stinger missile. He scored a direct hit on one plane, which *whumphed* into disintegrating fire, smoke and metal. Unfortunately, the trooper was a novice with the new American-made Stinger and did not realize that it required recharging with compressed gas; after his next two missiles, worth £50,000 each, flopped after just twenty metres the Commanding Officer ordered him to desist firing. The rest of the patrol had dived for cover.

Over the next fortnight SAS patrols continued their recces and probing missions. At the end of May, D Squadron seized Mount Kent, forty miles behind enemy lines, and held it for several days until reinforced by 42 RM Commando. This was despite aggressive – and courageous – patrolling from Argentine special forces in a sequence of sharp nocturnal firefights. Following their relief, D Squadron was in action again when five teams landed on West Falkland. The considerable enemy garrisons at Fox Bay and Port Howard enjoyed excellent radio-direction-finding equipment and responded vigorously. It was on West Falkland that Captain John Hamilton had lost his life.

Meanwhile, to reinforce SAS numbers in the Falklands, a troop from B Squadron was flown from Ascension in Hercules C130s; the troop was to join the Task Force by parachuting into the Atlantic, from which they would be plucked by Gemini inflatables. Tom Read wrote later:

We reach the convoy and quickly prepare for a static-line

jump from 1,000 feet, directly off the ramp. Whitecaps stretch from horizon to horizon. My dry suit will give me about five minutes in the freezing water before I lose consciousness. It has a hood and feet, but no hands. I stuff my training shoes inside my leggings because the rest of my kit is already bundled and packed into huge boxes to be dropped after us.

There are twenty-one of us on board, and seven jump on each pass because there are a limited number of inflatable boats to pick us up and ferry us to the warships. Timing is crucial, because three ships have maneuvered into a U-shape to act as a landing zone. The C-130 flies up through the middle and the green light flashes on. Another seven blokes go off the ramp. As I hook up my static line, Doomwatch Des is busy looking out the window, with his eyes bigger than portholes. He doesn't want to be here. Reports of enemy action in the area have him totally spooked.

On the ramp, I can see lads in the water and inflatable boats moving towards them. The pilot doesn't want to make another pass because he's worried he won't have enough fuel to get back to Ascension. Come on, don't lose your bottle now, I think, as the C-130 does a sharp turn and heads back towards the convoy.

Red light . . .

Green light . . .

Go!

The canopy swirls upwards and opens. Looking up, I make sure none of the lines are twisted and then ditch the serve chute, gone for ever in the sea. The last man is drifting dangerously close to one of the ships and almost bounces off the stern, unable to steer the round parachute.

A few feet from the water, I hit the release box on my chest and jettison the chute. I break the surface and let the water slow me down as my body surges under. The cold slaps me in the face like a punch and I get the worst ice-cream headache imaginable. From a thousand feet, the swells hadn't looked too bad, but now they're huge. One minute I'm in the bottom of a valley and the next I'm on top of a hill. Entire ships are disappearing in the troughs. Full credit to the marine coxswains, banging around in their dinghies – they surf off swells and risk capsizing to get to us within a few minutes. I feel the cold leaking through the suit and see the boat bouncing over the wash. Strong hands reach out and pull me on board.

The aircraft makes a final pass and drops the equipment. The boxes, wrapped in cargo nets, burst open on impact and the contents spill out. The seas are now so rough the navy won't risk sending the inflatables back out. Instead, they try using helicopters to winch boxes on board, but only manage to save a few.

As I climb the side nets on to the *Andromeda*, someone wraps a blanket around my shoulders. I turn to see my Bergen, rifle and webbing flop through the side of a net and sink to the bottom. Everything I'd personalized, my letters from Chris, a painting that Jason had sent me . . . all of it gone.

Taken down below, I have a shower, a scoff and then head for the Warrant Officers' Mess for a beer. The assault on Port Stanley airport has been overtaken by events. The land forces are within striking distance of the capital, so we are to relieve D Squadron patrols in the West Falklands.

It wasn't to be B Squadron's war. It was then tasked with ambushing the enemy reinforcement of the garrison at Fox Bay, but the enemy failed to turn up. By now it was becoming clear to all that the war was in its last days.

There remained one major SAS raid, which was mounted in East Falkland on the night of 13 June. To take the pressure off 2

Para, who were assaulting Wireless Ridge a few miles west of Port Stanley, the SAS volunteered to put in a raid to the enemy rear – from the sea. Two troops from D Squadron, one from G Squadron and six men from the 3 SBS rode into Port Stanley harbour on high-speed Rigid Raiders with the aim of setting fire to the oil-storage tanks. As troopers from the Regiment later conceded, the raid was more audacious than wise. Searchlights from an Argentinian ship in the harbour caught them as they approached, and the Argentinians opened up with every available weapon, including triple-barrelled 20mm Rheinmetall anti-aircraft cannon depressed to their lowest trajectory. These spewed out a constant stream of metal, which obliged the raiders to rapidly withdraw if they were not to suffer heavy losses.

The next morning, 14 June, it was all over. Mike Rose received a signal from the headquarters of the Argentine commander, General Menendez, asking to discuss surrender terms. By evening, the instrument of surrender had been signed.

The SAS campaign to liberate the Falklands had its price. A few days after the attack on Pebble Island, a helicopter cross-decking members of D and G Squadron from HMS *Hermes* to HMS *Intrepid* hit some airborne object, probably a giant petrel or albatross, which was then sucked into the air intake. The Sea King plummeted into the icy water with the loss of twenty SAS troopers and attached specialists, plus one of the aircrew. The dead included Squadron Sergeant Major Lawrence Gallagher and Pebble Island raider Paddy Ryan (Paddy 'R'). It was the heaviest loss the Regiment had suffered in a single day since the Second World War.

With the end of the Falklands campaign, the SAS returned home to Stirling Lines in Hereford. Although the Regiment had won a DSO, three MCs and two MMs, and chalked up some outstanding actions and important recces, the mood was sombre. The recent history of the Regiment had been in Black Ops; few, if any, of the SAS had fought against a regular army before, and it was obvious that too many mistakes had been made. And the loss of so many men in the Sea King crash touched almost everyone. An address by Peter de la Billière in the Paludrine Club at Stirling Lines served only to lower the mood further. After some preliminary remarks about the Regiment's victories in the Falklands, he began to berate B Squadron for being insufficiently gung-ho for the Rio Grande attack. At first there was stunned silence. Then, despite orders from the regimental sergeant major, the men began laughing derisorily. A clearly angered DLB strode stiffly from the room.

An SAS man through and through, Peter de la Billière wisely passed off the Paludrine Club fracas as evidence of the strong-mindedness of SAS troopers. That he harboured no grudge against his old regiment was amply proved in 1990, when the Iraqi president Saddam Hussein rolled his armour into Kuwait. General 'Stormin' Norman' Schwarzkopf, the American in command of the coalition gathered to evict Saddam, was notoriously no friend of special forces. Encountering a group of US special forces in the Gulf, Schwarzkopf barked: 'I remember you guys from Vietnam . . . you couldn't do your job there, and you didn't do your job in Panama. What makes you think you can do your job here?' The one British member of Schwarzkopf's planning staff, CENTCOM, knew what British special forces at least could do. For weeks de la Billière sought a role for 22 SAS, before finally persuading Schwarzkopf to sit down for a presentation by the Regiment on the benefits of its insertion deep behind the lines to cut roads and cause diversions to draw Iraqi troops from the front. Convinced, Schwarzkopf gave 22 SAS the go-ahead to cross the Iraqi border at the beginning of the air campaign against Iraq, scheduled for 29 January 1991.

The Regiment was as surprised as most people outside the US clique running the war when, at dawn on 17 January, hundreds of Allied aircraft and Tomahawk Cruise began bombarding targets in Iraq. Within twenty-four hours the Iraqi airforce was all but wiped out and Saddam's command and communications system heavily degraded. The only nagging area of doubt was Iraq's surface-to-surface missile capacity. Though an outdated technology, being little more than a Soviet version of Hitler's V2, the Scud was capable of carrying nuclear and bio-chemical warheads. On the second night of the air campaign, Saddam answered all the speculation about 'would he?' and 'could he?' by launching Scuds (with conventional warheads) at Israel. Although the Scuds failed to cause any injuries, they were politically lethal; if the Israelis retaliated, the fragile anti-Saddam coalition would likely blow apart. No Arab state could afford to be seen to side with 'Zionists' or their friends. Suddenly, the Scud-hunt was on, with the coalition diverting 30 per cent of its air capability to tracking Scuds and their mobile launchers in the vast Iraqi desert. Even the preternaturally upbeat Schwarzkopf could only say before the world's media on 19 January that seeking Scuds in the desert was like seeking the proverbial needle in a haystack.

Peter de la Billière, meanwhile, realized that the Scud menace offered 22 SAS a clear-cut mission in the war, signalling the Regiment that 'all SAS effort should be directed against Scuds'. That same day, the 300 troopers from A, B and D Squadrons already gathered in the Gulf were rushed 1,500 km from their holding area to a forward operating base just inside the Saudi border with Iraq.

The Regiment decided on two principal means of dealing with the Scud menace. Firstly, it would insert into Iraq three covert eight-man static patrols to watch roads (what the Regiment calls Main Supply Routes, or MSRs) and report on the movement of Scud traffic. When Scud sites and launchers were identified, US F15 and A10 airstrikes would be called down to destroy them, with the SAS identifying the targets using a tactical airlink or laser-designator.

Alongside the road-watch patrols, the Regiment would infiltrate into Iraq four columns of heavily armed 'Pink Panther' Land Rovers, Unimogs and Cannon motorcycle scouts. The columns were to penetrate the 'Scud Box', the area of western desert bordering Jordan which was thought to contain around fourteen mobile launchers.

The South and Central road-watch teams were inserted on 21 January, and both found that the spookily featureless desert offered no possibility of concealment. The South road-watch team aborted their mission immediately and flew back on their insertion helicopter. Meanwhile, the Central team called down an airstrike on two Iraqi radars, before they too 'bugged out', driving their Land Rovers through 140 miles of biting cold desert before reaching Saudi Arabia.

Road-watch North, codenamed 'Bravo Two Zero', was landed by Chinook at night 100 miles north-west of Baghdad. The weather was appalling from the start, with driving wind and sleet in what turned out to be the worst winter in the area for thirty years. As is traditional in the SAS, the decision on how to deploy was left to the patrol. Despite the urging of the Regiment's commanding officer and the regimental sergeant major, Peter 'Billy' Ratcliffe, Bravo Two Zero, led by Sergeant 'Andy McNab', decided not to take a 'dinky' (a short-wheel-base Land Rover) with them. They did decide to take an Everest of kit: water and rations for fourteen days, explosives, ammunition, extra clothes, maps, compasses, survival equipment, 203 rifles, guns, empty sandbags, LAW 66mm anti-tank launchers, communications gear, camouflage nets, Minimi machine guns – so much kit, indeed, that each man was carrying eighty kilograms of it.

As dawn broke on their first day, the Bravo Two Zero team saw that their map failed to contain some significant local features. Aside from a small farm across from the wadi they were lying in, there was an Iraqi S60 anti-aircraft battery less than a kilometre away. Unfortunately the ground was so hard they could not dig a hide, either for cover from the enemy or the cutting wind. The morning had not done with unpleasant surprises for Bravo Two Zero; when the patrol's signaller, Trooper Steven 'Legs' Lane went to use the PRC 319 radio he could not get communications with the Regiment's forward base at al-Jauf. Over the next hours, everybody had a go at 'fixing' the wireless; nobody could. At noon, McNab called the patrol together and explained he would instigate loss-comms drill, which involved the patrol relocating to the helicopter drop-off, where a helicopter would bring them in a new radio.

In the lying-up place in the wadi the next day, while the patrol waited to move out, they heard the jingle of sheep bells. Once before the sheep and their boy herder had come close to the wadi, but not so close as to see them. This time the boy herder reached the edge of the wadi, and looked down. The patrol froze. Sergeant Vince Phillips, the patrol second in command, believed he made eye contact with the boy, but wasn't certain.

The patrol had to assume they had been compromised. As Lane sent a message 'High possibility compromise. Request relocation or exfil' on the emergency guard-net, the rest of the team prepared to move out, gathering kit and gulping down water. Exiting the bottom of the wadi, they heard the sound of a tracked vehicle and a diesel engine. The SAS team thought a tank or Armored Personnel Carrier was being sent in after them and broke out their LAW 66mm rocket-launchers. Corporal Chris Ryan recalled:

There we were, waiting for this tank to come into view round the corner. Every second the squealing and grinding got louder. We were stuck, pinned like rats in the dead-end of the ravine. We couldn't tell what else might be coming at us over the flat ground above. The chances were that the Iraqis were deploying behind us, too; even at the moment, they were probably advancing on our position. A couple of hand grenades tossed over the edge would make a nice mess of us. Even so, if the tank came into view and levelled its gun on us, we'd have no option but to run up on to the plain, and chance it with the AA positions on the high ground.

By then it was 1700 hours, but still full daylight. Someone said, 'Let's get some water down our necks, fellers,' and everyone started drinking, because we knew that if we had to run for it, we'd need the liquid inside us. Other guys began frantically repacking their kit, pulling off the warm jackets they'd been wearing and stuffing them into their Bergens. A couple of the lads struggled out of their NBC suits and stowed them.

No one gave any orders about what to do. We just decided that if a tank or armored personnel carrier came round the corner, we'd try to take it out, and then go past it down the wadi, using the dry watercourse as our escape-route. The rockets wouldn't have been much use against a tank, but they might have disabled it by blowing off a track.

So there we were, getting water down our necks and having something to eat. Then I looked round at the tail ends of the rocket launchers in front of me and said, 'Hey, fellers – watch the fucking back-blast on these things. I don't want my face burned.' When a 66 is fired, the danger area behind the tube extends for twenty metres. There was silence for a minute. Then, suddenly, out of fear and tension, everyone started laughing. They couldn't stop. I thought, 'This is bloody ridiculous. There's a tank coming round the corner, and here we all are, giggling like schoolgirls.'

Dinger pointed at my German Army cap and shouted, 'Hey, Chris, you look like Rommel.'

'Fuck off, Dinger,' I yelled back. He was dragging desperately on his fag. 'Put that fucking thing out!'

'Ah – fuck the SOPs,' he said, and everyone laughed some more.

I checked my 203 magazines again, tapping them on the bottom to make sure the lip was properly engaged in the breech. I had the mags taped together in pairs, head to toe, so that I could load the second instantly by turning the empty one upside down. Each could hold thirty rounds, but I'd only loaded them with twenty-eight, to leave the springs a bit looser and cut down the chance of a stoppage. The spares were in my left-hand lower pouch.

Then suddenly round the corner came . . . not a tank, but a yellow bulldozer. The driver had the blade high up in front of him, obviously using it as a shield; he looked like an Arab, wearing a green parka with the hood up. We all kept still, lying or crouching in firing positions, but we knew the man had seen us. He was only 150 metres away when he stopped, stared, and reversed out of sight before trying to turn round. Obviously a local, he must have known that the wadi came to a dead-end, and his only purpose in coming up it had been to find out who or what was in there. We held our breath as the squealing and grinding gradually died away.

For a minute or two we felt more relief than anything else. Then it was, 'Get the radio away, Legs,' and everyone was saying, 'We've got to go. We've got to go.' Dinger lit another fag and sucked on it like a dying man. Now we felt certain that the local militia must be deploying behind us, and one or two of the lads were being a bit slow, so it was 'Get a fucking move on' all round. We'd already decided to ditch the surplus kit we couldn't carry, but we pulled our Bergens on and were ready for the off. As we were about to leave, I called, 'Get your shamags round your heads.' So we all wrapped our heads in shawls, in case we could bluff our way and pass as Arab soldiers, even for a few minutes.

As soon as Legs was ready, we started walking southwards, down the wadi, towards our emergency rendezvous point. Finding myself at the front, I led the patrol out. Call it arrogance, if you like, but I didn't trust anyone else to go first.

Dusk was already coming on, and I was hoping we could reach the drop-off point, less than two kilometres to the south, and put down enough fire to defend ourselves until dark fell – and then we'd have to wait until the chopper came in.

Moving out, I kept close in to the left-hand wall of the wadi, because that was the steepest, and in the lee of it we were out of sight of the AA guns. When I turned round, I found that the guys had opened up to a tactical spacing of maybe twenty metres between each; but I was thinking, 'If we have a nonsense here, we want to be tight together.' So I yelled back, 'Close up!'

The bulldozer had gone out of sight, but we were moving towards where we'd last seen it. All too soon the wadi began to flatten out, and on our left a long slope ran up to the plain above. As we came clear of the steep part of the wadi wall, I suddenly saw two Arabs on the high ground above us, guns down by their sides. They were barely 200 metres away, and were standing motionless. There was something oddly inert about their appearance; they showed no surprise and did not move as we walked into their view. Both were wearing dark overcoats on top of their dishdashes (native cotton robes), which reached down to their ankles. Also they had red-and-white shamags done up on top of their heads like turbans. I reckoned they were civilians or possibly militia.

'It's that sodding boy,' I said to myself. 'He's run like hell and tipped them off.'

'Close up!' I yelled again, because it was obvious the shit was going to go down. Next behind me was Bob Consiglio, and I shouted back to him, 'Fucking hurry! Catch up!'

We kept going. But the two Iraqis began to parallel us, moving forward. In case anybody hadn't seen them, I called back, 'We've got two on the high ground to the left, and they're walking down. Keep going.'

Behind me everyone started cursing. The tension in the patrol was electric. I felt fear rising in my chest. Afterwards, I realized that the two Iraqis were waiting for reinforcements to come up; also, they were probably a bit confused, not knowing who the hell we were. But at the time I was wondering if we could outrun them, or lose them somehow, without starting a firefight.

Then I blew it in a big way. I thought, 'I'm going to try the double bluff here,' and I waved at them. Unfortunately I did it with my left hand, which to an Arab is the ultimate insult – your left hand being the one you wipe your arse with. The reaction was instantaneous: one of them brought up his weapon and opened fire. Suddenly he was putting rounds down on us. We swung round and put a couple of short bursts back at them. Both dropped on to one knee to continue firing. As I stood there, I saw Vince take off down the wadi. In spite of the danger, there was something ridiculous about his gait: a pair of legs, going like the clappers under a Bergen, and not making much progress either.

'Stay together!' I yelled. 'Slow down!' We began to run, turning to fire aimed bursts. The secret is to keep them short – no more than two or three rounds at a time. Otherwise the recoil makes the weapon drift up, and the rounds go high. We ran and fired, ran and fired.

Within seconds a tipper truck with metal sides screeched to a halt beside the two Arabs, and eight or ten guys spilled out of it. Stan also saw an armored car carrying a .50 machine gun pull up. Somehow I never saw that; it may have been behind a mound from where I was standing. Some of the Iraqis began firing from the back of the truck, others from positions behind it.

Running and shooting, the SAS team found their Bergens too heavy and cumbersome and began ditching them. Eventually, Bravo Two Zero lost the pursuing Iraqis in the gloom of the early winter afternoon. Stopping to get their breath, the patrol decided to make for the Syrian border, 120 kilometres away, via the

Euphrates. The Iraqis, they calculated, would expect them to head south for Saudi. Bravo Two's decision to go for Syria may well have put the Iraqis off the scent; it certainly deceived SAS commanders at al-Jouf, because the emergency route the team had filed was different. Consequently, any search and rescue mission would look in the wrong place.

Bravo Two Zero walked fifty miles that night through sleet, pausing to rest only four times. Two of the team were in a bad way; Vince Phillips had injured his leg in the contact with the enemy, while Trooper 'Stan' was dehydrated because of sweat loss from his thermal clothing. Everybody else, meanwhile, was freezing to death.

Setting off again, the patrol staggered single file into the night. At the back of the patrol, McNab stopped to use his TACBE personal rescue beacon, and got a confused response from an American pilot. By the time McNab put the TACBE back in its pouch, Ryan, Phillips and Trooper Mal had disappeared into the night; McNab and the remainder of the patrol had no option but to carry on without them, hoping they would meet later. The sleet turned to snow. The wind-chill was starting to kill them; lying up in a hollow the next day McNab likened to 'lying in a freezer cabinet, feeling your body heat slowly slip away'. By dawn on 26 January McNab reckoned they might not survive another twenty-four hours in the open. They were next to the al-Haqlaniyya-Krabilah highway, so they decided to hijack a vehicle. With shamags wrapped around their swarthy faces, Trooper Bob Consiglio and McNab could pass for Arab. The plan then was for Consiglio to be an injured Iraqi soldier and McNab his Samaritan helper, who would stumble into the road and flag down a suitable car. McNab recalled:

> After about twenty minutes, vehicle lights came over the small crest and drove towards us. Satisfied that it was not a troop truck, we stood up. The vehicle caught us in its

290

headlights and slowed down to a half a few metres down the road. I kept my head down to protect my eyes and to hide my face from the driver. Bob and I hobbled towards it.

'Oh shit,' I muttered into Bob's ear.

Of all the vehicles in Iraq that could have come our way that night, the one we had chosen to hijack and speed us to our freedom was a 1950s New York yellow cab. I couldn't believe it. Chrome bumpers, whitewall tires, the lot.

We were committed. Bob was in my arms giving it the wounded soldier. The blokes were straight up from the ditch.

'What the fuck have we got here?' Mark shouted in disbelief. 'This is the story of our lives, this is! Why can't it be a fucking Land Cruiser?'

The driver panicked and stalled the engine. He and the two passengers in the back sat staring open-mouthed at the muzzles of Minimis and 203s.

The cab was an old rust bucket with typical Arab decoration – tassels and gaudy religious emblems dangling from every available point. A couple of old blankets were thrown over as seat covers. The driver was beside himself with hysteria. The two men on the back seat were a picture, both dressed in neatly pressed green militia fatigues and berets, with little weekend bags on their laps. As the younger of the two explained that they were father and son, we had a quick rummage through their effects to see if there was anything worth having.

We had to move quickly because we couldn't guarantee that there wouldn't be other vehicles coming over. We tried to shepherd them to the side of the road, but the father was on his knees. He thought he was going to get slotted.

'Christian! Christian!' he screamed as he scrabbled in his pocket and pulled out a keyring with the Madonna dangling from it. 'Muslim!' he said, pointing at the taxi driver and trying to drop him in it.

Now the driver sank to his knees, bowing and praying. We had to prod him with rifle barrels to get him to move.

'Cigarettes?' Dinger enquired.

The son obliged with a couple of packs.

The father got up and started kissing Mark, apparently thanking him for not killing him. The driver kept praying and hollering. It was a farce.

Driving towards Krabilah, McNab at the wheel, the SAS men in the taxi made good progress for nearly an hour. In the warmth and comfort of the car some of them began sleeping. They then hit a vehicle checkpoint, which they decided to bypass on foot. By now the dumped occupants of the taxi had raised the alarm. The Iraqis were hunting for McNab and his patrol.

On the other side of the checkpoint, McNab and Consiglio tried their old flag-down-a-car trick. They were spotted by an Iraqi police patrol, who opened fire. After a quick return salvo, the SAS men legged it into the night, heading towards the Euphrates and the border. An air raid proved a useful diversion, as the patrol cautiously edged along the alleyways of a town down to the Euphrates' bank. The river was in full spate, and McNab rated their chances of swimming across as slim. They were just ten kilometres from the border, so they decided to push along the bank looking for a crossing place. At seven kilometres from the border, an Iraqi patrol started blasting at the SAS men from the side of a wadi running into the Euphrates. A running firefight broke out. Bob Consiglio, a Swiss-born former Royal Marine, held off the Iraqis with his Minimi until he ran out of ammunition; separated from the remainder of the patrol, he ran down a track towards the Euphrates. A group of militiamen hidden in a clump of trees opened fire; one of their bullets felled Consiglio. Another round ignited a phosphorus grenade Consiglio was carrying. Awarded a posthumous Military Medal, Consiglio was the first SAS soldier of the campaign to die from enemy fire. Troopers Lane and Lance

Corporal 'Dinger', at the back of the patrol, edged down to the black Euphrates, where Lane urged Dinger to join him and swim across, with pieces of thrown-away polystyrene stuffed in their smocks for buoyancy. Lane emerged on the far bank in a state of collapse; Dinger hid him in a bankside hut and tried to warm him up. They were spotted and locked inside. Dinger broke through the roof, but was soon surrounded and captured. As he was taken away on a tractor-drawn cart, he saw Lane's body being brought out of the hut on a stretcher. Lane was dead.

While Lane and Dinger were swimming the Euphrates, McNab and Trooper Mike Coburn crawled across the bed of a wadi. As they emerged, a group of Iraqi police opened up. Coburn, by now left only with a bayonet in his armoury, was hit by rounds in the arm and leg. Captured, he was dragged through the mud to a Land Cruiser, to be taken away for interrogation. McNab, meanwhile, wormed along the ground, until he found an irrigation pipe and holed up. The next morning he was spotted by a labourer, who reported to the police. Screeching up in a Land Cruiser, the police pulled McNab out and bundled him into the back of a Land Cruiser. He was taken to the same barracks as Dinger. Like other captured Coalition personnel, they were subjected to days of torture.

On 26 January, the same day that McNab was dragged out of the water pipe, Chris Ryan and Mal split up when the latter decided to approach a shepherd's cottage and find some transport. A man in the cottage alerted the police. Mal was surrounded and captured. Now alone, Ryan struck out for the border, with only two packets of biscuits for food. Five days later, desperately short of water, he filled his bottles from a stream. Hiding away in a culvert, he sat down to slake his thirst:

I was desperate for a drink, and looking forward to one with incredible anticipation. But when I went to compress the plastic clip that held the buckle on my webbing pouch, I found that my fingers were so sore and clumsy that I could scarcely manage the simple task. Gasping with pain, I used all my strength to force the clips together. Then came a horrendous disappointment. Bringing out one bottle at last, I opened it and raised it to my lips – but the first mouthful made me gasp and choke. Poison! The water tasted vicious and metallic, as if it was full of acid. I spat it straight out, but the inside of my mouth had gone dry, and I was left with a burning sensation all over my tongue and gums. I whipped out my compass-mirror, pointed the torchbeam into my mouth and looked round it. Everything seemed all right, so I took another sip, but it was just the same. I remembered that when Stan had collapsed during the first night on the run I'd put rehydrate into my bottles, to bring him round, and I wondered if the remains of it had somehow gone off. Then I tried the second bottle, and found it exactly the same. I couldn't make out what the hell had gone wrong. Whatever the problem, the water was undrinkable, and I emptied the bottles out.

'Now I *am* fucked,' I thought. I was in a really bad state. It was eight days since I'd had a hot meal, two days and a night since I'd had a drink. My tongue was completely dry; it felt like a piece of old leather stuck in the back of my throat. My teeth had all come loose; if I closed my mouth and sucked hard, I could taste blood coming from my shrunken gums. I knew my feet were in bits, but I didn't dare take my boots off, because I feared I'd never get them on again. As for my hands – I could see and smell them all too well. The thin leather of my gloves had cracked and split, from being repeatedly soaked and dried out again, so that my fingers hadn't had much protection. I'd lost most of the feeling in the tips, and I seemed to have got dirt pushed deep under my nails, so that infection had set in. Whenever I squeezed a nail, pus came out, and this stench was repulsive.

With my extremities suppurating like that, I wondered what internal damage I might be suffering, and could only hope that no permanent harm would be done. With the complete lack of food, I'd had no bowel movement since going on the run, and I couldn't remember when I'd last wanted to pee. I yearned for food, of course, but more for drink – and when I did think about food, it was sweet, slushy things that I craved. If ever I found myself back among rations packs, I would rip into the pears in syrup, ice-cream and chocolate sauce.

I felt very frightened. First and most obvious was the danger of being captured – the fear of torture, and of giving away secrets that might betray other guys from the Regiment. Almost worse, though, was the fact that I could see and feel my body going down so fast. If I didn't reach the border soon, I would be too weak to carry on.

Setting off again, he stumbled towards the border, which he reached on the night of 30 January. Only he wasn't sure he was at the border:

I reached a refuse heap, where loads of burnt-out old cans had been dumped in the desert, and sat down among them to do yet another map-study. I couldn't work things out. Where was the town, and where was the communications tower which the map marked? Where, above all, was the bloody border?

I started walking again, on the bearing, and as I came over a rise I saw three small buildings to my front. With the naked eye I could just make them out: three square bulks, blacked out. But when I looked through the kite-sight, I saw chinks of light escaping between the tops of the walls and the roofs. As I sat watching, one person came out, walked round behind, reappeared and went back indoors. I was so desperate for water that I went straight towards the houses. Again, I was prepared to take out one of the inhabitants if need be. I was only fifty metres away when I checked through the kite-sight again and realized that the buildings were not houses at all, but sandbagged sangars with wriggly tin roofs. They formed some sort of command post, and were undoubtedly full of squaddies. Pulling slowly back, I went round the side and, sure enough, came on a battery of four anti-aircraft positions.

If I'd walked up and opened one of the doors, I'd almost certainly have been captured. Once more the fright got my adrenalin going and revived me.

On I stumbled for another hour. My dehydration was making me choke and gag. My throat seemed to have gone solid, and when I scraped my tongue, white fur came off it. I felt myself growing weaker by the minute. My 203 might have been made of lead, such a burden had it become, so much of the strength had ebbed from my arms. My legs had lost their spring and grown stiff and clumsy. My ability to think clearly had dwindled away.

At last I came to a point from which I could see the lights of a town, far out on the horizon. Something seemed to be wrong. Surely that couldn't be Krabilah, still such a distance off? My heart sank: surely the border couldn't still be that far? Or was the glow I could see that of Abu Kamal, the first town inside Syria, some twenty kilometres to the west? If so, where the hell was Krabilah? According to the map, Krabilah had a communications tower, but Abu Kamal didn't. The far-off town *did* have a bright red light flashing, as if from a tower – and that made me all the more certain that the place in the distance was Krabilah.

Morale plummeted once more. Like my body, my mind was losing its grip. What I *could* make out was some kind of straight black line, running all the way across my front. Off to my left I could see a mound with a big command post on

296

it, sprouting masts. Closer to me were a few buildings, blacked out, but not looking like a town.

I sat down some 500 metres short of the black line and studied the set-up through the kite-sight. Things didn't add up. With Krabilah so far ahead, this could hardly be the border. Yet it looked like one. I wondered whether it was some inner frontier-line which the Iraqis had built because of the war, to keep people back from the border itself. Suddenly I thought of the Int guy back at Al Jouf, unable to tell what the border looked like. 'What an arsehole!' I thought. 'He should have known. That's his fucking job.'

Whatever this line ahead of me might be, all I wanted to do was get across it. I was gripped by a terrific sense of urgency, but I forced myself to hold back, sit down and observe it. 'This is where you're going to stumble if you don't watch out,' I told myself. 'This is where you'll fall down. Take time over it.'

There I sat, shivering, watching, waiting. A vehicle came out of the command post and drove down along the line – an open-backed land-cruiser. Directly opposite my vantage-point two men emerged from an observation post, walked up to the car, spoke to the driver, jumped in, and drove off to the right. It looked as if the Iraqis were putting out roving observers to keep an eye on the border. I couldn't tell whether this was routine, or whether they suspected that enemy soldiers were in the area; but after a few minutes I decided that the coast was clear, and I had to move.

At long last I came down to the black line. Creeping cautiously towards it, I found it was a barrier of barbed wire: three coils in the bottom row, two on top of them, and one on top of that. Having no pliers to cut with, I tried to squeeze my way through the coils, but that proved impossible: barbs hooked into my clothes and skin and held me fast. I unhooked myself with difficulty, and decided that the only way to go was

297

over the top. Luckily the builders had made the elementary mistake, every twenty-five metres, of putting in three posts close to each other and linking them together with barbed wire. Obviously the idea was to brace the barrier, but the posts created a kind of bridge across the middle of the coils. I took off my webbing and threw it over, then went up and over myself, sustaining a few lacerations but nothing serious.

Still I could not believe I was clear of Iraq. The barrier seemed so insignificant that I thought it must only be marking some false or inner border, and that I would come to the true frontier some distance further on. The real thing, I thought, would be a big anti-tank berm, constructed so that vehicles could not drive across. Maybe this was why I had no feeling of elation; for days I had been thinking that, if I did manage to cross the frontier, it would be the climax of my journey, but now I felt nothing except utter exhaustion.

Ryan was in Syria. His marathon walk of 186 miles almost equals that of Jack Sillito in 1942.

While Bravo Two Zero were struggling their way to the frontier, the mobile fighting columns were having their own dramas. Three of the columns, which comprised a half-squadron each, were operating efficiently inside Iraq; however, Alpha One Zero, under an SBS major, seemed lacking in purpose. To the steaming ire of the regiment's commanding officer, the column couldn't actually find a way across the berm dividing Iraq from Saudi. At length, Alpha One Zero crossed into Iraq via a dash through a checkpoint. Almost immediately the column had a contact with the enemy. Its vehicles under cam-nets, the patrol had laagered up and Sergeant Cameron 'Serious' Spence was among those with drooping eyelids:

I sat there, taking my time over the smoke and the brew, until I felt my eyelids dropping. After three days and nights with scarcely a moment's shut-eye, I staked out my own patch around the forward wheel that Tom had vacated, ticking off those last few things I needed to know before I could sleep. Jeff was getting some kip at the next wheel. The visibility was good – out to ten kilometres, a mixed blessing. We were just about set for the rest of the day. All Tom had to do was clean his M16 and he was done, too. Buzz had taken the forward sentry position. Everything was as it should be. I adjusted my webbing under my head, got comfortable, and within seconds had lapsed into sleep.

After what passed for five minutes – I later found out it was an hour – I heard Buzz's voice go off in my head. He could only have whispered the warning, but it sounded like a fucking siren going off in some deep recess of my brain. The words tumbled over and over. There was something faintly hypnotic about them. For a moment, they held me in the grip of a dreamy kind of paralysis. Then, Tom was shaking me.

The words came back to me and I knew it was no dream.

Stand-to, stand-to. Enemy.

Fuck. A pang of fear hit me in the gullet, followed by a weird moment of doubt. Could this be some kind of wind-up? The fear redoubled and hit me again. Nobody, not even Tom or Buzz, would pull a stunt like this on our third day. This was for fucking real. I was up and out of the sleeping bag in a second, fumbling for my Bergen and my M16. For a few seconds more, chaos reigned, then we were taking up position. Suddenly, a vehicle appeared. It slowed, then stopped, sitting there 700 metres out; watching us, watching them. And then, it came towards us, and kept coming, until it drew up right outside our cluster of cam-nets. Two Iraqis got out. They paused to pick up their helmets, then divided. The driver moved for Tony's vehicle, the commander headed straight for the front of our Land Rover, where Tom and I had taken up station. The officer bent down and picked up the cam-net. That was when he saw me.

The last thing I remember thinking was that it shouldn't be like the fucking movies, but that's how it was – the whole thing moved in excruciating slow-time like a Sam Peckinpah Western.

I had a moment to register the look of blank surprise on the Iraqi's face as he came up under the cam-net and twigged me. He started to raise his weapon, but I fired, quick double-tap – *ba-bam* – and he went down. As he fell, his body was hit by at least six more rounds – bullets from other weapons that had been trained on him from the moment he'd got out of the vehicle – and he pirouetted in a macabre death-dance before hitting the dirt, face-down.

I heard more firing and saw bullets striking the second man. Several punched into his chest. One all but removed the side of his head. A voice in the back of my head started telling me over and over that I'd killed a man – *bam*, just like that. But it was a small voice. And it was rapidly drowned by a chorus of other thoughts. What about the GAZ? Who else was in there? Had Jeff made it with the phosphorus grenade?

Training, thank God, takes over. You're not left long with the moral consequences of your actions.

I was out from under the cam-net before I even knew it. As I moved towards the still-twitching body of the man I'd shot, I could see a flurry out of the corner of my eye as Buzz and Jeff tore into the back of the GAZ. Your training doesn't allow you to look, even though your instincts want to. I was on the body in a second, pulling it over, one hand tugging at his arms in the search for firearms, grenades, knives; you never know what the fucker might still have up a sleeve, even in his death-throes.

Secure.

I looked up and saw a similar scene being played out around the other body.

No doubt about it, they were both dead.

And then there's a blood-curdling cry from the GAZ.

I spun around to see Buzz and Jeff dragging something –
someone – out of the Iraqi vehicle. Another man had been in
the back, but they'd got the drop on him. As far as I could
tell, the guy was uninjured, but he was squealing like a stuck
pig all the same.

Jostling, blurred action as Buzz and Jeff threw their captive
to the ground, both of them yelling at the top of their voices:
'Shut the fuck up.'

The Iraqi doesn't get it and starts jabbering and wailing
louder than ever. And then he opens his eyes and sees the
muzzle of Buzz's Commando a moment before it grinds into
the thin skin between his eyebrows. At the same time, Buzz
is shouting again, only now the tone is different. The
shrillness that had been there in the initial adrenalin rush is
gone. There's depth and authority in his words. Be quiet, he's
telling him, or he'll blow his fucking brains to Babylon.

This time the Iraqi makes the connection and zips it.

Silence.

In the stillness that followed, there was a fraction of a
moment in which my heightened senses registered the
blueness of the sky and the sound of the cam-net flapping in
the wind behind me. And then it started all over again.
Shouts, movements, oaths, orders, as blokes from the other
vehicles pounded over to our two 110s to join the fray.

I left a group of the boys to go through the uniform of the
body at my feet as I searched the scene for Alec, Tony and
Graham. It was time for a fucking 'head shed' meeting, the
fastest we'd ever had. Two, maybe three minutes had elapsed
since the first shots had been fired. Everybody recognized the
situation for what it was. True, we had things under control,
but you could hear traces of panic in the shouts and rasped
commands around you.

The situation had turned to rat-shit and no mistake.

Back in al-Jouf the commanding officer was cock-a-hoop that Alpha One Zero had negotiated its first contact. The commanding officer's delight died when he realized that the major commanding the column was now heading south, away from its designated area of action. Turning to Regimental Sergeant Major Ratcliffe, the commanding officer informed him that he, Ratcliffe, would be relieving the major of his command. Never in the history of the Regiment has a squadron commander been relieved in the field and replaced by a non-commissioned officer.

The next day Ratcliffe flew into Iraq on the Chinook resupplying Alpha One Zero. He wrote later:

As I walked down the tail ramp I found myself buffeted by a strong wind that had sprung up from the north and which, because of the wind-chill factor, had sent the temperature plummeting well below zero. I could see at once why the men running down the nearby slope towards the Chinook didn't look much like the crack desert patrol I had last seen in Victor. They were mostly wrapped in their chemical-warfare suits with extra jackets on top, and had shamags, Arab headdress of the kind favoured by Yasser Arafat, wound around their heads and the lower parts of their faces. The noise from the two rotors, which continued to turn and had formed twin dust halos from the sand being sucked up from the desert floor, was almost deafening. RAF aircrew never switch off their engines during a supply run or insertion into hostile territory, in case they come under attack and have to make a quick getaway.

I grabbed one of the men as he trotted past, put my mouth close to where I thought his ear should be beneath the shamag, and yelled, 'Where's the OC?' He pointed up the slight incline down which they had come and shouted something I couldn't make out. I set off in the direction he had indicated, and on the way passed a strange-looking vehicle that had been parked with a couple of its wheels in a kind of natural ditch. It was giving off an awful stench which I vaguely recognized, but which I didn't have the time to investigate right then.

At the crest of the slope I came across another small gang of troopers gathered around two Land Rovers. They looked amazed suddenly to see the RSM, but I didn't give them time to ask me what I was doing there. Without preamble, I said, 'One of you go and find the OC and bring him here to me.'

A few minutes later the commander appeared. He looked at me quizzically, but before he could say anything I said, 'I'm sorry,' and handed him the CO's letter. There was enough moonlight for him to read it without a torch. When he'd finished he looked up, his face working with some powerful emotion which he somehow managed to keep bottled up. Then he walked away. I set off back for the chopper, wondering what he would do.

I needn't have worried. He fetched his Bergen and rifle and joined me at the tail ramp of the helicopter. The unloading had been completed. The Iraqi officer the patrol had captured the previous day was brought down and I went across and walked with him over to the helicopter. I could guess what he must be feeling, especially after seeing three of his fellow officers killed, and even felt a pang of sympathy for him.

While this was happening the outgoing OC had located his number two, Pat, and was explaining to him that he had been relieved of his command. Then the two men hugged each other as though they were brothers.

The worst part of my job was over. The pilots needed to get on their way as soon as possible, and I wanted to get started. Recognizing that there was no point in wasting more time, I hustled the patrol's former OC aboard the helicopter and gave Jim the thumbs-up signal. Now the handover was complete I couldn't help feeling sorry for the departing major. He had accepted the order without argument, and his behaviour had been impeccable.

Moments later the tail ramp winched shut, and with enough racket to wake every Arab – not to mention his goats, dogs and camels – within three miles, the engines wound up to full power and the Chinook was away into the star-studded sky.

After arranging the burning of the GAZ and the Iraqi bodies, Ratcliffe ordered the patrol fifty kilometres back towards the action. At the lying-up position, Ratcliffe told the half-squadron they were 'about to find out what it's really like to be involved in a war'.

Regimental Sergeant Major Peter Ratcliffe did not disappoint. On 8 February Alpha One Zero carried out a raid on a microwave Scud-control station, codenamed Victor Two, alongside the Baghdad–Amman highway.

I led my demolition team and six other men off to the left, to make use of whatever shadow cover was available close to the berm, and then headed north towards the road junction and the final jumping-off point for the target.

Pat and his three Land Rovers drove along the same route after us. The crew of the wagon carrying the Milan, which only had thirty metres to travel, had been told to move into position ten minutes after the rest of us had left.

The demolitionists were Mugger and Ken and a quiet Yorkshire corporal named Tom. A tall guy, very fit and strong, it was he who had driven the GAZ containing the bodies of the three dead Iraqis back to where I was flown in, apparently prepared to put up with the corpses in exchange for having a closed vehicle with a heater. As backup there was myself, Des and Captain Timothy, the young officer who had joined us from the infantry. Each of us carried one of the explosive charges that had been made up back in the LUP. I had the shaped charge for the fence and Des the charge for the wall, while Timothy had the charges we would use to blow the doors in the bunker. In addition, each of us was carrying a powerful high-explosive charge with which we would take out the switching gear.

When we reached our jumping-off point we were just 200 metres from the relay station. From there all we could see of the building was the wall around it and, behind it, the steel antenna soaring into the night sky. The wall seemed to be of concrete, grey in color apart from one section, a few metres wide, which appeared to be a different shade. From that distance, however, even with the moonlight, we couldn't make it out properly.

The six men who had moved forward with us – one of them with a LAW 80 – had already broken away and crossed the road to come up on the two trucks. To the right and less than fifty metres beyond them was the large bunker, where I could easily make out the enemy coming and going. Even though it was late there seemed to be quite a lot of activity. About 150 metres to our left the other bunker was now clearly visible. It too was brightly lit inside and had enemy personnel moving about. There were other, smaller buildings behind the left-hand bunker, and about 100 metres beyond the target was the large military encampment that we had spotted during the recce.

'A few more than the thirty guys we expected,' breathed Des.

'Yeah, but by the time they realize what's going on we'll be back at our LUP,' I answered softly. 'So let's just brass it out and get it over with.' I looked at the other five, then nodded. Time to go.

As we stepped out in single file, slightly crouched but

moving fairly quickly, I could see to our left, where the low growl of the Land Rovers had died away, that Pat had the wagons parked a few metres apart and facing the different directions from where trouble might be expected to come. We pressed on, slinking over the MSR and past the right-hand bunker.

Whether the Iraqis in the right-hand bunker actually saw us or not I don't know. But no one shouted or challenged us and in less than a minute we had reached the wall. Ken, whose job it was to blow this first obstacle, led the way, followed by Des, who was carrying the charges. Mugger, who would bring down the fence, was next, and then me with his charges. Behind me was Tom, who would blow the bunker's main door, and Captain Timothy carrying his charges.

Close to, we could see straight away what made one section a different shade from the rest of the wall. It was plastic sheeting. An already dodgy mission was growing stranger by the minute.

'Pull the stuff back and let's see what's behind it,' I hissed. At once Ken and Des peeled back one edge, then Des turned and said, 'The wall's already been blown. There's a bloody great hole here.'

'Well, let's get through it,' I said. We were crouched down by the wall, but with the moonlight we would be immediately visible to anyone who looked hard enough from the trucks, the bunkers, or even the smaller buildings to our left. It felt as though we were standing in the spotlights on stage in a packed theatre.

Within thirty seconds all six of us were through the gap and had pushed the plastic sheeting back in place. Inside, there was total chaos. The place had obviously suffered a direct hit from an Allied bomb or missile. In places the fence was twisted and flattened, and in others completely torn from its cement base. Of the main bunker there was almost nothing left. There were buckled steel girders and shattered concrete everywhere. Some of the wreckage was so precariously balanced that it looked likely to crash down at any moment.

I took a look around for an entrance to the three under-ground rooms, but the stairway and the rooms had been completely buried beneath the rubble. The whole site was extremely hazardous, and I realized that one or more of us could get badly injured simply walking in the ruins, especially since the moonlight on the wreckage left large areas in deep shadow. It was perfectly certain, too, that there wasn't any switching gear left for us to destroy. Curiously, I felt a sense of anti-climax. Still, there was one thing we could do.

'Des, you and Timothy dump all your explosives here and get back to the gap in the wall and wait for us there. Now we're here we'd better bring down the mast, if nothing else.' Since the mast was still up, it could still receive and transmit signals via the antennae and dishes on it – which meant the site could still get Scuds off towards Israel. Thinking quickly, I offloaded my own explosives and told Mugger, 'Let's blow the mast and get out of here.'

'These charges are not really suitable,' he replied mournfully. 'They're no good for cutting steel.'

This was too much. First we had intelligence that told us the place was defended, if at all, by about thirty Iraqis. Then Intel had failed to tell us that there were a military camp and fortified defensive positions around the relay station. Meanwhile, somebody had neglected to tell us, or RHQ, that the site had already received an extremely accurate air or missile raid. Finally, having successfully reached our target unseen with more than 100 pounds of explosive charges, we found that those charges probably would not do the one job that still needed doing. Well, we were bloody well going to do something, I thought.

'Surely you can do something?' I asked Mugger. He considered for a while, and finally nodded. 'If we pack a charge and a third of the other explosives around each of three of the mast's four legs, then it will give us about thirty-five pounds per leg. With luck that will do the job.'

'Okay. Let's do it,' I said. 'It sounds much too damned quiet out there for it to last.' By now we had been almost in the centre of an enemy installation for ten or fifteen minutes. It seemed incredible that nobody had noticed us, but how much longer could we trust our luck to last? I had a strong suspicion that the answer was 'not much', but the demolitionists were already on the case. Mugger, Ken and Tom quickly divided the explosives into three piles, then each of them grabbed one pile and headed in a crouch for one of the steel legs of the mast.

I waited between two of the legs, aware that these three guys were playing with high explosives that could blow us all to atoms in a millisecond if anything went wrong. So while I hoped that they wouldn't take too long, I also didn't want them to be foolishly hasty.

Ken was the first to finish, then, thirty seconds later, Tom came over to join us.

'What's keeping Mugger?' I asked.

'He's going to pull the three switches,' Ken answered. By now we were scarcely bothering to lower our voices.

'Right,' I told them. 'You two go and join Des and Timothy and all of you get through the wall and wait there. We'll be right with you.'

A minute later Mugger appeared out of the darkness and gave me a big grin. 'Okay, Billy,' he said. 'They're each on a two-minute delay, so let's head for the great outdoors.' He was, as usual, as cool as a cucumber and, like any artist, supremely happy in his work. I didn't need any extra prompting, and we lit out for the wall like greyhounds.

At which point our good fortune took a nosedive. We were through the tangled fence and close to the gap in the wall when all hell broke loose. There were several single shots followed by a burst of automatic fire, then the enormous *whoosh* of a Milan going in and, seconds later, a huge explosion as the missile struck home. Then everyone seemed to let rip together. Rounds were zipping overhead and we could hear them smacking into the other side of the wall.

There were bullets flying everywhere, riddling the sheeting covering the gap while, above, tracers created amazing patterned arches. We were safe enough on our side of the wall, but not for long. Behind us, no more than ten metres away, was over 100 pounds of high-explosive getting ready to blow in less than ninety seconds.

'What do you reckon, Mugger?' I asked.

'We haven't got much fucking choice, have we?' he replied.

I grinned at him. 'No. I suppose not. So let's go.' And with that I ducked round the plastic sheet and into the other area on the other side. The other four were all lying by the wall outside.

'Line abreast and back to the jumping-off point,' I yelled. 'And let's move it. It's all going to blow in a few seconds.'

Surging forward, we spread out like the three-quarter line in a rugby game and belted towards the dark, looming mass of the north end of the berm. Though I swear that not even the finest line-up ever made it from one end of a rugby pitch to the other at the speed we travelled that night. Of course, we were all as fit as professional athletes, and given the amount of adrenalin fizzing around in our muscles we'd have been good for a few world records – if anyone could have spared the time to clock us.

As Ratcliffe and his team reached the Land Rovers, Iraqis on

309

top of a nearby berm started popping them. The drivers started up, the gunners on the back loosing off Gimpies, Brownings and Mk19 grenade-launchers. A swerving Land Rover knocked Ratcliffe down, his rifle went flying into the dark. He was about to search for it – and the twenty gold 'escape' sovereigns hidden in the butt – when a voice yelled 'Jump on or we're fucking going without you.' He jumped on. Bullets snipped the bodywork as they roared away.

A motorcycle recce next day confirmed that the tower had fallen. Every SAS man had got out alive.

Regimental Sergeant Major Ratcliffe was later awarded the DCM for his bravery and leadership at Victor Two.

With the columns running short of supplies, the commanding officer of the Regiment organized a convoy of three-tonners to take in the goods. Escorted by spare B Squadron troopers in Pink Panthers, the resupply convoy arrived at the Wadi Tubal deep in Iraq. Assembled in the wadi were three full SAS sabre-squadrons, together with R Squadron reserves and headquarters' personnel. With the biggest gathering of the SAS in the field since 1942 around him, Peter Ratcliffe decided to mark the occasion by holding a meeting. Cameron Spence recalled:

Soon after I got back to our vehicle, word came down that Roger (Peter 'Billy' Ratcliffe) wanted all senior ranks to gather for a talk later in the afternoon in an area away from the resupply wagons.

'It can't be haircuts,' Nick said, preening himself in the reflection of his goggles.

'Or our beards,' Tom added, scratching the growth on his chin. 'We're at fucking war.'

'Maybe you're not allowed into theme parks with stubble,' Nick said. 'They think you're a bender or something.'

'Who knows?' I chipped in. A talk with the RSM was serious. Something was in the wind.

'Do you think this could be it?' Tom said, later. 'The big one.'

'Maybe,' I nodded. 'Let's just hope it's a worthwhile target.'

Later that afternoon, I grouped with the senior NCOs from A and D Squadron. While we waited for Roger to open the meeting, you could taste the excitement in the narrow gully where we'd all gathered. No question about it, this had to be the regimental work-out half of us had anticipated.

It was then that I glanced over my shoulder and saw Phil. I was still trying to work out why the Regimental Quarter Master Sergeant – our food-king – was at a planning conference that had all the makings of a war-party pow-wow when Roger stood on a boulder and the meeting kicked off.

It took a few minutes before we got the gist of what was happening here. It was a case of our ears working fine, but our sodding brains not believing the inbound message.

'Fuck,' I heard Tony say behind me. 'It can't be.'

I turned around. 'It is.'

One hundred kilometres inside Iraq, Britain's biggest war since Korea going on around us, and the warrant officers and sergeants of the Special Air Service had been called to a mess meeting.

It was serious business. Definitely no laughing matter. Top of the agenda was the forthcoming summer ball, followed by an outstanding mess account and the weighty matter of whether or not the sergeant's mess could afford a new suite and some nice blue curtains.

The motions were discussed, passed and the minutes recorded in a notebook so they could be transferred back to Hereford.

On my return to the vehicle, I stopped cursing and burst out laughing.

'What is it?' Nick asked.

I tried to get the words out, but the tears kept rolling down my face.

Nick, Tom and Jeff stared at me like I'd flipped. They must have been thinking: poor old sod. A month behind the lines and he's gone, a headcase.

Eventually, I managed to tell them about the meeting in the gully.

Their reaction was pretty much the same as mine. Disbelief. Anger. Laughter. Hysteria. It took us most of the rest of the afternoon to stop crapping ourselves.

Later, I managed to see this side-show in its true light. Who cared if it was British bureaucracy at its worst? It showed that even in the enemy's backyard, we were in control. Totally relaxed. Life went on and nothing was going to interfere with it.

The SAS had some new curtains to choose. Saddam could go swivel.

On 23 February the SAS columns were ordered to return to Saudi Arabia. The Coalition's ground offensive had started, and there was no longer a role for the SAS behind the lines. Crossing the border back into Saudi Arabia, some of the drivers looked at their mileage clocks; the pinkies, Unimogs and motorcycles had done more than 1,500 miles. Some of the men had been behind Iraqi lines for forty-two days. Even the cynical General Schwarzkopf was impressed by the achievements of 22 SAS, to the extent of writing them a personal letter of commendation (see Appendix III). Alpha One Zero's destruction of the mast at Victor Two was only one hit in a list that included the same unit's wrecking of a military fibre-optics network, Delta Two Zero's laser-painting of two Scuds for an F-15 airstrike, Delta Two Zero's demolition of a Scud-control tower, a D Squadron patrol's 'painting' of a Scud convoy for another US airstrike, plus its own Milan guided-missile attack on the convoy. (Troopers from the same half-squadron also made a bug-out to rival Bravo Two Zero's, going five days across the desert, despite Lance Corporal Taff Powell having a bullet in the guts.) After the SAS entered the Iraqi desert, Scud launches fell by 50 per cent.

David Stirling died on 5 November 1990. That evening his body was laid to rest in a London chapel, with his SAS beret and DSO on top of the coffin, next to his Knight Bachelor. The founder of the SAS missed by only weeks the regiment's deployment as behind-the-lines desert raiders in Iraq, in what turned out to be a glorious reprise of L Detachment's raiding half a century before. Even the 'pinkie' Land Rovers of 22 SAS, festooned with kit and guns and attended by soldiers in shamags, were strangely reminiscent of L Detachment's jeeps and men.

An historic circle had been turned. The SAS had returned to the desert, the place of its birth. But the wheel kept on turning. After a decade of 'Green Ops', from the Falklands to the Gulf, the SAS returned to the shadow war of 'Black Ops', courtesy of the conflagrations in the Balkans and, especially, the invasions of Afghanistan and Iraq. During a six-year campaign in Iraq as part of 'Task Force Black', the SAS was credited with capturing 3,000 insurgents, and killing 350 to 400. Snatching Al-Qaeda operatives from the backstreets of Baghdad might seem a world away from L Detachment's blowing-up of Luftwaffe planes in the Western Desert, but David Stirling would have appreciated the similarity: both campaigns were for strategic ends and both had decisive impacts. L Detachment severely hampered the operational efficiency of the Afrika Korps, 22 SAS degraded the capability of Al-Qaeda in Iraq. More than that, the make-up of the SAS soldier then and now is near identical, what Stirling (see Appendix II) characterized as the 'unrelenting pursuit of excellence', the maintaining of 'the highest standards of discipline', the brooking of 'no sense of class', and the holding of a sense of 'humility and humour'.

313

These virtues have a price, which is sometimes paid in blood. At least nine SAS soldiers died in Iraq, their names joining those on the roll of honour inscribed on the regimental clock at Stirling Lines. The clock has a verse from *The Golden Road to Samarkand* by James Elroy Flecker inscribed on its base:

> We are the Pilgrims, master; we shall go
> Always a little further: it may be
> Beyond that last blue mountain barred with snow
> Across that angry or that glimmering sea . . .

Individual pilgrims may have failed to 'beat the clock', but the SAS – the world's most famous and most imitated special forces unit – most surely has. The SAS worked in 1941 and it works today. It will work tomorrow.

APPENDIX I

An SAS Chronology

July 1941:
The SAS, then designated 'L Detachment, SAS', raised in North Africa by Lieutenant David Stirling.

November 1941–January 1943:
SAS patrols raid Axis airfields and installations in the Western Desert, destroying over 250 aircraft on the ground. Stirling, now Lieut. Col., captured January 1943. A second SAS regiment is created by the founder's brother, Bill, and a large waterborne element developed, known as the Special Boat Section.

February 1943–December 1943:
1 SAS renamed Special Raiding Squadron (SRS) and placed under the command of Lieut. Col. Paddy Mayne. The Special Boat Section becomes the Special Boat Service. SRS raids in Sicily and Italy, 2 SAS fights in Italy.

January 1944:
SAS units, less SBS, formed into SAS Brigade under command of Brigadier R. W. McLeod.

June 1944:
SAS parachute into France before D-Day. SAS order of battle for D-Day:

HQ SAS Brigade

1st SAS Regt   2nd SAS Regt

3rd (French) SAS Regt   4th (French) SAS Regt

5th (Belgian) SAS Regt

1944–45:

1, 2, 3, 4 and 5 SAS serve in France, Belgium, Holland, Italy and Germany.

October 1945:

SAS regiments disbanded. 3 and 4 SAS go to French Army, 5 SAS to Belgian Army.

1949:

21 SAS (Artists' Rifles), a TA unit, raised in London.

1950:

Major J. M. Calvert raises Malayan Scouts (SAS) to fight the communists in Malaya.

1952:

Malayan Scouts redesignated 22 SAS.

1958:

Battle of the Jebel Akhdar, Oman.

1963–6:

Borneo Confrontation.

1964–7:

SAS deployed in Aden.

1970:

SAS personnel deployed in Northern Ireland.

1972:
Battle of Mirbat, Oman.

1975:
Balcombe Street siege, London.

1976:
SAS deployed in strength in Northern Ireland.

1980:
22 SAS lift Iranian Embassy siege, London.

1982:
The Falklands War.

1987:
Peterhead prison siege.

1988:
Operation *Flavius* results in the shooting dead of three suspected IRA terrorists, Gibraltar.

1990:
Death of David Stirling.

1991:
Gulf War.

1997:
Operation *Tango*, Bosnia.

1998:
SAS deployed to Serbia and Kosovo.

2000:
Operation *Barras*, Sierra Leone.

2001–:
Afghanistan.

2003–9:
Iraq, including participation in 'Task Force Black' to remove insurgents from streets.

APPENDIX II

David Stirling: 'The Philosophy of the SAS'

To understand the SAS role it is important first to grasp the essential difference between the function of Airborne Forces and Commandos on the one hand and that of the wartime Special Operations Executive on the other. Airborne Forces and Commandos provided advance elements in achieving tactical objectives and undertook tactically scaled raids, while the SOE was a *para*-military formation operating mainly out of uniform.

In contrast, the SAS has always been a strictly military unit, has always operated in uniform (except occasionally when seeking special information) and has functioned exclusively in the *strategic* field of operations. Such operations consisted mainly of: firstly, raids in depth behind the enemy lines, attacking HQ nerve centres, landing grounds, supply lines and so on; and, secondly, the mounting of sustained strategic offensive activity from secret bases within hostile territory and, if the opportunity existed, recruiting, training, arming and coordinating local guerrilla elements.

The SAS had to be capable of arriving in the target area by air and, therefore, by parachute; by sea, often by submarine and foldboat; or by land, by foot or jeep-borne penetration through or around the enemy lines. To ensure surprise the SAS usually arrived in the target area at night and this required a high degree of proficiency, in all the arrival methods adopted for any particular operation.

Strategic operations demand, for the achievement of success, a

319

total exploitation of surprise and of guile – accordingly, a bedrock principle of the Regiment was its organization into modules or sub-units of four men. Each of the four men was trained to a high level of proficiency in the whole range of the SAS capability and, additionally, each man was trained to have at least one special expertise according to his particular aptitude. In carrying out an operation – often in the pitch-dark – each SAS man in each module was exercising his own individual perception and judgement at full strength. The SAS four-man module could be viable as an operational entity on its own, or be combined with as many other modules as an operation might require.

In the early days of the SAS, Middle East HQ sometimes tended to regard us as a baby Commando capable of 'teasing' the enemy deep behind the lines during the quieter periods but available, in the circumstances of a major defensive or offensive confrontation, to undertake essentially tactical tasks immediately behind or on the flank of an aroused enemy. It took some further successful raids to persuade HQ to acknowledge that our role should remain an exclusively strategic one.

In today's SAS the importance of good security is thoroughly instilled into every man. Certain delicate operational roles require the Secret Service to invest in the SAS Command highly classified intelligence necessary for the effective planning of these operations and, just as importantly, for special training. For such intelligence to be entrusted to the SAS, its security disciplines have to be beyond reproach.

As the SAS was operating at a distance of up to 1,000 miles from Army HQ, an exceptionally efficient wireless communication was essential. Frequently we would require interpretation of air photographs of target areas, taken while an SAS unit was already deep in the desert on its way to attack them. An effective communication system became even more important to the SAS in Europe. (Their own dedicated and special communications are still an essential feature of SAS operations.)

Recruitment was a problem, as we had to depend on volunteer recruitment from existing Army units. Not unnaturally, Commanding Officers were reluctant to see their most enterprising individuals transfer to the SAS, but eventually Middle East HQ gave us firm backing and we were usually able to recruit a few volunteers from each of the formations which had undergone general military and desert training. We always aimed to give each new recruit a very testing preliminary course before he was finally accepted for the SAS. Today the SAS is even more ruthless in its recruitment procedures.

Once selected, our training programme for a man was an exhaustive one and was designed to give him thorough self-confidence and, just as importantly, equal confidence in his fellow soldiers' capacity to outclass and outwit the enemy by use of SAS operational techniques.

We kept a careful track record of each man and capitalized whenever possible on the special aptitude he might display in various skills such as advanced sabotage technique, mechanics, enemy weaponry, night-time navigation and medical knowledge, etc. This register of each man's special skills was vital to make sure that each of our modules of four men was a well-balanced entity. Historical precedents, demonstrating how vital this concept could be to the winning of wars, were ignored and we, therefore, had to start again nearly from scratch. Luckily, the British, for one, now acknowledge the validity of the strategic raid, hence the continuing existence of the SAS regiment. The SAS today fully recognizes its obligation to exploit new ideas and new development in equipment and, generally, to keep a wide open mind to innovation and invention.

From the start the SAS regiment has had some firmly held tenets from which we must never depart. They are:

1. The unrelenting pursuit of excellence;
2. Maintaining the highest standards of discipline in all aspects

of the daily life of the SAS soldier, from the occasional precision drilling on the parade ground even to his personal turnout on leave. We always reckoned that a high standard of self-discipline in each soldier was the only effective foundation for Regimental discipline. Commitment to the SAS pursuit of excellence becomes a sham if any *single one* of the disciplinary standards is allowed to slip;

3. The SAS brooks no sense of class and, particularly, not among the wives. This might sound a bit portentous but it epitomizes the SAS philosophy. The traditional idea of a crack regiment was one officered by the aristocracy and, indeed, these regiments deservedly won great renown for their dependability and their gallantry in wartime and for their parade-ground panache in peacetime. In the SAS we share with the Brigade of Guards a deep respect for quality, but we have an entirely different outlook. We believe, as did the ancient Greeks who originated the word 'aristocracy', that every man with the right attitude and talents, regardless of birth and riches, has a capacity in his own lifetime of reaching that status in its true sense; in fact in our SAS context an individual soldier might prefer to go on serving as an NCO rather than have to leave the Regiment in order to obtain an officer's commission. All ranks in the SAS are of 'one company' in which a sense of class is both alien and ludicrous. A visit to the sergeants' mess at SAS HQ in Hereford vividly conveys what I mean;

4. Humility and humour: both these virtues are indispensable in the everyday life of officers and men – particularly so in the case of the SAS which is often regarded as an elite regiment. Without frequent recourse to humour and humility, our special status could cause resentment in other units of the British Army and an unbecoming conceit and big-headedness in our own soldiers.

APPENDIX III

J. M. Calvert: 'Future of SAS Troops' 1945

Subject: Future of SAS Troops

HQ SAS Tps/80/17/G

Lt Col W. Stirling
Lt Col D. Stirling, DSO
Lt Col R. B. Mayne, DSO
Lt Col B. M. F. Franks, DSO MC
Lt Col I. G. Collins
Lt Col E. C. Baring
Lt Col The Earl Jellicoe
Lt Col D. Sutherland
Lt Col D. Lloyd Owen, MC
Major J. Verney, MC
Major R. Farran, DSO, MC

The Director of Tactical Investigation, Maj Gen Rowell, has been ordered by the Chief of Imperial General Staff that his directorate should investigate all the operations of the Special Air Service with a view to giving recommendations for the future of the SAS in the next war and its composition in the peacetime army. The actual terms of reference were:

'An investigation of SAS technique tactics and organization without prejudice to a later examination of all organizations of a similar nature which were formed and operated in various theatres of this last war'.

323

Brigadier Churchill is Deputy Director of Tactical Investigation and lives at Flat 110, 4 Whitehall Court, London, SW1 (Whitehall 9400 Ext 1632), just behind the War Office. The officer immediately concerned is Lt Col C. A. Wigham. Lt Col Wigham has in his possession all the reports on SAS operations in western Europe. The reports on SAS operations in Italy and in the Mediterranean theatre are also being obtained and forwarded. I have given Lt Col Wigham your names so that he may either have a talk with you to obtain your views and to find out about incidents which are not clear in the reports, or to ask you to write your views to him.

We all have the future of the SAS at heart, not merely because we wish to see its particular survival as a unit, but because we have believed in the principles of its method of operations. Many of the above-named officers have had command of forces which have had a similar role to that of the SAS, as well as being in the SAS at one time.

The object of this investigation is to decide whether the principles of operating in the SAS manner are correct. If they are correct, what types of units should undertake operations of this nature, and how best to train and maintain such units in peace, ready for war. I will not start now by writing about the principles of SAS, which have been an intrinsic part of your life for the past few years, but I will mention what I think are some of the most important points which need bringing out. The best way to do this is to consider the usual criticisms of the SAS type of force.

1. *'The Private Army'*
From what I have seen in different parts of the world, forces of this nature tend to be so-called 'Private Armies' because there have been no normal formations in existence to fulfil this function – a role which has been found by all commanders to be a most vital adjunct to their plans. It has only been due to the drive and initiative of certain individuals backed up by senior

commanders that these forces have been formed and have carried out their role.

2. 'The taking up of Commanders' valuable time'

This has often been necessary because it has very often only been the Comds of armies who have realized the importance of operations of this nature, and to what an extent they can help their plans. The difficulty has been that more junior staff officers have not understood the object or principles of such forces. They have either given us every help as they have thought us something rather wonderful, or they have thought we were 'a bloody nuisance'. I feel that the best way to overcome this is, that once the principle of the importance of Special Raiding Forces operating behind the vital points of the enemy's lines is agreed to, it should become an integral part of the training of the army at the Staff College, military colleges, and during maneuvers, etc. Students should be asked not only what orders or directors or requests they have to give to the artillery, engineers, air, etc., but also what directives they would give to their raiding forces. There should be a recognized staff officer on the staffs of senior formations whose job it is to deal with these forces, i.e. the equivalent of a CRE or CRA. This should also be included in the text books FRS, etc.

3. 'These forces, like airborne forces, are only required when we pass to the offensive, which – judging by all previous wars – is when the regular army has been nearly wiped out in rearguard actions whilst the citizen army forms, i.e. about 3 years after the beginning of the war.'

The answer here, I feel, is that it is just when we are weak everywhere that forces of this nature are the most useful, and can play a most vital part in keeping the enemy all over the world occupied. Also there is little difference between the roles of SAS and 'Auxiliary Forces' who duck when the enemy's offensive rolls over them and then operate against the enemy's L or C from previously constructed bases. An SAS formation, by its organization and training, is ideally suited to operate in this defensive role.

4. *'Overlapping with SOE and other clandestine organizations'*

My experience is that SOE and SAS are complementary to each other. SAS cannot successfully operate without good intelligence, guides, etc. SOE can only do a certain amount before requiring, when their operations become overt, highly trained, armed bodies in uniform to operate and set an example to the local resistance. SOE are the 'white hunters' and produce the ground organization on which SAS operates. All senior officers of SOE with whom I have discussed this point agree to this principle.

5. *'SAS is not adaptable to all countries.'*

This has already been proved wrong. SAS is probably more adaptable to changes of theatres than any regular formation. Also, as I have said in 4 above, SAS work on the ground organization of SOE. It is for SOE to be a world-wide organization with an organization in every likely country. Then when necessary, SAS can operate on this organization using their guides and intelligence knowledge, etc.

6. *'Volunteer units skim the regular units of their best officers and men.'*

Volunteer units such as SAS attract officers and men who have initiative, resourcefulness, independence of spirit, and confidence in themselves. In a regular unit there are far less opportunities of making use of these assets and, in fact, in many formations they are a liability, as this individualistic attitude upsets the smooth working of a team. This is especially true in European warfare where the individual must subordinate his natural initiative so that he fits into a part of the machine. Volunteer units such as the Commandos and Chindits (only a small proportion of the Chindits were volunteers although the spirit was there) have shown the rest of the army how to fight at a time when it was in low morale due to constant defeat. A few 'gladiators' raises the standard of all. Analogies are racing (car, aeroplane, horse, etc.), and test teams.

7. *'Expense per man is greater than any other formation and is not worthwhile.'*

Men in units of this nature probably fight 3 or 4 times more often than regular units. They are always eager for a fight and therefore usually get it. If expense per man days *actually in contact with the enemy* was taken into account, there would be no doubt which was the more expensive type of formation. I have found, as you will have done, the 'old familiar faces' on every front where we have seen trouble. I consider the expense is definitely worth it without even taking into account the extra results. One SAS raid in North Africa destroyed more aeroplanes in one day than the balloon barrage did during 6 years of war.

8. *'Any normal battalion could do the same job.'*

My experience shows that they definitely cannot. In Norway in 1940, a platoon of marines under a sergeant ran away when left on its own, although they had orders to stay, when a few German lorries appeared. Mainly owing to the bad leadership of this parade-ground sergeant, they were all jittery and useless because they were 'out of touch'. A force consisting of two Gurkha Coys and a few British troops, of which I was one, was left behind in 1942 in Burma to attack the enemy in the rear if they appeared. The Commander, a good Gurkha officer with a good record, when confronted with a perfect opportunity (Japs landing in boats onto a wide sandy beach completely unaware of our presence), avoided action in order to get back to his Brigade because he was 'out of touch' and could not receive orders. By avoiding action, the unit went into a waterless area and more perished this way and later by drowning than if he had attacked.

My experience with regular battalions under my command in Burma was that there were only 3 or 4 officers in any battalion who could be relied on to take positive action if they were on their own, and had no detailed orders. This 'I'll 'ave to ask me Dad' attitude of the British Army is its worst feature in my opinion. I found the RAF and dominion officers far better in this respect. I have not had experience with the cavalry. They should also be better. Perhaps cavalry could take on the SAS role successfully? I admit that with training both in Burma and North Africa there were definite improvements amongst the infantry, but in my opinion, no normal battalion I have seen, could carry out an SAS role without 80 per cent reorganization. I have written frankly and have laid myself open to obvious criticism, but I consider this such a vital point I do not mind how strongly I express myself. I have repeated this for 5 years and I have nowhere seen anything to change my views, least of all in Europe.

I have mentioned some points above. You may not agree with my ideas but I write them down as these criticisms are the most normal ones I know. Other points in which the DTI wants to obtain information are:

1. *Obtaining of recruits.* Has anybody got the original brochure setting out the terms and standards required?
2. *Obtaining of stores and equipment.* Here again, I imagine SOE has been the main source of special stores. My own HQ is producing a paper on this when in England.
3. *Signal communication.* This is of course one of the most important parts of such an organization and it has, as in other formations, limited the scope of our operation.
4. *Foreign recruits and attached civilians.*
5. *Liaison with RAF and Navy.*
6. *Command.* How is an organization of this sort best commanded and under whom should they be?

7. Suggestions re survival in peacetime including auxiliary formation, command, technical development, etc.

You may expect a communication from Lt Col Wigham. Please give your views quite candidly. They certainly need not agree with those I have written down. I am sending Lt Col Wigham a copy of this letter so that it may give you something to refer to if necessary. I hope, from the army point of view, and for all that you have worked for and believed in during the last few years, that you will do everything you can to help Lt Col Wigham to obtain all the information that he requires. We can no longer say that people do not understand if we do not take this chance to get our views put before an impartial tribunal whose task it is to review them in the light of general policy, and then make recommendations to the CIGS. Send along any reports or documents you have got. Lt Col Wigham is thirsting for information.

[Mike Calvert]
Brigadier,
Commander,
SAS Troops

Sloe House,
Halstead, Essex.
12 Oct 45.
JMC/LGM.

APPENDIX IV

General H. Norman Schwarzkopf: 'Letter of Commendation for the 22 Special Air Service (SAS) Regiment'

SUBJECT
Letter of Commendation for the
22 Special Air Service (SAS) Regiment.

1. I wish to officially commend the 22 Special Air Service (SAS) Regiment for their totally outstanding performance of military operations during Operation Desert Storm.

2. Shortly after the initiation of the strategic air campaign, it became apparent that the Coalition forces would be unable to eliminate Iraq's firing of Scud missiles from western Iraq into Israel. The continued firing of Scuds on Israel carried with it enormous unfavorable political ramifications and could, in fact, have resulted in the dismantling of the carefully crafted Coalition. Such a dismantling would have adversely affected in ways difficult to measure the ultimate outcome of the military campaign. It became apparent the only way that the Coalition could succeed in reducing these Scud launches was by physically placing military forces on the ground in the vicinity of the western launch sites. At that time, the majority of available Coalition forces were committed to the forthcoming military campaign in the eastern portion of the theater of operations.

Further, none of these forces possessed the requisite skills and abilities required to conduct such a dangerous operation. The only force deemed qualified for this critical mission was the 22 Special Air Service (SAS) Regiment.

3. From the first day they were assigned their mission until the last day of the conflict, the performance of the 22 Special Air Service (SAS) Regiment was courageous and highly professional. The area in which they were committed proved to contain far more numerous enemy forces than had been predicted by every intelligence estimate, the terrain was much more difficult than expected and the weather conditions were unseasonably brutal. Despite these hazards, in a very short period of time the 22d Special Air Service (SAS) Regiment was successful in totally denying the central corridor of western Iraq to Iraqi Scud units. The result was that the principal areas used by the Iraqis to fire Scuds on Tel Aviv were no longer available to them. They were required to move their Scud missile firing forces to the north-west portion of Iraq and from that location the firing of Scud missiles was essentially militarily ineffective.

4. When it became necessary to introduce United States Special Operations Forces into the area to attempt to close down the north-west Scud areas, the 22 Special Air Service (SAS) Regiment provided invaluable assistance to the US forces. They took every possible measure to ensure that US forces were thoroughly briefed and were able to profit from the valuable lessons that had been learned by earlier SAS deployments into Western Iraq.

I am completely convinced that had US forces not received these thorough indoctrinations by SAS personnel, US forces would have suffered a much higher rate of casualties than was ultimately the case. Further, the SAS and US joint forces then immediately merged into a combined fighting force where the synergetic effect of these fine units ultimately caused the enemy to be convinced that they were facing forces in western Iraq that were more than tenfold the size of those they were actually facing. As a result, large numbers of enemy forces than might otherwise have been deployed in the eastern theater were tied down in western Iraq.

5. The performance of the 22 Special Air Service (SAS) Regiment during Operation Desert Storm was in the highest traditions of the professional military service and in keeping with the proud history and tradition that has been established by that regiment. Please ensure that this commendation receives appropriate attention and is passed on to the unit and its members.

H. NORMAN SCHWARZKOPF
General, US Army Commander-in-Chief.

SOURCES AND ACKNOWLEDGEMENTS

Peter de la Billière, *Looking for Trouble*, HarperCollins, 1995. Copyright © Peter de la Billière 1995

Paul Bruce, *The Nemesis File: The True Story of an SAS Execution Squad*, Blake Publishing Ltd, 1995. Copyright © Bruce/Davies 1995

Roy Close, *In Action with the S.A.S.: A Soldier's Odyssey from Dunkirk to Berlin*, Pen and Sword Military, 2005. Copyright © Roy Close 2005

John Cochrane, quoted in *Being the Story of 'Apple' of the Commandos and Special Air Service Regiment*, J. E. Appleyard, Blandford Press, 1946

Frank Collins, *Baptism of Fire*, Corgi Books, 1998. Copyright © Frank Collins 1997

Johnny Cooper, *One of the Originals: The Story of a Founder Member of the SAS*, Pan Books Ltd, 1991. Copyright © J. Murdoch Cooper 1991

Virginia Cowles, *The Phantom Major: The Story of David Stirling and the SAS Regiment*, The Companion Book Club, 1959. Copyright © Virginia Cowles, 1958

Corporal Davey, quoted in *A History of the SAS Regiment*, John Strawson, Guild Publishing/Book Club Associates, 1984. Copyright © John Strawson 1984

'David', quoted in *SAS: The Soldiers' Story*, Jack Ramsay, Macmillan, 1996. Copyright © Macmillan/Carlton 1996

Geordie Doran with Mike Morgan, *Geordie Fighting Legend of the Modern SAS*, Sutton Publishing Ltd, 2007. Copyright © Mike Morgan 2007

Roy Farran, *Winged Dagger*, Collins, 1948. Copyright © Roy Farran 1948

Roy Farran, *Operation Tombola*, Collins, 1960. Copyright © Roy Farran 1960

Derrick Harrison, *These Men Are Dangerous: The Early Years of the SAS*, Grafton Books, 1990. Copyright © D. I. Harrison 1957

John Hislop, *Anything But A Soldier*, Michael Joseph Ltd, 1965. Copyright © John Hislop 1965

Robin Horsfall, *Fighting Scared*, Weidenfeld & Nicolson, 2002. Copyright © Robin Horsfall 2002

George, The Earl Jellicoe, Imperial War Museum, Sound Archive

Jon E. Lewis (Ed.), *The Mammoth Book of SAS & Special Forces Thirty Missions of Ultimate Danger Behind Enemy Lines, from WWII to Afghanistan and the Iraq War*, Constable & Robinson Ltd, 2004. Copyright © J. Lewis-Stempel 2004

David Lloyd Owen, Imperial War Museum, Sound Archive

Fitzroy Maclean, *Eastern Approaches*, Pan Books Ltd, 1956. Copyright © Fitzroy Maclean 1949

J. Fraser McLuskey, *Parachute Padre Behind German Lines With The SAS France 1944*, SPA Books, 1985. Copyright © SPA Books Limited 1985

Andy McNab, *Bravo Two Zero: The True Story of an SAS Patrol behind Enemy Lines in Iraq*, Corgi Books, 1995. Copyright © Andy McNab 1993

Malcolm Pleydell, Imperial War Museum, Department of Documents

Malcolm Pleydell, *Born of the Desert*, Greenhill, 2006.

Jack Ramsay, *SAS: The Soldiers' Story*, Macmillan, 1996. Copyright © Macmillan/Carlton 1996

Peter Ratcliffe, *Eye of the Storm*, Michael O'Mara Books Ltd, 2001. Copyright © Peter Ratcliffe 2000

Tom Read, *Freefall*, Little, Brown and Company, 1998. Copyright © Livvy Publishing Ltd 1998

Chris Ryan, *The One That Got Away*, Century 1995. Copyright © Chris Ryan 1995

Gilbert Sadi-Kirschen, *Six Friends Arrive Tonight*, Nicolson Watson, 1949.

Pete Scholey, quoted in *SAS: The Soldiers' Story*, Jack Ramsay, Macmillan, 1996. Copyright © Macmillan/Carlton 1996

James Sherwood, quoted in *The Imperial War Museum Book of War Behind Enemy Lines*, Julian Thompson, Sidgwick & Jackson, 1998. Copyright © Julian Thompson 1998

David Smiley, *Arabian Assignment*, Leo Cooper, 1965. Copyright © David Smiley 1965

Cameron Spence, *Sabre Squadron*, Penguin Books Ltd, 1998. Copyright © Cameron Spence 1997

J. S. Spreule, quoted in *A History of the SAS Regiment*, Guild Publishing/Book Club Associates, 1985. Copyright © John Strawson 1984

John Strawson, *A History of the SAS Regiment*, Guild Publishing/Book Club Associates, 1985. Copyright © John Strawson 1984

Trooper Takavesi, quoted in *SAS: The Soldiers' Story*, Jack Ramsay, Macmillan, 1996. Copyright © Macmillan/Carlton 1996

Wilfred Thesiger, *The Life of My Choice*, Fontana, 1987. Copyright © Wilfred Thesiger 1987

Julian Thompson, *The Imperial War Museum Book of War Behind Enemy Lines*, Sidgwick & Jackson, 1998. Copyright © Julian Thompson 1998

INDEX